For Jim, Ted, and Alfie.

Pursuing Meaning

Emma Borg examines the relation between semantics (roughly, features of the literal meaning of linguistic items) and pragmatics (features emerging from the context within which such items are being used), and assesses recent answers to the fundamental questions of how and where to draw the divide between the two. In particular, she offers a defence of what is commonly known as 'minimal semantics'. Minimal semantics, as the name suggests, wants to offer a minimal account of the interrelation between semantics and pragmatics. Specifically, it holds that while context can affect literal semantic content in the case of genuine (i.e. lexically or syntactically marked) context-sensitive expressions, this is the limit of pragmatic input to semantic content. On all other occasions where context of utterance appears to affect content, the minimalist claims that what it affects is not literal, semantic content but what the speaker conveys by the use of this literal content—it affects what a speaker says but not what a sentence means. As Borg makes clear, the minimalist must allow some contextual influence on semantic content, but her claim is that this influence can be limited to 'tame' pragmatics—the kind of rule-governed appeals to context which won't scare formally minded horses. *Pursuing Meaning* aims to make good on this claim. The book also contains an overview of all the main positions in the area, clarification of its often complex terminology, and an exploration of key themes such as word meaning, mindreading, and the relationship between semantics and psychology.

Pursuing Meaning

EMMA BORG

OXFORD
UNIVERSITY PRESS

OXFORD
UNIVERSITY PRESS

Great Clarendon Street, Oxford, OX2 6DP,
United Kingdom

Oxford University Press is a department of the University of Oxford.
It furthers the University's objective of excellence in research, scholarship,
and education by publishing worldwide. Oxford is a registered trade mark of
Oxford University Press in the UK and in certain other countries

First published 2012
First published in paperback 2015

Published in the United States of America by Oxford University Press
198 Madison Avenue, New York, NY 10016, United States of America

British Library Cataloguing in Publication Data
Data available

Library of Congress Cataloging in Publication Data
Data available

ISBN 978–0–19–958837–4 (Hbk.)
ISBN 978–0–19–873898–5 (Pbk.)

Contents

Preface

This book examines some recent answers to the questions of how and where to draw the divide between semantics (roughly, features of the literal meaning of linguistic items) and pragmatics (roughly, features emerging from the context within which such items are being used). In particular, this book attempts a defence of what is commonly known as 'minimal semantics' (aka 'semantic invariantism' or 'insensitive semantics'). Minimal semantics, as the name suggests, wants to offer a pretty minimal account of the inter-relation between semantics and pragmatics. Specifically, it holds that while context can affect literal semantic content in the case of genuine (i.e. lexically or syntactically marked) context-sensitive expressions (e.g. indexicals, demonstratives, tense markers), this is pretty much the limit of pragmatic input to semantic content.[1] On all other occasions where context of utterance appears to affect content the minimalist claims that what it affects is not literal, semantic content but what the speaker conveys by the use of this literal content—it affects what a speaker says not what a sentence means. So minimalists are fond of making claims along the following lines: the sentence 'Snow is white' means that *snow is white,* the sentence 'Ted is ready' expresses the proposition that *Ted is ready,* and the sentence 'there is nothing to eat' is true iff *there is nothing to eat.* For the minimalist, then, the semantic content of these sentences is not (as some theorists contend) a pragmatically enriched content such as *snow is white in some contextually determined respect,* or *Ted is ready to play football,* or *there is nothing appropriate to eat in the kitchen.* Though a speaker may convey a more complex content such as one of these, this is held to be a feature of pragmatic speaker meaning not semantic sentence meaning.

Notice that minimalism does not claim that pragmatics has *no* effects on semantics. This claim has been made (e.g. see Katz 1977, and more recently Garcia-Carpintero 2006) and indeed, depending on how we define our terms here (a point I'll return to in Chapter 1) this can be seen

---

[1] The qualification 'pretty much' is to allow for pre-semantic pragmatic processes, like word disambiguation; see Borg 2004a, Chapter 2.

as precisely the claim made by opponents of minimalism such as Sperber and Wilson, Carston and Travis.[2] To claim that pragmatics has no role to play at all within the semantic realm is very likely to lead to the claim that the subject matter of semantics is sub-propositional or non-truth-evaluable content. The reason for this is pretty easy to see: consider the sentence 'I'm here now'. Unless one is able to look to a specific context in which this sentence is uttered it will be impossible to deliver values for the context-sensitive terms 'I', 'here' and 'now'. Yet without such values any content we can recover for the sentence (perhaps in terms of a Kaplanian character) is bound to fall short of propositional, truth-evaluable content. The minimalist wants to preserve the idea that semantics trades in truth-evaluable content, thus she is driven to allow some contextual influence on semantic content, though her hope is that this influence can be limited to 'tame' pragmatics—the kind of rule-governed appeals to context which won't scare any formally minded horses.

The niche the minimalist wants to carve out for herself is then, we should recognize from the outset, potentially precarious. The problem is as follows: on the one hand, it seems clear that that we need (i) a level of content which is determined simply by word meaning and structure, where this is context-invariant yet not necessarily propositional content. We need this kind of context-invariant core to linguistic meaning to explain how it is possible to understand or learn a language in the first place, to make language a vehicle for successful communication, to account for features of our comprehension like its systematicity and productivity (to be explained below, see Chapter 1.1), and so on. On the other hand, it also seems clear that we need (ii) a level of significantly pragmatically enriched and necessarily propositional content to deliver what the speaker actually conveys in a given context (after all, it's that content which we are really concerned to recover in communicative exchanges). The problem for minimalism, and what makes her position potentially precarious, is the question of why on earth we should think that in addition to these two levels of content we also need (as it seems the minimalist wants) (iii) an

---

[2] Note that one might think to include the 'radical minimalism' of Kent Bach on this list of approaches which bar all pragmatic input to semantics, but this would be a mistake, since though Bach treats provision of referents for demonstratives as a pragmatic process resulting in a content beyond that yielded by semantics alone, he does allow that 'pure indexicals', like 'I' and 'tomorrow', have their referents provided as part of semantics not pragmatics. Thus he does permit some contextual input to semantics, even though, as we will come to see, this input is limited.

intermediary level of purely lexico-syntactically determined but also necessarily propositional sentence-level content?[3] Given this fundamental worry, the arguments against minimalism then come primarily in two forms: (a) arguments to the effect that a minimal level of truth-evaluable content is not necessary, i.e. that the minimal propositions that minimalism posits are explanatorily redundant (and thus should be rejected by any respectable, parsimonious approach to semantics), and (b) arguments to the effect that lexico-syntactically determined content on some or perhaps all occasions falls short of propositional content, so that in at least some cases there are no such things as the miminal propositions minimalism requires.[4] This book is an attempt to rebut both these lines of argument and to show that minimalism is a feasible and attractive semantic theory.

Chapter 2 introduces and rejects the claim that minimal propositions are explanatorily redundant, while Chapters 3–6 focus on the idea that minimal propositions do not exist. The reason for this weighting towards the argument of non-existence is due to the relative power of the arguments: if minimal propositions don't exist one can't be a minimalist, if minimal propositions exist but have no work to do one can be a minimalist, though the task is then clearly to try to find some useful work for minimal propositions to do (I'll suggest some of this work in Chapter 2; see also Borg 2009b for a further suggestion). Distinguishing these two very different kinds of arguments against minimalism will also help to clarify the terrain of relevant opposition here. For, as we will see in Chapter 2.6, it is important to make clear which of these arguments is at work in attacks on minimalism, for a failure to appreciate exactly where theorists are disagreeing can lead to people simply talking past one another. Thus Chapter 2 will close with an overview of at least some of the possible dimensions along which parties to the debate either agree or disagree.

Now, as excessively well-informed readers may know, minimal semantics is actually a position I have defended before (see, e.g. *Minimal Semantics*, Borg 2004a) and although no familiarity with this earlier

---

[3] Ultimately, of course, the minimalist will reject this way of phrasing the issue, for her claim will not be that there is an 'additional intermediary' level of lexico-syntactically determined and always propositional content. Rather her claim will be that well-formed sentences always reach the level of truth-evaluable content; i.e. that (i), at least as far as well-formed sentences are concerned, is always propositional content. However I think it is dialectically useful, in setting up the problem for minimalism, to think of these as three distinct levels or kinds of content.

[4] See Recanati's 2004: 86 distinction between contextualism and quasi-contextualism.

work is presumed in what follows, a perfectly reasonable question to ask at this juncture is why I (or anyone else for that matter) should want to devote another monograph to the defence of this position (or indeed, much more pertinently, why you or any one else should devote your time to reading it?) Well, the first point to note is that (incredible as it may seem) *Minimal Semantics* hasn't actually succeeded in convincing everyone (or maybe even anyone) that minimalism is simply the best account on the table. Indeed, it seems as if minimalism hasn't even managed to hang on to those few friends it once had (e.g. see the apparent shift from minimalism to contextualism/indexicalism between Cappelen and Lepore 2005 and Cappelen and Hawthorne 2009, or compare the Soames of 2002 with the Soames of 2005). So, since minimalism remains a theory I'm partial to, a first reason for writing this book is to have another go at convincing others of its attractions (and conversely, of course, to stress the pitfalls of alternative accounts in the area).

Secondly, it seems to me that what is really at issue in the debate between minimalism and competitor accounts, like contextualism (of which *much* more below), is sometimes obscured in work on this topic. What I take to be really crucial to minimalism is the denial of what King and Stanley 2005 call 'strong pragmatic effects'—i.e. a denial of the idea that a context of utterance could come to affect semantic content when there is *no* syntactic trigger for such a contribution. For me, what is central to minimalism is the claim that propositional semantic content runs exhaustively off syntax and lexicon. The claim, which is often taken to be absolutely definitive of minimalism (see, e.g. Cappelen and Lepore 2005), and which minimalism does indeed also want to make, that what is found at the lexico-syntactic level is generally or largely context-insensitive (i.e. the claim that our language is not populated by massive numbers of hidden or surprise indexicals) is then, I believe, somewhat secondary and, as I'll try to spell out in Chapters 1 and 2, emerges from minimalism's commitment to a formal, syntax-based route to semantics rather than being a fundamental assumption of the approach.[5] If this is right, then accounts which posit hidden or surprise indexicals turn out not to be competi-

---

[5] There is an important caveat here, concerning distinct ways in which the claim that there are a limited number of context-sensitive expressions may be interpreted; see Chapter 1, n.4.

tors to minimalism in anything like the sense in which contextualist theories (i.e. those positing strong pragmatic effects) are. Furthermore, the questions of how we conceptualize the terrain and what the core commitments of our theories are taken to be matter here because they serve to delimit the range of options open to a minimalist in the face of putative counterexamples to her theory. So one of the claims I'll make in Chapter 2 (and indeed throughout) will be that, when properly understood, minimalism turns out to have a wider arsenal of defensive weapons available to it than is sometimes supposed.

A third reason to revisit this topic is that the terrain which minimalism seeks to occupy looks rather different today than it did when I was writing the last book. At the time of writing *Minimal Semantics* it seemed to me that the really exciting news (exciting at least to those of us with quiet social lives) was the emergence, and growing popularity, of accounts which allowed pragmatic processes to contribute to what was traditionally thought of as semantic content (i.e. to the first complete or truth-evaluable proposition recoverable on the basis of a sentence) in ways which didn't depend on lexico-syntactic context-sensitivity. This claim perhaps first emerged with Atlas and Kempson's position that sentences containing 'not' were semantically underdetermined, requiring contextual completion to settle questions of scope (see Atlas 1977, Kempson 1975). However, the idea crystallized and generalized with the Relevance Theorists (such as Sperber and Wilson 1986, or Carston 2002) who claimed, for instance, that the literal content of a sentence like 'Peter's bat is grey' as uttered in a given context, c, makes reference to a contextually determined relation between Peter and the bat (so a speaker literally asserts that *The bat owned by Peter is grey,* or *The bat chosen by Peter is grey*, etc.), and the work of Recanati (e.g. 2002, 2004), who argued, for instance, that a sentence like 'It's raining' at least sometimes needs the contextual provision of a place prior to capturing the proposition literally expressed by the speaker, even though such a need is not syntactically realized (see also Searle 1980, Perry 1986, among others). All these positions (and many more) shared a fundamental assumption that the citadel of semantic content was pragmatically permeable in ways not dreamt of in standard formal semantics (for instance, see Kamp 1981, Taylor 2001, Jaszczolt 2005). This 'contextualist' stance provided a new and extremely challenging opponent to traditional formal semantics and thus *Mini-*

mal Semantics presented primarily a two-headed debate between minimalism and contextualism.[6] Now, however, an exclusive concentration on varieties of contextualism looks inadequate, for alongside contextualist opponents to minimalism, there now stand a range of further positions against which the minimalist must bear arms. Thanks in large part to the work of Jason Stanley, various forms of indexicalism are now on the table as clear alternatives to minimalism, while, thanks to the work of John MacFarlane, Stefano Predelli, Max Kölbel, and Peter Lasersohn (among others), various forms of semantic relativism are proving increasingly popular. Despite the current economic downturn, the shopper in the market for a semantic theory has perhaps never had it so good. Thus a proper defence of minimalism needs to say something about the full range of opposition it now faces and this will be the task of Chapter 1.

A fourth reason to re-tread this ground concerns the growing consensus view that what matters to minimalism is the truth of what Bach calls 'propositionalism'—the view that every well-formed sentence, perhaps relativized to a context of utterance, is capable of expressing a proposition—but that propositionalism is obviously false. Without propositionalism, minimalism risks imminent collapse into one of its competitor accounts, for the claim becomes the weak one that, while *some* element of content is recoverable on the basis of lexicon and syntax alone, there is no reason to think that what this determines is a complete proposition. That is to say, without a commitment to propositionalism, we have the simple two-level model sketched above, with on the one hand lexico-syntactically determined, context-independent but often or always non-propositional content and, on the other, pragmatically determined and always propositional content.[7] For min-

---

[6] In Borg 2004 I used the label 'dual pragmatics' for what I'll here term 'contextualism'. The previous title perhaps had the benefit of being more informative, as it explicitly recognized the double role the account assigns to pragmatic processes, with an appeal to context occurring once within what traditionally counts as the semantic domain (to deliver the literal proposition expressed), and once post-semantically, to deliver implicatures. However, the title 'contextualism' has far greater currency in the current debate, thus I'll use it in what follows.

[7] This is why the clear blue water we might have hoped to preserve between minimalism and its foes becomes somewhat muddied given something like Bach's 'radical minimalism'. On this approach lexico-syntactic content is held to determine completely semantic content, but semantic content is allowed to fall short of propositional content; for instance, the sentence 'Jill is ready' is held to express a mere propositional radical or fragment outside a context of utterance. Yet allowing that pragmatic processes are required to get one to a proposition seems essentially to agree with opponents of minimalism that the lexico-syntactic route to content is, on at least some occasions, inadequate. See Chapters 2, 3, and 5 for further discussion.

imalism to offer a genuine alternative to its competitors then it seems it must hold fast to the idea that what a semantic theory trades in is essentially truth-evaluable, propositional items, maintaining that the literal propositional content of any well-formed sentence can be recovered simply on the basis of the syntactic form and lexical content of that sentence. So, in Chapter 3 I want to focus on the most usual reason theorists in this area give for thinking propositionalism must be false, namely the existence of so-called 'incomplete expressions'. Thus, the objection goes, while we might be willing to think that a sentence like 'Flintoff is ready to start bowling at Ponting' does succeed in expressing a proposition simply on the basis of its syntactic constituents, it seems much less obvious that the content of a sentence like 'Flintoff is ready' achieves propositional status as it stands. Rather it seems that we need to know from a context of utterance what Flintoff is being claimed to be ready for. However, as I'll argue in Chapter 3, there are moves a minimalist can make in the face of putatively incomplete expressions and thus, I'll suggest, such cases do not suffice to show that propositionalism is wrong.

However, the preservation of propositionalism in the face of putatively incomplete expressions may seem like cold comfort to the minimalist if it turns out that the recovery of the propositions (some) sentences express still requires access to rich features of a context of utterance such as speaker intentions. The worry for Chapter 4 then will be that, contrary to the minimalist's idea of a purely formal, syntax-driven route to semantic content, at heart the recovery of semantic content (in a range of cases) goes via consideration of what a speaker is thinking. That is to say, despite the veneer of formality in which minimalism dresses itself, it may turn out that it is just as steeped in what I'll term (in an obviously unbiased way) 'the dark magic of pragmatics' as any other account.[8] Seeing why the minimalist shouldn't go swimming in the murky waters of mindreading, and how she can give an account of the semantic content of even apparently intention-sensitive expressions (such as demonstratives) without taking the plunge, will be the task of Chapter 4. Here I'll suggest that the minimalist hold strictly apart reference-fixing/iden-

---

[8] Neale 2007 uses the term 'the magic of pragmatics', the epithet 'dark' is my own addition.

tification, on the one hand, and grasp of semantic content, on the other, maintaining that access to speaker intentions, though required for the former ability, is not necessary for the latter. This move is one which I originally advocated in Borg 2004a and an aim of this chapter will be to show that this position remains the most attractive one for the minimalist to pursue, even given the existence of two other possible approaches which would cohere with the overall minimalist approach.

These then are some of my reasons for returning once more to the breach of the current debate about semantic theorizing to fight once again for the minimalist cause ('we few, we happy few' and all that). However, what really got me started on writing this book was an interest in how the kind of minimal semantics for sentence meaning I was advocating related to claims about the meanings of the words that give rise to those sentence meanings. For it seems clear that the minimalist picture carries with it certain fundamental assumptions about the nature of word meanings. This can be seen by asking how exactly the minimalist model differs from accounts like the semantic occasionalism of Charles Travis (which will be looked at in more detail in Chapter 1). On Travis' (broadly Wittgensteinian) account, there is no such thing as determinate content outside a context of use, for it is only when words and concepts are put to use in a given context that they come to have a fixed meaning. Now this kind of radical use-based approach is (as we will see more clearly in Chapter 1) diametrically opposed to minimalism, yet it seems that the occasionalist need not in fact have any problem with accepting what are usually taken to be the key tenets of a position like minimalism. For minimalism claims, first, that the meaning of a sentence is fully determined by the meaning of the words it contains and the way they are put together, and second that only a few of the words contained within a natural language are marked at the lexical or syntactic level as belonging to the same semantic category as overtly context-sensitive expressions like 'I' or 'that'.

Yet the occasionalist too, it seems, will claim that the meaning of a sentence is fixed by the words it contains and the way they are put together and that only a few words in our language belong to the same semantic category as expressions like 'I' or 'that', which are context-sensitive *in the sense of* looking to a set of established contextual parameters to fix their value in a context of utterance.[9] Where the occasionalist parts company with the minimalist then is in the view taken of word meanings and what it is for a term to be context-sensitive. For on the occasionalist model what words in general offer us is something which constrains but certainly does not determine the contribution that that word might make to any sentence in which it appears, with such determination occurring only at the point of use. That is to say, though only a few words are context-sensitive in the sense of behaving like 'I' or 'that', all or almost all words are context-sensitive in the sense of having their propositional contribution fixed only within a context of use. As Travis 2008: 154 maintains, though 'blue' speaks of what it would be for something to be blue (so it is not suitable for, say, calling something red or a table), this doesn't specify how 'blue' is to be understood outside a particular context of use. For instance, it doesn't tell us whether a use of the term will be true in a given context if the object it is attributed to is blue on its outside, or inside, or writes in blue ink, or is sad, etc, etc.

So, if the minimalist view is to hold itself apart from the use-based occasionalist view it must come replete with a view of the contribution words make to sentences *not* as open-ended, web-like things which stand in need of contextual precisification prior to fixing their input to larger linguistic units, but *rather* as discrete, probably atomistic, blob-like things.[10] If we are to get propositional, truth-evaluable content from words and the ways they are put together, what those words contribute had better (in general) be determinate, context-invariant content which, when combined in the right way, is capable of yielding truth-evaluable content. Thus, while it is right to think that minimalism is primarily a theory of the semantic content of sentences, it is clear that the approach is nevertheless inherently bound up with a theory of word contents.

The particular way in which the debate about word meanings hooves into view in this book is as follows: in Chapter 4 I propose a

---

[9] That such a Wittgensteinian-style approach coheres with a 'weak' notion of compositionality is stressed by Dancy with respect to his 'semantic particularism', an approach which bears strong affinities to Travis' occasionalism. As Dancy 2004: 192 writes 'It is, I think, agreed on all hands that the meaning of the [linguistic] whole is determined by the meanings of its parts and the way in which they are there combined.'

[10] I'm grateful to Jonathan Dancy (pc) for the terminology of minimalism's 'blobby' approach to word meaning.

certain account of the semantic contribution made by overtly context-sensitive expressions like 'this' or 'that' (expressions whose contribution seems to depend on the intentional states of the speaker). I
claim that the semantic content a hearer is required to entertain
when faced with an utterance of a sentence like 'That is red' in a
given context c, will contain a singular concept in subject-position,
the content of which is exhausted by the object to which the speaker
refers. However I also allow that all that is required, from the perspective of linguistic understanding, is that the hearer be able to
think about that object under the token-reflexive description (which
gives the character of the concept) 'the actual object referred to by
the speaker with this token of "that"'. Specifically the hearer does
not need to be able to identify the object in some more substantial,
non-linguistic sense (e.g. having perceptual knowledge of the object).
However, once we have this picture of the semantic content of singular expressions as possessing both content and character (so that at
the level of both language and thought we have a distinction between
the object referred to and the rule by which it is secured) it seems
natural to ask why one would think that semantic content needs to
go beyond the level of character-based content? Since the minimalist position allows that grasp of semantic content here doesn't come
replete with further skills (like the ability to perceptually identify the
referent, or reidentify the object later on), why not hold that what is
involved in the grasp of semantic content is grasp of a context-
invariant, stable, character-based content only, with the step to 'fill
in' this fragment of content with a referent actually coming only
with respect to the *use* of the expression (being part of speaker meaning not semantic content)?[11]

In this way, all tokens of 'that is F' would have the same (non-propositional) semantic meaning (a character-based content), though this
meaning could then be used to pick out an indefinite number of different objects in distinct contexts of use. Furthermore, as we will see
in Chapters 5 and 6, this thought generalizes: so, for instance, as far as
predicates are concerned, why should we think that their lexical content is given by some kind of direct appeal to a feature of the world

---

[11] In the case of 'this' and 'that' (though not 'I' or 'tomorrow') I think this is pretty close to the view
espoused by Bach (see Bach 1992b). See also Garcia-Carpintero 2006.

(e.g. holding that 'blue' refers to *the property of blueness*)? Why not instead hold that the lexical entry for 'blue' doesn't yet get us to the world, but instead yields up a context-independent fragment of content which can then be applied to the speaker's environment in a context of use (so that one token of 'blue' might be true only if an object is blue on the outside, while another might be true only if the object in question writes in blue ink, etc.) What, the thought is, does letting the world into our *semantics*, in the way conceived of in minimalism, really buy us over an approach which treats application to the world as occurring only at the point of use?

This, it seems, is another incarnation of the general objection (canvassed above) that though there is a need for lexico-syntactically determined, context-invariant content and though there is a need for context-sensitive, propositional utterance-level content, the need for lexico-syntactically determined, context-invariant *propositional* content (i.e. the level of literal, truth-evaluable sentence-meaning which minimalists want) is much less obvious. But notice that the angle of the objection here is rather different to the form it has in some other debates between minimalism and its opponents. For instance, the objection from context-shifting to be looked at in Chapter 1 is an instance of what we might call an 'argument from above': that is to say, an argument which focuses on the richness of communicated content and uses this as a basis for arguing against the need for a propositional, lexico-syntactically determined content. (To connect to an earlier point, note that an argument from above can at most show that minimal contents lack explanatory value, while arguments from below seek to show that minimal contents are impossible in some or all cases.) So we find that, say, 'tall' must mean *tall for a four-year-old* in one context, though it must mean *tall for a basketball player* in another, or that 'Jill is ready' expresses the proposition that *Jill is ready for her exam* in one context but *Jill is ready for lunch* in another, or that 'rain' requires a contextually determined location, and so on and so forth. The thought here is that the content we intuitively take the speaker to have asserted must be *richer* than the minimalist supposes, thus austere minimal content should be rejected as it fails to match our intuitions about communicated content.

The concern in question above though is a form of what I'd call an 'argument from below': that is to say, an argument to the effect that, when we look at the contents delivered simply by syntax plus lexicon we find no reason to think that they reach the level of propositional, truth-evaluable contents (and indeed, we find good reason to think that they do not or cannot reach this level). So, the thought is, lexico-syntactically determined content must be *poorer* than minimalism supposes. As Collins 2009: 55 puts it:

Semantic theory *does* target invariance in the interpretation of linguistic structure, but we lack good reason to think that such…linguistic structures encode anything worth calling a proposition, minimal or not.

In recent work Noam Chomsky has presented just such an argument from below, contending that words in general do not make the kind of context-independent, world-involving contribution to the meaning of larger linguistic units in which they appear which an approach like minimalism assumes. Chomsky's arguments for this claim are two-fold: first, he contends that the kinds of simple, broadly referential lexical axioms (such as ⌈'London' refers to London⌉) which minimalism might think to adopt are simply not possible (at least within any genuinely scientific explanation of natural language). Second, he contends that any such world-involving lexical axioms will be irrelevant to a semantic theory for the work a semantic theory needs to do can be understood in entirely internalist terms. In Chapter 5 we will look at Chomsky's reasons for thinking that broadly referential lexical axioms are impossible and I will argue that these arguments are mistaken. I will also suggest, contrary to Chomsky, that part of the work we want a successful semantic theory to do can only be understood in broadly externalist terms (specifically, if we want a semantic theory to move beyond the level of syntax to semantics in the first place and to accommodate the normative aspects of linguistic meaning we must incorporate an externalist dimension of some sort within our semantic theory). However, as we will see in Chapter 6, it also seems that Chomsky and others are right to think that there is a non-trivial internalist burden on semantics: at least some of the work we require from a semantic theory concerns not word-world connections but complex intra-linguistic phenomena. As Pietroski 2005: 264 suggests:

[A] theory with axioms like '*easy* means EASY' or 'x satisfies *easy* iff x is easy'…may be a poor theory of meaning. Even if such axioms/theorems are true, it is a tendentious hypothesis that they are formulated in the right way for purposes of explaining how humans understand language.

The evidence to be explored here includes the need to explain semantic relations like synonymy and polysemy, together with those patterns of syntactic distribution for expressions which seem to demand semantic level explanation. As we will see, accommodating this intra-linguistic burden seems to call for lexical entries which treat the content of words as complex and structured (and honed within a context of utterance), as opposed to the simple, atomistic content supposed by minimalism. In response to this challenge, however, I will argue that, even if it is right to lay the demand for an explanation of these features at the door of semantics (something I remain somewhat sceptical of in some cases) a theory of lexical content can accommodate these features *without* moving away from atomistic, broadly referential lexical axioms.

My positive proposal in Chapter 6, then, will be in terms of what I'll call 'organizational lexical semantics', an account which sees lexical entries for simple terms as atomic and broadly referential in nature, but which allows that further information may nevertheless be associated with such entries within the lexicon. However, for reasons we'll look at, this kind of approach to lexical semantics may be thought, prima facie, to sit uncomfortably with the minimalist approach to sentence-level semantics, thus I will explore the relationship between minimalism and organizational lexical semantics, arguing that there is nothing in the driving ethos of minimalism which would rule out adopting an approach to lexical complexity like that found in organizational lexical semantics. Finally, this will bring us back full-circle to consider once again the issue of propositionalism and I'll argue once more (with reference to explicitly non-propositional approaches to semantics such as Kent Bach's radical minimalism) that there are good reasons to preserve the idea that all well-formed declarative sentences are capable of expressing truth-evaluable content without rich appeal to a context of utterance.

In many ways, then, the overall conclusion of this monograph is the same as the conclusion of Borg 2004a—namely that, though there are bullets to be bitten in pursuit of a minimal semantics, these bullets are less fatal than is often supposed and indeed are less damaging than those to be targeted at the opposition. However, I hope that, even though I'm aiming to get to the same place, the journey through the countryside of a currently pretty lively debate in philosophy of language will be diverting enough to readers, whether they have or haven't read the last book. Seven years (and two children) on, minimal semantics still seems to me to be the best game in town and thus a game that it is worth encouraging others to pursue.

Emma Borg
8 July 2011

Acknowledgments

I started thinking about the connections between minimalism and Chomsky-style internalism during AHRC Research Leave and Chapter 5 borrows heavily from the paper written during that time. I'm thus very grateful to the AHRC for making it possible to start thinking about the things which eventually prompted me to write this book. The rest of the book was made possible by the award of a Philip Leverhulme Prize, which funded two years of research leave. I would like to express my gratitude to the Leverhulme Trust: the funding of (relatively) early career researchers, via the Philip Leverhulme Prizes, provides invaluable support to the academic profession in this country. Furthermore, the method of funding involved encapsulates, I think, the kind of trust-based relationship which should lie at the heart of the partnership between funding bodies and those whom they fund. At the start of this project I couldn't have told the Leverhulme Trust that this (or indeed any other) book was the one I was going to write, and it is very much to their credit that they didn't ask me.

Beyond financial support, two other areas of support have been crucial. First, I'm immensely grateful to all the really smart people who have provided input and advice during the course of writing this book. These include, first, my colleagues in the Philosophy Department at Reading, particularly Jonathan Dancy, Brad Hooker, Galen Strawson and Jussi Suikkanen, together with all those graduate students who attended a seminar series I ran on material from the book. I also ran a second seminar series on the material while acting as the White Distinguished Visiting Fellow in Philosophy at the University of Chicago in Spring 2011. I'm very grateful to Josef Stern for the invitation to come to Chicago and to him, Chris Kennedy, Jason Bridges, Jason Merchant, Aidan Gray, and all the others who attended the seminar for insightful comments and questions. The attempt to spell out what I was really trying to do and to defend the project during these seminars was an immense help to me. Beyond this, many others have helped in the development of this work, including Zac Abrahams, Kent Bach, Herman Cappelen, Robyn Carston, John Collins,

Thiago Galery, Manuel Garcia-Carpintero, Nat Hansen, Sanna Hirvo-nen, Claire Horisk, Larry Horn, Kasia Jaszczolt, Ernie Lepore, Stephen Neale, François Recanati, Stefano Predelli, Barry Smith, Rob Stainton, Nathan Salmon, Agustin Vicente, and Daniel Whiting. I would like to single out for particular thanks Lenny Clapp, Rob Stainton and an anonymous reader for OUP, all of whom read drafts of the entire manuscript and whose perceptive comments throughout resulted in many improvements. This book has had a longer gestation period than it might otherwise have had, since it was written either side of a year's maternity leave and during a period as Head of Department. I'm thus conscious that those who helped in the early parts of the project may have slipped under the radar. So apologies to anyone that I have inad-vertently failed to thank by name: thank you anyway.

Various parts of the book have been presented at various places (as detailed below) and thanks are also due to the organizers and audi-ences on these occasions for helpful feedback and discussion. Various parts of the book have also appeared elsewhere (as detailed below) and I would like to thank the editors and publishers of these works for allowing material to re-appear here.

Finally, it would have been impossible to write this book without the help and support of people on the home front. Liz Hughes pro-vided invaluable and much appreciated childcare, my Mum has helped out in many a crisis, and Jim, Ted and Alfie have all been extremely patient (at least most of the time). Now that the book is finished I hope to spend more time with them all.

Chapter 1 contains material from 'Meaning and Context', in *The Later Wittgenstein on Language*, ed. D. Whiting. Palgrave Macmillan, 2009: 96–113. The paper was presented in the Royal Institute of Philosophy seminar series at Cardiff University, 2008, and Brighton University 2010.

Chapter 2 draws on 'Minimal Semantics and the Nature of Psycho-logical Evidence', in *New Waves in Philosophy of Language*, ed. S. Sawyer. Palgrave Macmillan, 2009: 24–40. This paper was presented at the Joint Session of the Mind and Aristotelian Societies 2008.

Chapter 4 appears in the conference proceedings for the ILCLI International Workshop on Semantics, Pragmatics, and Rhetoric, San Sebastian, 2009. It also appeared in *Manuscrito* 32: 85–122, special edition on semantics/pragmatics. Versions of the paper were presented at the Institute of Philosophy at the London School of Advanced Studies (2006), the relevance reading group at UCL (2008), Nottingham research seminar (2008), Cambridge Linguistics Society (2008), ILCLI SPR (2009), the CSMN workshop on context and intentions (2009).

Chapter 5 is reprinted by courtesy of the Aristotelian Society: 2009. It was presented at the Joint Session of the Mind and Aristotelian Societies (2009), the Florence G. Kline Workshop on Meaning, University of Missouri-Columbia (2009), and a workshop on minimal semantics, University of Valladolid (2008).

Chapter 6 was presented at the Context and Levels of Locutionary Content workshop, IFL, Lisbon (2009) and a version appeared in the conference proceedings for this event. It was also presented at a CSMN workshop on 'Word Meaning' (2010) and a workshop on 'Words and Concepts', Granada (2010).

CHAPTER I

Surveying the Terrain

This essay is an exploration of the way(s) in which context contributes to meaning and the position I'm going to argue for is that context contributes in only a very constrained way to semantic content. Specifically, I'm going to argue that it is possible to recover the proposition literally expressed by a well-formed declarative sentence (its semantic content) simply on the basis of knowledge of the lexical entries for the expressions involved and an understanding of the syntactic construction of that sentence, plus, for sentences which contain genuinely context-sensitive elements, a merely minimal conception of the context within which the sentence was produced. What one does not need to know in order to grasp semantic content is rich additional information such as what a speaker uttering a sentence intends to convey, nor does one need substantial (non-linguistic) identifying knowledge about which events, objects or properties were salient in a given context of utterance. What I'll be arguing for, then, is a variety of what is commonly known as 'minimal' (or 'insensitive' or 'invariant') semantics. As we will see in this and subsequent chapters, minimalism faces a number of problems, however the aim of this essay is to show that none of these problems are insurmountable and, furthermore, to argue (contrary to the claims of recent views like indexicalism, contextualism and semantic relativism, all to be looked at below) that the kind of austere account of semantic theorizing which minimalism recommends provides the only true alternative to a full-blooded use-theoretic approach to meaning. If one wishes to resist the allure of use-based theories then, I'll contend, minimalism provides the only firm ground upon which to stand.[1]

---

[1] So why might one want to resist a use-based approach? The topic won't be broached directly in what follows, but traditional problems include trying to spell out the notion of use involved (whose use, when, and why?), explaining the normative dimensions to semantic content, and showing how features like language acquisition and shared meaning are possible. We will look at some of the positive reasons for pursuing a formal, minimalist approach below (§1).

The first aim of this chapter is to introduce minimal semantics and to sketch the landscape within which it belongs. To this end, I'll start in the next section by defining minimalism via four key claims, two of which are directly inherited from the general school of formal semantics (to which minimalism belongs) and two of which are particular to minimalism (though I'll suggest they also emerge, though in a less direct fashion, from minimalism's formal heritage). Once we have an initial characterization of minimalism and have explored the motivation for the view, we will then turn, in §2, to the problem which many have taken to sound the death-knell for a minimalist approach, namely what Cappelen and Lepore 2005 have called 'context shifting arguments'. Context-shifting arguments seek to show that a sentence which doesn't appear (relevantly) context-sensitive at the surface level must in fact be context-sensitive in some less obvious way. This covert context-sensitivity is apparently revealed by our intuitions about shifts in truth-value for the sentence across shifts in its context of utterance. As we will see (in §3) the responses context-shifting arguments elicit can be thought of as lying on a spectrum, ranging from fairly standard formal semantics at one end (in the guise here of minimalism) through to full-blooded use-based theories at the other (in the guise here of occasionalism). Seen in this way, however, I'll argue that it becomes less than clear that the intermediate positions (of indexicalism, contextualism and relativism) between the two ends of the spectrum, are truly viable. The general problem is that all seem prey to an internal tension, at once recommending that we take the phenomenon thrown up by these examples seriously and yet recommending that we don't take it so seriously as to lead us to adopting a use-based approach to meaning. Yet, as I'll argue in §4, it's not obvious that this is tenable: once we open the door to context-shifting arguments, taking them to be of genuine semantic significance, we may well find that there is no principled reason to shut it again until we have reached the Wittgensteinian end of the spectrum.

The conclusion of this chapter will then be that, although it is right that if one wants to defend a version of standard formal semantics in the current environment (as I do) one needs to bear arms against a much more diverse range of foes than was once the case, still it turns out that the newer stances on how and where to draw the semantics/ pragmatics divide are essentially slippery and run a real risk, on closer inspection, of sliding back into the embrace of either standard formal approaches or standard use-based approaches. Thus although theoretically there are a number of distinct positions available to the theorist between brute formalism and full-fledged use-theoretic approaches, in reality the positions which we can really motivate here are the all too usual suspects at either end of the spectrum. The rest of this essay, then, will be an exercise in showing that, contrary to what seems to be an almost consensus view in recent literature, minimalism remains a live option as the correct approach to semantic theorizing.

(1) Minimal semantics

According to minimal semantics, natural language sentences mean things, the things they mean are in some sense complete (that is to say, they are propositional, truth-evaluable contents), and these literal meanings are determined entirely as a function of the lexical elements a sentence contains together with its syntactic form. Thus minimalism claims that well-formed sentences like 'La neige est blanche', 'Everyone likes chocolate' and 'Two plus two equals four' possess literal linguistic meanings (semantic content), meanings which (in some, broad sense) make claims about the way the world is, and furthermore that the semantic content each has is (more or less) that which it appears to wear on its sleeve (see Chapters 3 and 6 for discussion of the caveat 'more or less' here). Roughly speaking, then, according to minimalism, these sentences express the propositions *that snow is white, that everyone likes chocolate*, and *that two plus two equals four*. There are of course issues about exactly how the minimalist story is to be told, e.g. in terms of truth-conditions or propositions. In Borg 2004a I advocated a truth-conditional version, however since I take propositions to be the bearers of truth-conditions, the two approaches don't seem hopelessly antagonistic to me. In what follows, then, unless it is germane, I'll gloss over the debate between propositions vs. truth-conditions, taking minimal content to be either propositional or truth-conditional in nature. There are also fundamental questions to be addressed here about exactly what it is for content to reach the level of propositional or truth-conditional content. The assumption I will make below is that, at a minimum, content of this kind must be truth-evaluable as it stands. That is to say, it specifies a content which, held up against a world, is capable of being true or false (this point is explored further in Chapter 3, §3.3, see also Cappelen and Hawthorne 2009).

It seems that, at the outset, minimalism looks fairly innocuous: what could be wrong with claiming that sentences express the (propositional-level) content that their lexico-syntactic form tells us that they express? Of course however, as in all things, the devil is in the detail, and in spelling out that detail minimalism has come to seem to many to be an entirely implausible theory. Thus, in this section I would like to spell out the precise claims I take minimalism to be committed to and sketch at least some initial motivation for accepting those claims (with further motivation hopefully being supplied over the course of the book, as we see how well minimalism copes with apparent counterexamples to the theory).

In what follows I'm going to take minimalism to be defined by the following four claims:[2]

i. Semantic content for well-formed declarative sentences is truth-evaluable content.[3]

ii. Semantic content for a sentence is fully determined by its syntactic structure and lexical content: the meaning of a sentence is exhausted by the meaning of its parts and their mode of composition.

---

[2] The following definition of minimalism differs from that advocated in Cappelen and Lepore 2005 in the following ways: C&L reject (i)—see next note—and (iv), and they take (iii)—understood as the claim that there are no indexical expressions beyond the intuitively obvious ones—to be the defining feature of minimalism. Differences between the minimalism of this book (and of Borg 2004a) and Cappelen and Lepore 2005 will surface at various points in what follows, primarily in Chapter 2, §6, and Chapter 3.

[3] As we will see below, this clause can be understood as the requirement that all well-formed sentences express propositions, a requirement that Kent Bach has termed 'propositionalism'. However, not all minimalists agree that minimalism is committed to propositionalism. For instance, Cappelen and Lepore (both in print and in person) deny that propositionalism is relevant to the discussion of minimalism (see, for instance, their 'Reply to Bach'). However, to my mind, such a denial makes the dialectic here odd: once Cappelen and Lepore jettison the idea that what semantics trades in must reach the level of a proposition (where this means something truth-evaluable), then it becomes unclear to me why they bother arguing (as we will see that minimalists do) that sentences like 'Jill is ready' or 'Steel is strong enough' (for which there is at least a prima facie appearance of sub-propositionality prior to contextual input) do in fact express propositions. If semantics isn't in the business of always churning out propositions for sentences, why have the fight about these kinds of sentences at all? Furthermore, if minimalism isn't committed to propositionalism then, I think, it becomes extremely hard to hold the position apart from opposing views (like contextualism) which specifically hold that there is a context-invariant element to sentence meaning (often characterized as a potentially incomplete logical form, e.g. see Sperber and Wilson 1986) though this at least sometimes falls short of propositional content. In what follows, then, contrary to Cappelen and Lepore, I'll follow Bach in taking minimalism (as opposed to what Bach terms 'radical minimalism') to be committed to propositionalism. See also Chapter 2, §6.

iii. There are only a limited number of context-sensitive expressions in natural language.[4]

iv. Recovery of semantic content is possible without access to current speaker intentions (crudely, grasp of semantic content involves 'word reading' not 'mindreading').

Since minimalists do allow that there are some genuinely context-sensitive expressions in natural language they do not hold that semantic content is entirely context-invariant (as does, say, Katz 1977; hence the label of 'semantic invariantism', often adopted for what I'll term 'minimalism', is not, I think, fully transparent), but they do think that the input of context to literal content is severely restricted. Specifically, context can only come to affect semantic content when it is called for by something in the lexico-syntactic form of the sentence and the kinds of lexico-syntactic elements which call for contextual input are themselves limited.

Turning to claims (i) and (ii) first: the kind of approach to semantics put forward in these two principles is, I take it, simply that already enshrined in the general formal approach to semantics extant in the work of theorists like the early Wittgenstein, Frege, Russell, Carnap, Davidson, and Kaplan (among many others).[5] The thought is that semantic content attaches to formally specified (i.e. syntactically described) objects, specifically the logical forms taken to underlie the surface structure of natural language sentences. Furthermore the route to meaning is taken to travel exclusively through the syntax and the lexicon: there is a level of syntactic structure which, together with the lexical content attaching to words, provides the complete input to a semantic theory, which in turn

---

[4] This tenet is, as it stands, ambiguous. The way it has standardly appeared in discussions of minimalism (e.g. Cappelen and Lepore 2005) is as the claim that natural languages do not contain vast numbers of hidden or surprise indexicals, i.e. that Kaplan was more or less right in his list of indexical and demonstrative terms. Understood in this way, I take (iii) not to be a fundamental assumption of minimalism but to fall out of minimalism's commitment to a formal route to semantic content. This point will be discussed further below (§4.1). However, (iii) can also be understood in a different way, as the denial of the occasionalist claim that word meanings themselves are context-sensitive (i.e. that working out what contribution 'red' makes to a sentence in which it appears is something which can only take place given a context of utterance). In this latter guise, it relates to the assumptions that minimalism makes about word meanings themselves (namely, that they are stable, probably atomic, context-invariant entities) which will be the focus of discussion in Chapters 5 and 6. Until Chapter 5, I'll read (iii) in its standard incarnation (unless otherwise indicated), as the denial of the kind of indexicalism posited by Stanley 2000 and others.

[5] A detailed attempt to construct a formal theory for a natural language can be found in Larson and Segal 1995.

is capable of generating an account of the meaning of every well-formed sentence of a natural language. That formal, syntactic structures play a key role in the delivery of content is, the formal theorist avers, shown by facts about our linguistic competence such as its productivity and systematicity. So, as is well known, formal theorists like to stress the fact that, despite the limited cognitive resources which subjects can devote to language comprehension, nevertheless people are able to produce and comprehend entirely novel sentences (our understanding is productive). Or again, if a normal subject understands a sentence like 'Jill loves Bill' we can also predict that they will understand the sentence 'Bill loves Jill' (our understanding is systematic). These surprising facts about our linguistic competence are explained if we assume that semantic content is delivered via recursively specified rules operating over syntactically described objects. In other words, they are explained if formal structures lie at the heart of a theory of meaning.[6]

   The assumption embedded in (i) and (ii) is that sentences are capable of conveying information, of making claims about the world, and that it is this relatively invariant sentence-level content (rather than what is said by a speaker who utters that sentence, which may vary across different contexts of utterance) which is the proper subject matter of semantics. The idea that a semantic theory should be concerned with generating meanings for sentences (relativized to contexts of utterance) and that these meanings will be in some way complete, i.e. truth-evaluable, probably has its roots in Frege (cf. 1967: 338) and it is often phrased in terms of the idea that declarative sentences are capable of expressing propositions.[7] Clearly, phrasing things in this way opens the door for a metaphysical discussion about the

---

[6] The controversial point here is, of course, whether or not there is an *exclusively* syntactic and lexical route to sentence-level semantic content and, as many theorists have pointed out, it looks as if facts about compositionality (productivity/systematicity) can only support the claim that semantic content is *in part* determined via formal operations over syntactic forms. Thus while appeals to compositionality might perhaps form the basis of arguments against thorough-going use-based accounts (like that of Travis 1989, 2008, or Dancy 2004), it doesn't seem it can form the basis of an argument against the kinds of intermediary positions (indexicalism, contextualism and relativism) to be looked at below.

[7] For a more recent treatment see Cappelen and Hawthorne's 2009: 1 outline of what they call 'the Simple View', which includes the claims that:

   T1: There are propositions and they instantiate the fundamental monadic properties of truth *simpliciter* and falsity *simpliciter*.
   T2: The semantic values of declarative sentences relative to contexts of utterance are propositions.

See also Neale 2007: 368–9, n.68

nature and status of propositions, however, in what follows, I'm going to keep that particular door mostly shut (see Chapter 3, §3.6 for some further discussion). For though I will follow convention here and talk of sentences expressing (or failing to express) propositions, what I will mean by this claim is simply that sentences do (or do not) express truth-evaluable content. This, it seems to me, is the key property traditionally ascribed to propositions, regardless of the range of other properties which they may or may not be held to possess (for discussion of this range of properties, together with an account of propositions highly conducive to the minimalist perspective, see King 2007). Thus when I talk of propositions here it is this issue of truth-evaluability which will be at issue. Furthermore, as we will see, it's this issue—of the truth-evaluability or otherwise of lexico-syntactically determined content—which is at the heart of the contemporary debate between minimalism and its opponents (as well, of course, as being central in the historic debate between formal and use-based approaches to semantics).

So, why might we think, with our formal ancestors, that purely lexico-syntactically described objects (sentences) are (at least sometimes) capable of expressing truth-evaluable, propositional contents? Well, first I think we should note that much of the evidence we have for the existence of propositions in the first place comes from consideration of natural language sentences. It is because it seems so natural to treat 'Snow is white' or 'Two plus two equals four' as conveying information which represents the world as being a certain way, where this information is capable of being true or false depending simply on how the world in fact is, that I think we are led to posit the existence of proposition-like content at all. Or again, because it is natural to allow that two sentences, possibly in two different languages, can express the same content and thereby make the same claim about the world that we are tempted to think about positing a propositional content which the sentences share. Secondly, it seems we are happy to infer from sentences like 'Ted believes England won the Ashes in 2009' and 'Alfie believes England won the Ashes in 2009' that there is something both Ted and Alfie believe. Furthermore, given some knowledge of the world and of cricket, we can judge that what they both believe is true. Yet this kind of practice seems to entail that the sentences in the scope of 'believes' express a certain kind of content (a truth-evaluable content), attributable here to both subjects. Third, it is standard practice to think that arguments, expressed via natural language sentences, can be valid or invalid, sound or unsound, or that one sentence (not just one speaker) can contradict another, yet all of these properties assume that sentences (not merely utterances) are capable of expressing proposition-like content. Finally, we might note that it is often claimed that only propositions can be reasons for belief, yet it seems that we give our reasons (both in internal monologue and public dialogue) via declarative sentences (see Williamson 2000: 194–200). We use the connective '__because__' which is well formed just in case well-formed declarative sentences flank both sides and we expect that if a non-indexical declarative sentence gives our reasons in one context, then the very same sentence can be used correctly to give our reasons in another. If it is true in c_2 that Jim bought the scarf in c_1 because it was blue, then it will still be true in c_3 that Jim bought the scarf in c_1 because it was blue. Reasons for belief and evidence for theories seem to be the kinds of stable, repeatable contents we want to be able to express using the stable, repeatable vehicles of well-formed sentences, not the kinds of context-bound, potentially unrepeatable contents we can only express from within a context of utterance. So, while there certainly could be *arguments* to show us that sentences are not, in fact, capable of expressing truth-evaluable claims (and much of this book will be preoccupied with such arguments), my claim is that our *default* position is that at least some sentences do express truth-evaluable, propositional content.

Now, obviously, if one were to reject the idea that sentences express propositions there are two opposing positions one might take: either one might claim that *some* well-formed declarative sentences fail to express propositions (the topic of Chapter 3) or one might take the view that *all* well-formed sentences fail to express propositions (the topic of Chapters 5 and 6). My argument throughout will be that none of the arguments looked at suffice to show that there are well-formed declarative sentences which fail to express complete propositions. Furthermore, it should be noted that there are questions to be asked of the weaker position here that at least some sentences fail to express propositions. For, although this claim seems prima facie more attractive than the stronger claim that no sentences express propositions (since the weaker stance would be able to accommodate the pre-theoretical points above), it clearly requires a criterion by which we tell which sentences do, and which sentences do not, express propositions.[8] Yet, as we will see below (Chapter 3, §3.1 and Chapter 6, §6.1) it is far from clear that there is any such workable criterion available here. For instance, many theorists have suggested that a sentence like 'Flintoff is ready' fails to express a proposition because it doesn't answer the question of what he is ready to do. Yet this kind of failure to answer further questions is ubiquitous: for instance, although apparently more 'complete' than our original sentence, 'Flintoff is ready to bowl at Tendulker' also leaves a range of further questions unsettled (ready to bowl what kind of ball? Ready to bowl where and in what way?, etc.) Thus if it is this property which is the hallmark of a lack of propositional content, we seem destined to deny such content to all natural language sentences (with the proposed weaker position then collapsing into the stronger one). Prior to considering the arguments in favour of the view that some or all well-formed declarative sentences fail to express propositions, there are then immediate questions to be asked of them. First, if we adopt the stronger view that no sentences express propositions, how do we accommodate the pre-theoretical views on linguistic content (which link sentences and propositional content in at least some cases)? Second, if we adopt the weaker position that at least some sentences fail to express propositions, what criterion can we supply for holding apart sentences which do express propositions from those which don't? In advance of consideration of the actual arguments for failures of what we will come to call 'propositionalism', I think these kinds of considerations do at least provide a prima facie motivation for exploring the theoretically simple and parsimonious view (endorsed by minimalism) that all well-formed natural language sentences are capable of expressing propositions.

While the first and second tenets of minimalism embody claims which, it seems, one might expect from any traditional variety of formal semantics, the third and fourth tenets have the potential to set minimalism apart. The third tenet of minimalism is that there are a limited number of context sensitive expressions in natural language.

---

[8] Those who have found the weaker claim more attractive include Bach 1994, Carston 2002, and Soames (post-2002).

For instance, though 'this' and 'that' and 'now' are held to be lexically marked as context-sensitive, words like 'love', 'cricket' and 'eleven' are not. Cappelen and Lepore 2005: 2 put the claim as follows:

The most salient feature of semantic minimalism is that it recognizes few context sensitive expressions, and, hence, acknowledges a very limited effect of the context of utterance on the semantic content of an utterance. The only context sensitive expressions are the very obvious ones [i.e. those listed by Kaplan on the first page of *Demonstratives*] plus or minus a bit.

As this quote shows, Cappelen and Lepore take this to be the most noteworthy aspect of minimalism (note also that the above passage is the first element in their initial characterization of minimalism). However, while I agree that minimalism is committed to limitations on the number of indexicals in natural language, I also think such limitations are best seen as emerging from other things to which minimalism is committed, rather than being a basic assumption of the theory itself.[9] Specifically, as I see it, minimalism's limitation on the number of indexical expressions emerges from the fact that it is committed to preserving a formal route to meaning and, as I'll argue below (in §4.1 with respect to indexicalism), allowing too liberal an appeal to syntactic context-sensitivity risks undermining this allegiance to formality. The grounds for minimalism's limitations on indexicality matter, I think, because (as I'll argue in Chapter 3) taking it as a fundamental commitment of minimalism risks skewing the debate between minimalism and its opponents. However, whether or not the limitation on indexicality is a basic assumption of minimalism or something which emerges from other commitments it undertakes, it is nevertheless the case that all versions of minimalism subscribe to the view that natural languages contain only very limited sets of lexico-syntactically marked context-sensitive expressions, so this gives us one of the defining features of the position.

The final feature which I'll take to be definitive of (at least my variety of) minimalism also emerges from the commitment I see

---

[9] There is an important caveat here concerning the two distinct readings of (iii) (as initially noted in n.4). For while I take (iii) not to be a fundamental assumption of minimalism on its standard reading (where it denies the existence of a plethora of hidden or surprise indexicals, thought of along broadly Kaplanian lines), (iii) *is* a fundamental assumption of minimalism if read as the denial of all-pervasive context-sensitivity within lexical entries for simple expressions (i.e. where the context-sensitivity in question is not Kaplanian indexicality but the more nebulous context-sensitivity of the occasionalist, whereby word content itself can be fixed only within a context of use). This latter reading comes to the fore in the second part of the book.

minimalism as having undertaken to formalism in semantics. The final claim is that recovery of semantic content should be possible without appeal to current speaker intentions. That is to say, when we talk of semantic content as being delivered for sentences *relativized to contexts of utterance* (as we must in order to accommodate overt context-sensitivity) the kinds of contexts in play will be formal, Kaplanian ones, given by ordered sets of objective parameters (like time and world of utterance) which do not include the intentional states of the speaker.[10] The argument that a minimalist should embrace this constraint is two-fold: first, it might be argued that such a condition is really definitive of what it is to pursue a formal route to meaning itself. The guiding principles of formal semantics were held to be that semantic content gives us a level of content which attaches to sentences, which is dictated by syntax and which is free from the vagaries of what someone might intend to convey by uttering a given string of words. Yet allowing that access to speaker intentions is necessary to recover the semantic contribution for at least some expressions runs counter to this formal ethos and risks undermining the idea that semantic content is formally tractable. Furthermore, if semantics has the tools needed to look to speaker intentions in some cases, we might wonder why it doesn't use them in all cases (thereby allowing semantic content to cleave more closely to communicated content)? That is to say, if we allow that I need to know what you are thinking in order to recover the semantic contribution of an utterance of 'that' (because I need to work out to which object you intend to refer), why shouldn't it also be the case that I need to know what you are thinking in order to recover the semantic contribution of, say, 'red' as well (because I need to know if you intend to mean red on the inside, red on the outside, etc.) There are then, I think, general reasons, to do with minimalism's commitment to formalism and the wish to avoid a slide towards use-based theories, which suggest that the context against which semantic content is determined should be one which makes no reference to current speaker intentions.

A second reason for maintaining that semantic content should be recoverable without access to current speaker intentions

---

[10] It is somewhat misleading to call contexts 'Kaplanian' here, for though the Kaplan of *Demonstratives* does seem to understand contexts in the formal way envisaged above, the Kaplan of *Afterthoughts* is pretty clear that speaker intentions can be treated as part and parcel of a context.

concerns the connection between minimalism and modularity. As I've argued elsewhere (Borg 2004a), a primary motivation for believing that semantic content must be amenable to treatment via a formal, syntax-driven theory is that only in this way could our semantic competence be underpinned by a genuine Fodorian module (see Fodor 1983), where what is essential to a Fodorian module is that it be a computational device, a Turing machine. As I argued in Borg 2004a Chapter 2, there are good reasons for believing that our linguistic abilities, up to and including recovery of semantic content, are modular, for they fit the profile of properties associated with modular capacities (e.g. speed, automaticity, encapsulation) as given in Fodor 1983.[11] Yet, if we want to tell a Fodorian, modular story about our semantic competence then, on the one hand, semantic content must be recoverable via purely lexico-syntactic means and, on the other, the processes operating over those syntactically described items must themselves be formal, computationally tractable operations.

The problem then is that, while Fodorian modules are computational, syntax-driven devices, mindreading is an abductive, syntax-independent process par excellence. For instance, to work out if, in moving his cricket bat thus and so, Flintoff is preparing for a defensive shot, or to cut the ball, or perhaps even to whack the fielder at silly mid-off, one needs to know a wealth of information about the situation, including information about what Flintoff wants or believes. Furthermore, learning something new about the situation can always change our views on the best interpretation of Flintoff's actions (background information about Flintoff's batting style may lead me to believe he is intending an over-ambitious slog, but learning what the fielder at silly mid-off has just said may cause me to revise this judgement). The reasoning involved in the attribution of mental states is thus, it seems, inductive, defeasible and content-driven (see Fodor 2000, Borg 2004b for a fuller discussion of this point). However mindreading works then, the suggestion is that it works in a way not to be captured within a computational module (see especially Fodor 2000).

---

[11] However, see Robbins 2007 for an objection to some of the empirical data used to support my position in Borg 2004a.

One reason to be a minimalist, then, is that minimalism is the kind of semantic theory which stands a chance of fitting within a modular story of our linguistic competence and there is independent reason to think a modular story about our linguistic competence is right. However, minimalism fits within a Fodorian module only on the condition that it involves deductive reasoning processes alone. So minimalism, as I construe it, should be constrained to account for linguistic understanding in terms of discrete, deductive, syntax-driven reasoning processes, rather than via the murky world of content-driven inference to the best explanation. A truly formally respectable minimalist must, I think, treat current speaker intentions as *verboten* at the semantic level. Indeed it seems to me that this is simply one way of spelling out the intuitive idea (voiced, for instance, in Neale 2007) that a properly formal semantics must be one which steers clear of the 'magic of pragmatics' (see also Recanati's 2004: 57 comments on 'cheating'). From this perspective, a theory is free of the magic of pragmatics if it offers an account of our semantic competence which is computationally tractable. That is to say, if it maintains that semantic content can be recovered on the basis of limited, encapsulated information about lexical content and grammatical structure, rather than requiring appeal to, potentially, anything a subject believes.[12] So, my variety of minimalism will see the semantic contribution of context as doubly constrained: on the one hand, all versions of minimalism agree that context contributes to content only when syntactically triggered and hold that the expressions which can perform this kind of triggering are pretty limited. In addition to this, however, my more stringent version of minimalism will also hold that what context is able to supply is a set of objective parameters (such as world and time) and not rich, intensional aspects of the context of utterance, such as speaker beliefs or intentions. It is this doubly constrained version of minimalism which I'll seek to defend in the rest of this essay.

We have seen, then, how minimalism is to be defined and we've touched on some of the reasons for embracing the conditions minimalism imposes. In the next section I want to turn to introducing the

---

[12] I should note that this is not to say that accounts which treat recovery of semantic content as a branch of general, defeasible pragmatic reasoning need treat recovery of semantic content as particularly difficult or time-consuming or effortful, but simply to note that they make use of reasoning processes which are paradigmatically human and which resist attempts to explicate them in less complex systems.

competitor accounts to minimalism, via consideration of the kind of context-shifting arguments that have done so much to shape debate in this area. Before that, however, I want to close this section by considering the overall plausibility of minimalism. For even if minimalism can, as I'll argue in the rest of this book, overcome the problems which opponents raise for it, we might ask: are there actually any reasons for thinking minimalism might be right?

A first point to note with respect to minimalism is that, at least prima facie, it seems to possess a fair degree of intuitive appeal. Pre-theoretically the idea that sentences convey information which is capable of being true or false, and that the information a given sentence conveys is simply a function of, more or less, the words it contains and the way they are put together, seems pretty appealing. Now, as we are going to see time and again in what follows, adopting this kind of simplistic approach to semantic content leads the minimalist to make predictions about semantic content which diverge from the attributions of content which ordinary speakers make to the things they say in conversational exchanges. So, for instance, minimalism claims that the sentence 'There is nothing to eat' means that *there is nothing to eat (in some universal domain)*. Yet of course what someone conveys when they utter this sentence is likely to be a much narrower content like *there is nothing to eat in the fridge* or *there is nothing appealing to eat in the kitchen*. Furthermore, this point is entirely general: take any sentence of natural language and minimalism is likely to predict a literal meaning for it which is at odds with the content likely to be conveyed by an utterance of that sentence. So why, the question is, would anyone want an account of semantic content which departs so radically from our intuitions about what is said in conversational exchanges, which sets so little store by what speakers take themselves to mean? Well, I think the answer to this question is three-fold. First, I think it is not right to portray minimalism (as it sometimes is) as running counter to all pre-theoretical intuitions about utterance-level content. Given the right context (i.e. one where subjects are asked to reflect on 'literal' or 'strict' meaning) ordinary interlocutors can and do grasp exactly the kinds of contents minimalism predicts. We are all used to the sarcastic or uncooperative response to something we have said which picks up not on obvious features of the conveyed content but instead insists on the minimal, literal interpretation of our words.[13] Children, legislators, and philosophers often seem to operate precisely with the kind of strict, syntax-based model of meaning which minimalism suggests, so to claim that the readings the account predicts fail to match *any* of our intuitions about utterance content would be far too strong.

What is right, then, is that minimalism predicts sentence-level contents which usually fail to match ordinary interlocutors intuitions about what is said by utterances of those sentences. However (and this brings us to the second reason for accepting a semantic theory which fails to respect typical judgements about speech act content), as I tried to argue at length in Borg 2004a (§2.5 and elsewhere) and as I'll stress again in Chapter 2, §1, there are good reasons to think that it is simply a mistake to require a *semantic* theory to be answerable to intuitions about *speech act* content, for semantic content is one kind of thing (a repeatable, codifiable, rule-governed kind of thing) while speech act content is another kind of thing altogether (a potentially unrepeatable, nebulous, context-governed kind of thing). The sentence 'It's raining' can convey that it is raining here, raining there, that it is my favourite weather in Palo Alto today, that precipitation is occurring somewhere in the States, that the drought is over and the ducks will be happy, or any of an indefinite number of things beside. Though clearly there must be a connection between the meanings sentences have and the things we can say using them—roughly, it must be in some way because sentence s means p that we can use it to say q—still there is simply no reason to believe we can isolate some one (or just a few) of the things that can be conveyed by a sentence and treat them as yielding the literal content for that sentence.[14] Speech act content is, in the jargon, a massive interaction effect and thus the project of starting with intuitions about speech act content and trying to abstract out accounts of semantic content from there is doomed from the start. So, I would urge, the fact that minimalism predicts semantic contents which

---

[13] Think of the recalcitrant student who, under threat, promises 'I will definitely hand in my next essay', but, when found not to have submitted it by the deadline, seeks to avoid sanction by claiming that they didn't state when they would hand it in, or the child who is told 'You must give some of that to your brother' and who subsequently parts with the tiniest crumb of their cake to comply, and so on.

[14] I'd reject, then, the view of Soames 2002 and Cappelen and Lepore 2005 that minimal contents are those conveyed by *every* utterance of a sentence, holding instead that the minimal proposition which gives a sentence's meaning may not be asserted at all by a speaker uttering that sentence; see Borg 2007.

diverge from intuitive attributions of speech act content is not, in and of itself, a reason to impugn the theory.

The third reason for accepting minimalism despite the fact that it sets so little store by intuitions about speech act content is that moves away from an exclusively lexico-syntactic route to semantic content (which seem to be necessary if we want a semantic theory that fits better with speaker intentions) would leave us (with apologies to Paul Churchland) all at sea in pragmatic space. This is a point we will return to below, in §4.2, but to advertise in advance, the claim will be that if we dissolve the syntactic walls on what counts as semantic content we will be left with no way to reconstruct any walls at all. That is to say, we will lose all distinction between literal meaning and speech act content. If we open the door to let a little bit of (not syntactically-demanded) pragmatic content inside the citadel of semantics we will, the suggestion is, at once be overwhelmed by a tsunami of pragmatic content, eroding entirely the semantics/pragmatics distinction. Thus, to the extent that we want to preserve a distinction between literal meaning and speaker meaning at all, we should simply be sanguine about the fact that semantic content fails to track speech act content.

It seems to me then that we do have good reason to want the kind of strict, syntax-driven semantics which minimalism offers us. Contrary to some claims, such an approach does fit with at least some pre-theoretic intuitions, second the idea that semantics should in general capture intuitions about speech act content is ill-conceived and third, if we jettison the lexico-syntactic borders on semantic content we will be left unable to reconstruct a semantics/pragmatics divide at all. Finally, as argued in Borg 2004a, it seems that only an intention-insensitive semantics like minimalism could fit within a computational, Fodorian module for linguistic comprehension and production. Given this, the rest of this book will be concerned with the question of whether or not such a strict, minimal semantics is possible.

(2) Context-shifting arguments

To begin to get a feel for the terrain within which our discussion will take place I want to look at how a variety of positions have grown up in response to what Cappelen and Lepore 2005 label 'context shifting arguments' (or CSAs).[15] An example of this form of argument is as follows: imagine a fridge which contains only a small puddle of milk on its floor. Two conversations concerning the fridge then take place:

> *Scenario 1:*
> Hugo is dejectedly stirring a cup of black coffee. Noticing this Odile says 'There is milk in the fridge'.
>
> *Scenario 2:*
> Hugo has been cleaning the fridge. Odile opens the fridge door and says 'There is milk in the fridge'.

The intuition which drives much of the current debate in this area is that what Odile says can differ in truth value between these two scenarios. As Travis (from whom the example is taken) 1989: 18–9 notes:

Although there is no ambiguity in the English words 'There is milk in the refrigerator', or none relevant to the differences between the two speakings, Odile's words in the first case said what was false, while in the second case they said what was true. Both spoke of the same state of the world, or the same refrigerator in the same condition. So, in the first case, the words said what is false of a refrigerator with but a milk puddle; in the second case they said what is true of such a refrigerator.

Or again, imagine two utterances of 'Jill is tall', one in the context of a discussion about two-year-olds and one in the context of a discussion about basketball players. Here again it seems that the truth-value of what is said by these utterances can change across these contexts of utterance, even while Jill's height remains the same (specifically, Jill might be tall for a two-year-old but not tall for a basketball player). What CSAs show, it seems, is that sentences which are not overtly context-sensitive (or at least, which are not overtly context-sensitive in relevant respects) can nevertheless shift in truth-value across changes in conversational context, even when the state of affairs in the world

---

[15] It is perhaps misleading to say that these positions have 'grown up in response to CSAs', for not all of the arguments used to motivate the newer positions take the form of CSAs. For instance, incompleteness arguments (to which we will turn in Chapter 3) certainly play a role, while in semantic relativism much of the emphasis has been on the possibility of faultless disagreement (see Kölbel 2003, Lasersohn 2005). Finally, even where arguments which look closer to those identified as CSAs by Cappelen and Lepore are in pole position, it may be a mistake to characterize them as arguing for context-sensitivity on the basis of an intuitive change in truth-value; for instance, DeRose 2009, Chapter 2 stresses that he is concerned with cases where a sentence and its contradiction ('A knows that p'/'It is not the case that A knows that p') both seem intuitively true.

which they describe remains unchanged. CSAs then seek to demonstrate a change in semantic content or in methods of assessment via a
change in a subject's intuitive assessments of truth and falsity for utterances of type-identical sentences (where no obviously indexical
expression in the sentence is responsible for such a change).

(3) The current positions in logical space

Although questions can be raised about some putative examples of
CSAs, it seems indisputable that in many cases they highlight a phenomenon which stands in need of explanation. The question then is
obviously how one chooses to accommodate that phenomenon. As
we will see below, Travis takes examples like these as the stepping off
point for a radically context-sensitive account of meaning, which he
attributes to the later Wittgenstein (e.g. see Wittgenstein *Philosophical
Investigations* §117, §514, Travis 1989, Chapters 1 & 6); however this is
just one possible response. In fact, in broad outline, it seems that there
are three possible directions to go in search of an explanation here:
first, one may seek to keep one's syntax and semantics as standardly
conceived of in formal semantics and look to pragmatics to take on
the explanatory burden (the position of minimalism); second, one may
keep semantics and pragmatics as standardly conceived and look to
syntax to carry the burden (indexicalism); third, one may seek a purely
semantic level explanation of these cases (contextualism, relativism,
and occasionalism). So let's look now at how each of these solutions is
supposed to work.

(3.1) Minimalism

As we saw above, minimalists allow context to contribute to semantic
content on some occasions. However they reject the idea that CSAs
show us that contextual contributions to semantic content run deeper
than the intuitively obvious context-sensitive expressions. Instead,
minimalists are minded to give a wholly pragmatic explanation of (at
least some) CSAs (for the full range of responses available to the minimalist, see Chapter 3). So, when we hear 'There is milk in the fridge'
as true relative to one context and false relative to another, with no

change in the state of the fridge, what we are sensitive to is held to be the pragmatic speaker meaning the agent communicates, not the semantic content which gives the literal meaning of the sentence itself. The parallel here is of course to Grice's explanation of implicature— just as someone may utter a sentence which literally means that *it is a lovely day* and thereby convey some quite different proposition (say that *it is a horrible day* if the speaker is being ironic), so a speaker can utter a sentence with a very general literal meaning, say just that *There is milk in the fridge,* and thereby pragmatically convey a different proposition, say that *There is milk in a form suitable for coffee in the fridge.* To explain a range of CSAs then the minimalist imposes a firm distinction between semantic content (attaching to sentences relativised to contexts of utterance) on one side and pragmatic speaker meaning (attaching to utterances) on the other. The rich contributions of context to content which we see in CSAs fall squarely, the minimalist claims, on the side of speaker meaning. However, the strategy of passing the explanatory burden (as far as CSAs are concerned) over to pragmatics in order to preserve the commitment to (i–iv) above has not met with universal approval. So we might ask what other avenues are open to us in the light of CSAs?

(3.2) Indexicalism[16]

Indexicalism shares two foundational assumptions with minimalism— it assumes that semantic content is propositional (tenet (i)) and that it is wholly determined by lexico-syntactic form (tenet (ii)). Thus contextual contributions to semantic content must be limited to those

---

[16] We should note that what I am going to call 'indexicalism' here often goes under the title of 'contextualism', especially in debates about epistemic vocabulary; so, for instance, I would characterize DeRose's 1992 epistemic contextualism as epistemic indexicalism. Also, as we will see below, what Cappelen and Lepore 2005 call 'contextualism' I would prefer to call 'indexicalism'. Furthermore, Schaffer 2011, when concentrating solely on taste predicates and epistemic modals, defines 'contextualism' as any position which holds that the propositions expressed in these cases contains information about whose standards of taste are involved or whose epistemic state is in question. He then identifies two main versions of contextualism: 'indexicalism', by which he means the kind of predicate indexicalism I'll attribute below to Rothschild and Segal, and what he terms 'variabilism', which includes both Stanley-type approaches positing syntactically realized but phonetically null variables and what I'll below term 'contextualist' positions which posit syntactically unrealized but semantically demanded variables. Finally, what I'll below term 'semantic relativism' is labelled 'perspectivalism' by Schaffer and is grouped as belonging under the general heading of 'minimalism' since, as we will see, the approach agrees with mini-

licensed by syntactic elements. However, unlike minimalism, indexicalism seeks to offer a semantic level account of the changes in truth
value in CSAs, thus it aims to offer a semantics which fits our intuitive
judgements of content in a way which minimalism does not. These
two apparently opposing desiderata are met by rejecting the third
tenet of minimalism above (i.e. expanding the amount of lexico-
syntactically licensed context-sensitivity in our language). For an
indexicalist, if our intuitions suggest that the content of a sentence
shifts, in various respects, across shifts in context of utterance, then this
is compelling evidence for the existence of lexico-syntactic context-
sensitivity in that sentence. Exactly what form this additional syntactic
context-sensitivity takes is then a fairly open matter. For instance
Stanley 2002, 2005 argues that associated with each nominal are
two hidden, context-sensitive variables which are jointly responsible
for the kinds of shifts in truth-value we witness in CSAs (Stanley 2002
takes these variables to cohabit with the noun, while Stanley 2005
takes them to occupy their own distinct terminal node). In contrast to
this kind of hidden indexical view, Rothschild and Segal 2009 treat
predicate expressions themselves as context-sensitive. On this kind of
'predicate indexicalism' there is no need to posit phonetically hidden
indexicals, instead axioms are provided directly for predicates which
treat them as context-sensitive terms on a par with standard indexicals.
So, roughly, an utterance of 'That is red' in context c expresses a distinct syntactic item 'red$_c$' and an object satisfies 'red$_c$' iff it is red according to the contextual standard of redness operative in c.

Finally, it seems that we might opt not to posit hidden indexicals
nor to redefine expressions as indexicals, but rather to treat the properties terms express as the source of the additional context-sensitivity
witnessed in (at least some) CSAs. So for instance, Hawthorne 2004

---

malism on the existence of minimal propositions (though relativism/perspectivalism requires additional
parameters to move from this proposition to a truth-value).

So, what motivates my potentially confusing use of vocabulary? Well, a first point to note is that it is
simply not possible to use these terms in a way that coincides with all recent uses. For instance, contextualism as given by Recanati 2004 fits the characterization I propose in the next section, where it will be
argued that it is the possibility of free—i.e. not lexico-syntactically required—enrichment which is the
hallmark of contextualism (note also that Recanati 2004 uses 'indexicalism' for positions like Stanley's, as
I do, though Recanati 2010 labels Stanley-style positions 'I-minimalism'). My definition of 'contextualism' also seems to fit the profile of relevance theory, which is often taken as a paradigm example of a
contextualist approach (see Carston 2002). Finally, since the idea of hidden or covert indexicality predates
the contextualist-minimalist debate (e.g. in hidden-indexical treatments of belief reports) it seems better
to me to retain the old term indexicalism for this pre-established position and keep the newer term,
contextualism, for the newer idea of free pragmatic enrichment.

and Stanley 2005b treat epistemic vocabulary as picking out subject-sensitive properties. Whether or not someone knows that p is held to be due in part to their own practical situation: I might know that p in a low stakes context but fail to know that p in a high stakes one. Treating predicates as expressing context-sensitive properties increases the amount of context-sensitivity in our language and it does so, broadly speaking, via the syntax of the language (e.g. it is because a sentence contains the word 'know' that a sentence like 'Alfie knows that he has hands' can change in truth-value across changes in context of utterance). However note that (unlike other versions of indexicalism) this kind of property indexicalism need not be particularly syntactically revisionary. A Stanley- and Hawthorne-style account need at most amend the lexical entry for relevant expressions to reveal the context-sensitive nature of the properties picked out and indeed it need not even posit this degree of change (e.g. a disquotational axiom like ['know' means *know*] could appear unchanged in a property indexical theory).

Although they differ in details, all three of these positions seem to me to deserve classification as forms of indexicalism because all preserve the basic idea that context contributes to content only via something in the lexico-syntactic form of a sentence while maintaining that the phenomenon thrown up by CSAs must be explained at the semantic level. Thus indexicalists are driven to find syntactic or lexical context-sensitivity where we might not immediately expect it.[17]

(3.3) Contextualism

While indexicalism rejects one of minimalism's basic claims—that the class of lexical or otherwise syntactically marked context-sensitive items in a natural language is highly constrained—contextualism (also) rejects another. Specifically (as I construe it) contextualism rejects the second tenet of minimalism above, the idea that the route to semantic

---

[17] One reader suggested that it might be better to use the term 'variabilism' (see Schaffer 2011) for what I here call indexicalism, picking up on the idea that, in relying on binding arguments (of the kind to be looked at below, see §4) such positions argue for the existence of hidden variables. However, as noted above, I want to treat approaches like Stanley's (which do call for hidden variables) as belonging to the same overall camp as those which treat nouns as indexical expressions in their own right (as do Rothschild and Segal), yet in this latter case no hidden variables are posited. Thus in the context of this way of grouping positions I don't think using the label of 'variabilism' would be helpful.

content runs exclusively via lexico-syntactic elements.[18] According to contextualism, the standard mechanism for handling context-sensitivity (drawn from the framework developed by Kaplan and Perry and exploited to differing extents in minimalism and indexicalism) is radically inadequate. Instead, to properly account for the depth and range of context-sensitivity in the propositions we literally express on occasions of utterance, we must allow pragmatic features a much freer reign within the semantic realm (see Carston 2002, Recanati 2004). The proposal of contextualism is thus that pragmatic properties get to act *twice*: once in the usual Gricean, post-semantic way to deliver implicatures, but also once in a non-standard, inherently semantic way to deliver the proposition literally expressed by a sentence as relativized to a given context.[19] So where we have an intuitive change in content across changes in context, as in a CSA, the claim is that this can reflect a change in semantic content, even if there is no context-sensitive lexico-syntactic element which alone can explain this change. For context can contribute to semantic content *simply* because that is what is demanded by the context. I'll use the term 'free pragmatic enrichment' as the label for pragmatic effects on semantic content which are driven solely by pragmatic, contextual demands concerning appropriate interpretation, that is to say, for pragmatic effects on semantic content which are not required by any lexico-syntactic

---

[18] Note that Cappelen and Lepore 2005 define contextualism in a different way: for them, moderate contextualism is the view that some expressions, beyond the obvious, are context-sensitive, while radical contextualism is the claim that all expressions in a natural language are context-sensitive. The debate between minimalism and contextualism is thus construed as one about the *number* of context-sensitive expressions and not about the *mechanisms* of context-sensitivity. For reasons I've set out elsewhere (Borg 2007) I think this is not the most helpful way to frame the debate and I would instead retain the term 'indexicalism' for what they term radical/moderate contextualism; the issue is raised again in Chapter 3, §2.

[19] This is why I labelled the position 'dual pragmatics' in Borg 2004a. We should also note that the vocabulary here (as in so much of this debate) is tricky, for one could hold that semantic content is what one gets simply from paying attention to the lexico-syntactic features of a sentence, but maintain that this potentially falls short of truth-conditional or propositional content, with the latter being delivered only via pragmatic processing (i.e. one could reject the first assumption attributed to minimalism above). For instance, this is the way that Sperber and Wilson 1986 often frame the debate. Similarly we find Bach 2006 proposing what he terms 'radical minimalism' whereby semantic content is determined by lexicon and syntax, but what is thereby determined may fall short of a complete proposition. Although probably Sperber and Wilson and certainly Bach would object to the characterization of their positions as ones where pragmatics has non-syntactically triggered effects on semantics (instead characterizing it as having effects on *explicatures*—Sperber and Wilson's term—or *implicitures*—Bach's term), both would agree that pragmatic enrichment is at least sometimes necessary to arrive at a truth-evaluable content. To my mind, this warrants including both accounts in this section; see also Borg 2007. The issue of propositionalism will be returned to in Chapters 2 and 3.

element in the sentence.[20] So, when Odile utters 'There is milk in the fridge' in the first kind of scenario above, what she literally asserts may be that *there is milk in the fridge in a form suitable for coffee*—the context acts to enrich the proposition literally expressed even though this is not demanded by any lexico-syntactic element of the sentence. Thus the datum provided by CSAs is given semantic level explanation not by broadening the occasions on which appeal to the standard mechanisms of indexicality is made (as in indexicalism) but by altering our view of the way in which contextually determined content can enter into the semantic arena.

(3.4) Semantic Relativism

Our fourth move agrees in many ways with the earlier position of indexicalism, for it adopts a broadly Kaplan-Perry-style picture whereby sentences are true or false relative to a number of contextually determined parameters. Where it differs from indexicalism and contextualism (and why it is a more radical position than either of these two) is in the role played by contextually determined material. Specifically, while our previous accounts have treated contextually determined content as contributing to the proposition expressed by a sentence as uttered in a given context (with the disagreements being, first, how often this happens—the debate between minimalism and indexicalism—and, second, how it happens—the debate between minimalism/indexicalism and contextualism), the relativist account treats contextual material (in at least some cases) as contributing to the parameters against which a proposition is assessed for truth or falsity. Relativism, then, either rejects or insists on a more nuanced understanding of the first and third tenets of minimalism, namely that semantic content is propositional content and that there are only a limited number of context-sensitive expressions in natural language.[21]

---

[20] The term 'free pragmatic enrichment' is from Recanati 2004, see also his 2002: 316 discussion of 'top down' pragmatic effects. For further exploration of free enrichment and its relation to minimalism and contextualism, see Chapter 2, §5.

[21] Specifically, relativism rejects the first tenet of minimalism if by 'proposition' we mean a content which is truth-evaluable as it stands, without adversion to rich contextual parameters (parameters beyond, say, world and perhaps time). Relativism rejects the third tenet of minimalism if 'context-sensitive expression' is taken to include any expression whose evaluation requires appeal to contextual features (though, as we will see below, it is consistent with the third tenet if 'context sensitive term' is taken to mean expressions whose propositional contribution is contextually determined, as with standard indexicals).

To see how this proposal works consider the debate between eternal-ism and temporalism about propositions: according to advocates of eternalism propositions incorporate relevant times into their content.[22] So if I say 'Fido is hungry' at t_1, then the proposition I express can be thought of as consisting of three elements: <Fido, hunger, t_1>. (Nothing here turns on the suggestion that we treat propositions as actually consisting of objects, properties and times.) Asserting the same type sentence at a different time, t_2, results in a different proposition being expressed, one consisting of <Fido, hunger, t_2>. Advocates of temporalism, on the other hand, argue that propositional contents are themselves timeless: our two utterances of 'Fido is hungry' express one and the same proposition, simply consisting of the ordered pair <Fido, hunger>, what differs is the time against which the proposition should be evaluated for truth. In the first case, we get the value True if Fido is hungry at t_1, and in the second if he is hungry at t2. Both eternalism and temporalism then yield the same results, but in temporalism time features not as a part of the propositional content but as a parameter against which a propositional content is assessed. Following this model, then, and faced with CSAs, the advocate of relativism suggests increas-ing in some way the parameters usually accepted as relevant to deter-mining truth for a proposition.[23]

One way to account for CSAs on this approach would be to allow a massive increase in the number of relevant parameters. For instance, there could be a contextually determined parameter of richness against which the unique propositional content expressed by the sentence 'Jill is rich' could be assessed for truth or falsity. Thus one and the same proposition, that *Jill is rich*, might be true with respect to one contex-tually determined parameter (say, rich-for-average-Senegalese-citizens) but false relative to a different one (say rich-for-UK-royalty). On this sort of approach we might end up with every (or perhaps almost every) term requiring a distinct parameter against which an utterance of it in a sentence could be assessed: an utterance of 'That is a table'

---

[22] See MacFarlane 2009 for a similar introduction to his position of 'nonindexical contextualism' and Recanati 2008 for a discussion of the connections between temporalism and relativism.

[23] We should note that the motivation for semantic relativism has not in general come from considera-tion of CSAs. Though these arguments are to the fore in some cases (cf. Predelli 2005), other proponents of relativism focus their attention on the predicates of taste and the possibility of faultless disagreement (see Kölbel 2003, Lasersohn 2005), on debates about epistemic vocabulary (see MacFarlane 2005) or on future contingents (see MacFarlane 2003).

might be sensitive to different parametric values for *tablehood*, 'She is my wife' might be sensitive to different contextually determined standards for counting as a wife, and 'milk in the fridge' could be true or false relative to different parametric values for counting as containing milk.[24] Alternatively, one might seek to add just one or two more abstract parameters which could serve to cover all the more specific instances required. So for instance MacFarlane 2007a: 246 (see also Predelli 2005) suggests:

> The 'counts-as' parameter is so called because it fixes what things have to be like in order to *count as* having the property of tallness (or any other property) at a circumstance of evaluation.

So, we have one proposition, say *that Jill is rich*, but this is true/false depending on whether Jill *counts as* rich in the relevant context.

Finally, a third version of the relativism approach would be to posit an added parameter which makes reference to the person assessing a given proposition. In this way, we would not require public parameters (such as a contextually salient standard of richness) set within a context of utterance, but would instead allow that propositions are true or false only relative to an assessor (and their standards). So, for instance, the proposition expressed by a single utterance of 'Star Wars is good' could be true as assessed by me and false when assessed by you. Notice that the claim is not (the fairly innocuous one) that when I utter the sentence I'm asserting the proposition that *Star Wars is good according to me*, while you are asserting the different proposition that *Star Wars is good according to you*. This approach would be tantamount to indexicalism or contextualism. Rather the claim is that the unique content of a sentence relativized to a single context of utterance can be true if assessed by me and false if assessed by you. This makes content relative not merely to additional parameters from within the context of utterance (as do the first and second versions of relativism canvassed above) but to features within a context of assessment. So, for instance, MacFarlane 2003 holds that the sentence 'There will be a sea-battle tomorrow' is neither true nor false when uttered, but it becomes true or false when someone evaluates that utterance the following day. In this way, we don't simply have a non-standard parameter for truth

---

[24] MacFarlane 2009 notes this proliferation but doesn't see it as overly damaging, at least when construed merely as a claim about the number of parameters semantics might require.

(like, say, a standard of taste), rather we have it that a single utterance content can shift in truth-value across different acts of assessment.[25] This version of the relativist view, then, gives rise to a kind of radical or full-blown relativism and we should note that moves to motivate relativism are likely to differ depending on how radical the relativist view espoused is (see Kölbel 2008: 4; Recanati 2008: 44–5; we will return to the question of the motivation for relativism in §4.3).

However, regardless of the number of parameters proposed, or their precise nature, the key idea remains the same: a single proposition is assessed for truth on each occasion, with what changes being something in the contextually determined parameters against which that proposition is assessed for truth. It is because context matters for assessments of truth though it doesn't contribute to propositional content that the relativist proposal counts as increasing the amount of context-sensitivity in our theory but *not* as increasing indexicality.

(3.5) Occasionalism

The final approach to be outlined in response to the phenomenon thrown up by CSAs follows the approaches of contextualism and relativism in counselling a purely semantic level explanation. However it differs from these accounts in how far it is willing to move from the model of meaning deployed in previous accounts (see Travis 1989, 2008, Dancy 2004, Chapter 11). For whereas all our previous approaches preserved aspects of the standard formal model for explaining context-sensitivity, occasionalism embraces a very different way of thinking about meaning and its relation to context. According to occasionalism there is simply no such thing as determinate content outside a context, for it is only in use that words and concepts come to have particular conditions of application. As Travis (1985: 187–8) writes:

[T]ypically, an (e.g.) English expression is such that, with its meaning (unambiguously) fixed, there are a variety of distinct (perhaps better: distinguishable) things to be said in using it on some production of it or other... If there

---

[25] MacFarlane 2007: 22: 'To be a relativist, then, is not to relativize propositional truth to "nonstandard parameters" like standards of taste, but to adopt a certain view about how the *accuracy* of certain acts or states is to be assessed'. See also Kölbel 2008: 4.

is nothing which is *said* in a sentence, in particular, nothing which is said to be so, then, one would think, the sentence as such, even under the best of circumstances, could not be true. That not being its business, one would also expect that there could not be a (substantive) condition for its truth ... Given that a variety of distinct things might be said to be *so* in some speaking of the sentence (at a fixed time), no one of these, and so it seems, nothing, is what we could sensibly require to *be* so if the sentence, as such, is to be true. There would seem no motivated way of selecting some one particular condition for the truth of the sentence.

This view of meaning is one which Travis 2008: 254 traces back to the later-Wittgenstein:

The point of the discussion of language games, with which [*Philosophical Investigations*] begins, is that naming, or referring ... underdetermines conditions for correctness of wholes, notably, where relevant, conditions for their truth. Wholes with given referents, embedded in different language games, would be true under any of many very different sets of conditions ... [T]rue and false are in the first instance evaluations of particular historical events—speakings of words on particular occasions, in particular circumstances—and of the fittingness of the words for those circumstances.[26]

While this may sound at first blush like contextualism, the position is in fact more radical than many under the contextualist banner would wish to endorse.[27] For Travis takes underdetermination to be a feature of representation in general, hence it holds for language and for thought. There can thus be no idea of 'filling out' a linguistically expressed content to get to the complete content the speaker had in mind, for this kind of context-independent content is non-existent. One reason for thinking this is that, just as the overt elements of the utterance are open to different contextual understandings, so any attempt to fill out or

[26] See also Dancy 2004: 197. For the Wittgensteinian connection, see for instance *Philosophical Investigations* 432: 'Every sign by *itself* seems dead. *What* gives it life?—In use it is alive.' There are of course interesting exegetical questions here concerning how accurate it is to call occasionalism 'Wittgensteinian' (see Bridges 2010); however, I will leave these exegetical issues to one side

[27] We might note that Cappelen and Lepore 2005 take Travis to be a central proponent of what they term 'radical contextualism' (which they define by the claim that all terms in natural language are context-sensitive). However (as indicated in Borg 2004a: 224) I think that contextualism and occasionalism are best held apart, for despite similarities in the kinds of arguments deployed, Travis' account is better seen from a Wittgensteinian perspective rather than a contextualist one. As discussed below, contextualists assume there is such a thing as determinate context-independent content, their complaint is that lexico-syntactic content alone falls short of such determinacy. However for an occasionalist this is the wrong way to look at things, since content per se emerges only in use (see here Wittgenstein's discussion of 'shadows', reported in Moore 1954).

expand what is expressed will itself be open to different contextual understandings. So, if we have an utterance of 'The apple is red', which a contextualist might claim expresses a contextually enriched proposition like *the apple is red on its skin*, Travis' concern is that the contextual expansion *on its skin* is no less in need of contextual interpretation than the original elements were. As he writes (1989: 36): 'only in appropriate circumstances do words make sense; only in a suitable home or in suitable surroundings do they express a thought with content definite enough to permit, *inter alia*, evaluation in truth-involving terms'.[28]

These five positions give us, I think, the main responses to the issues thrown up by CSAs. As I conceive of them, they lie on a scale moving from a pretty standard formal perspective at one end through to a pretty standard use-based perspective at the other.[29] In the current arena theorists have, it seems, managed to combine bits of a formal approach with bits of a use-based approach and thereby to hold out the promise of a

[28] Or again, as Travis 2008: 152 writes in response to Cappelen and Lepore: 'For [a radical contextualist (RC)] semantics is emphatically not in the business of predicting what proposition would be expressed in some given utterance of a sentence. Nor do RCs think such things *are* predictable (as a function of a set of parameters, for example). Exactly not... To an RC, such an idea simply fails to see what the phenomenon of occasion-sensitivity in fact is'.

[29] That these positions lie on some kind of scale is not a novel idea (see, for instance, Recanati's excellent overview of essentially the same territory in *Literal Meaning*); less well explored, I think, is the idea of the instability of the mid-ground in this scale, to be explored below. It may however be, as a reader objected, that speaking of these positions as lying on a single, one-dimensional scale ultimately risks oversimplifying matters here. For as we have seen (and will continue to see in the next section) the dimensions along which the competitor positions differ from minimalism are themselves very different. Thus the notion of nearness to/distance from minimalism/occasionalism can be no more than a rough, intuitive heuristic. That said, however, it does seem clear to me that indexicalism is much closer in spirit to minimalism than other competitor accounts, though perhaps the differences between minimalism on the one hand and contextualism and relativism on the other are too disparate to be shoe-horned into a single scale. For while, as we will see below, contextualism steps away from minimalism/indexicalism by allowing elements from a context of utterance to contribute to semantic content even when they are not syntactically demanded (i.e. it rejects minimalism's second clause that semantic content be fully realized by lexico-syntactic features), relativism keeps the idea that all semantic content is lexico-syntactically realized but maintains that that semantic content is then only truth-evaluable relative to additional contextual parameters (thus rejecting or refining the first and third tenets of minimalism, see n.34). So a better model might be to think of the positions as related in the following way:

Be this as it may, however, the central argument of this chapter remains that any step away from minimalism on the grounds of arguments about intuitive speech act content alone is destined ultimately to deliver one directly to the door of occasionalism.

seductive account of natural language semantics, one which both respects the idea of a formal core to meaning but which might nevertheless cleave tightly to intuitions about communicated content. Now of course there is much more we could do to spell out each of these positions, including looking in proper detail at the arguments each can muster in its own defence. However, instead of doing this, I want to ask a more general question concerning the stability of the positions between minimal semantics and occasionalism. My worry is that, having bought into the intuitions which motivate use-based theories sufficiently to abandon standard formal semantics, the accounts on offer can give us no principled reason to stop short of a full-blown use-theoretic approach. If this is right then it may turn out that, despite the initial impression of a range of possible positions here, it is really the old warhorses of formal semantics and use-based theories of meaning which remain standing.

(4) Reassessing the middle ground

As I framed the debate in the last section, minimalism and occasionalism lie at opposite ends of the spectrum on accounts of linguistic meaning: minimalism holds that there is a meaning for sentences (relativized to contexts of utterance to accommodate genuine, syntactically marked context-sensitivity) and this meaning is truth-evaluable or propositional. This minimal semantic content is (at least for sentences not containing genuinely context-sensitive expressions) insensitive to the use to which a word or sentence is being put. Occasionalism, on the other hand, holds that meaning emerges only within a context of use, there is necessarily no such thing as 'that which a sentence says to be so' (Travis 2008: 151). The positions which lie between minimalism and occasionalism can then be seen as progressive movements away from the view of formal semantics that it is sentences (relativized to contexts of utterance) which possess semantic content and towards the Wittgensteinian view that meaning is properly a property of utterances (i.e. of language in use). So indexicalism takes a small step along this road by preserving the idea that semantic content is wholly lexico-syntactically determined but relaxing the range of expressions which are treated as genuine indexicals in natural language. Contextualism takes a much bigger step and allows pragmatically determined features to contribute to the proposition expressed by a sentence as uttered in a given context *whenever* they are required (whether this requirement comes from syntactic elements or purely contextual needs). The relativist then takes a bigger step again by locating the context sensitivity in question not within the content of a proposition at all, but as part of a contextually determined framework within which questions of truth and falsity can be asked (perhaps going so far as to allow that this framework can differ across acts of assessment, if a full-blown relativist position is adopted). Thus it seems as if we have a range of options for handling the way in which context contributes to content (at least so far as CSAs are concerned) between hard-nosed formalism on one side and full-blooded use theoretic approaches to meaning on the other. Furthermore, given that in philosophy, as in life, compromise is often the best policy it may well seem that one of these intermediate positions gives us the most plausible solution to the phenomenon revealed by CSAs. However I want to suggest that this appearance may be illusory for, regardless of the specific arguments which have been given for and against different intermediary positions, there is reason to think that the entire middle ground in this debate is unstable.

(4.1) Indexicalism

Turning first to indexicalism, I think a first point to note with respect to this approach is that it is not, in principle, inimical to minimalism in the way that contextualism and occasionalism are. For indexicalism seeks to preserve the central tenet of formal semantics that there is an exclusively lexico-syntactic route to semantic content, whereas these other approaches reject this claim. In principle, then, the idea of positing hidden indexicals, or relocating expressions within the category of context-sensitive terms, or treating properties as context-sensitive is something a minimalist could allow. The issue for the minimalist instead comes, I believe, with the question of the motivation for, and following this, the scope of application for, this kind of manoeuvre. However, regardless of whether or not an appeal to indexicalism might be warranted in some limited cases (a point I will return to in Chapter 3), still minimalists and occasionalists alike agree that it does not provide a plausible explanation in the majority of cases. Thus Travis 2008: 115 writes:

There are several respects in which the present phenomena are *unlike* central cases where the parameter approach seems promising. One difference is this. In central cases, such as 'I' and 'now', pointing to given parameters seems to be a part of the terms meaning what they do. It is a part of the meaning of 'I', and its use in English, that it is a device for a speaker to speak of himself. That suggests speakers as a relevant parameter....By contrast, it is not part of what 'green' means, so far as we can tell, that speakings of it speak of, or refer to, such-and-such parameters. If its contribution, on a speaking, to what is said *is* a function of some parameters—say, implausibly, the speaker's intentions—saying so is not part of what 'green' means. The parameter approach does not *automatically* suggest itself here as it did with 'I'.

Cappelen and Lepore in their 2005 defence of minimalism reinforce this intuitive rejection of the indexicality approach by setting out tests for genuinely indexical expressions which they argue standardly context-sensitive terms (words like 'this' and 'I') pass while terms not standardly treated as context-sensitive (words like 'man' and 'red') fail. Thus they argue there are strong reasons to resist the claim that these latter words are really disguised indexicals. (For some concerns about the tests proposed by Cappelen and Lepore see Gross 2006, Cappelen and Hawthorne 2009.)

However the point I would like to make here is that there also seems to be a somewhat more abstract concern with indexicalism, for it seems to need both to take CSAs seriously and yet to fail to take them quite seriously enough. On the first point, indexicalism counsels taking CSAs seriously for it is these kinds of examples which push us away from the intuitive picture of a fairly limited class of indexicals in natural language and towards a much more pervasive model of the context-dependence of our language. Thus it is CSAs which push us to a picture where syntax is largely hidden from view and context-sensitivity is endemic in language. However having taken them seriously in this way, indexicalism then suggests that the appeal to context which CSAs throw up can be entirely handled by syntactic means, but I think we need to ask what could motivate this claim.

First, I think we need to ask why the indexicalist wants to hold on to the idea (from formal semantics) that lexico-syntactic elements fully determine semantic content. For this principle has some bite while syntax is taken to be relatively objectively specifiable, so that it can provide a clear constraint on what can count as semantic content and in turn can play the role of an epistemic guide to that content.[30] Yet on the indexicalist picture this independence of syntax is undermined, for on this model syntactic claims are in part determined by semantic intuitions: we posit hidden indexicals or move nouns to the class of indexicals, etc. because we want to capture the intuitions about meaning thrown up in CSAs.[31] But if syntactic form is, in this respect, dictated by semantic intuitions then there doesn't seem to be any point in hanging on to the idea that syntax determines semantics: syntax doesn't serve to constrain what we can find at the semantic level (since, crudely speaking, we are allowed to fiddle with our syntax to get it to deliver what we want in our semantics) nor can it provide an independent epistemic route to semantics since the relevant syntax is covert and can be established (if at all) only by using fairly recherché tests. Indeed, it is worth noting that at least some indexicalists, such as Rothschild and Segal, offer no motivation for a syntactically context-sensitive analysis of words like 'red' beyond the existence of CSAs; syntactic analysis in these cases apparently depends *entirely* on semantic intuitions.

Of course, it must also be noted that other indexicalists, most notably Stanley, have gone to some lengths to offer independent motivation for the variables they posit. The main argument here is Stanley's 'binding argument' (e.g. Stanley 2000) which states that the variables

---

[30] We might also note that the idea that syntax determines semantics is weight-bearing in attempts to specify a language module as a purely computational system; see Borg 2004a for one such attempt.

[31] One objection here might be that it is a mistake to think of syntax in general as not being determined by semantic intuitions, after all arguments for proposed syntactic analyses turn at heart on which readings of a sentence speakers take to be available and which they take to be unlawful. However, while this point is well-taken and we must indeed be careful not to overstate the objectivity of syntax, it also seems that the kinds of intuitions appealed to in standard syntactic arguments are of a different order to the ones in play in CSAs and related arguments. In the former case, we appeal to type-level intuitions: can a sentence of this form be interpreted in this way? Can an expression in this position give rise to this kind of reading? So, for instance, in an agentless passive such as 'The boat sank', there is a debate to be had about whether or not there is a hidden, syntactically represented argument for the agent. Evidence in support of this claim includes the fact that addition of *by*-phrases is licensed (e.g. 'the boat was sunk by the captain') and that such passives can control PRO subjects (e.g. 'the boat was sunk to collect the insurance'); see Roeper 1987, Stanley 2002b, Glanzberg 2009. This sort of evidence can be collected for sentences at the type level and no appeal to a specific context of utterance is required. On the other hand, the semantic intuitions elicited in CSAs seem far more context-bound (e.g. is an utterance of 'Jill is tall' true in a context where two-year-olds are under discussion, is it true when a speaker is intending to talk about basketball players?)

posited by indexicalism must be syntactically real since they are available for binding in sentences containing quantifiers. So, for instance, a natural reading of 'Every student answered every question' is *every student x answered every question y put to x*, but to get this reading, the suggestion is, we need to suppose that there are bound variables in the structure of quantified noun phrases. However, it seems that this argument plays something of a post-facto role in Stanley's work: it is supposed to provide support for the existence of the hidden variables which semantic intuition (in the form of responses to CSAs) tells us must be there (see, e.g. Stanley 2005: 235). So it is intuitions about meaning which lead to claims about syntax and this seems to undermine the idea that syntax is independent of semantics (in the kind of way which would make trying to hang on to the idea that syntax determines semantics worthwhile).

Furthermore, it is not at all clear that the syntactic arguments to which Stanley appeals in support of his hidden variables can do the work required. For instance, in general, binding seems to be the weakest and most easily manufactured of all syntactic relations, thus in lieu of any stronger syntactic evidence we may doubt that binding alone can show syntactic realization.[32] This concern is reinforced by Cappelen and Lepore's 2005: 74 observation that the binding argument over-generates, e.g. indicating incorrectly that there are contextual variables operating in mathematical predicates, since one can say 'Everywhere I go, $2 + 2 = 4$'.[33] Responding to this concern, Stanley 2005: 244 appears to suggest that arithmetical predicates do not contain bound variables as they do not in fact give rise to bound readings. However, in responding in this way, as Collins 2007: 833 notes, Stanley runs the risk of slipping from a syntactic support for his variables to a semantic one:

[Stanley] suggests that arithmetical nominals do not contain covert variables because their semantics do not require domain restriction. But we are after

---

[32] Schaffer 2011 appeals to three tests: binding, control and collection. However, not all three tests are available in all cases and he treats binding as the most important of the three.

[33] Soames 2009: 12–15 notes another important respect in which Stanley's argument would seem to overgenerate, for since it holds that all nouns carry hidden variables it will be the case that even a quantifier phrase with a long, complex restricting clause will contain more information than is available at the surface level. Yet Soames notes (2009: 15): 'That strikes me as redundant...Of course, no matter how long [the restricting clause] is, we could always have said more, but surely this is no reason to think that we have in effect already said more by including unpronounced variables in our sentence.'

a *syntactic* reason to think that covert variables exist. Even if one were to sideline the other problems, which look quite recalcitrant, to posit an empty adjunct to capture a semantic reading is not to furnish a syntactic reason. Overall, Stanley's argument here, as far as I can see, is premised upon the silent assumption that the nature of syntax should be read off our stable semantic intuitions.

As Collins puts the worry later (2007: 842) 'The problem for the proposal is that, *derivationally*, the [variable] complex has no place in LF structure: it is parachuted in from semantics'. Our first concern for indexicalism, then, is with the nature of the evidence it invokes to justify the increase in syntactic context-sensitivity: fundamentally, the reasons for the syntactic posits are semantic ones (i.e. the drive to come out with a semantic interpretation which matches our intuitions of what a speaker uttering the sentence has said) but such semantic reasons are simply the wrong kinds of reasons to motivate syntactic claims.

Secondly, as has been stressed by Stephen Neale, it is not clear what the added syntactic complexity which indexicalism posits adds to the explanatory story here—once we allow that it is pragmatics which is in the driving seat for delivering content for sentences like 'the apple is red', what does it add to require that these pragmatic processes be chained to syntactic constituents? As Neale 2007: 82 writes:

However we proceed, the heavy lifting is done by pragmatic inference because interpreting utterances of sentences containing aphonic 'indexicals' is a pragmatic, richly inferential matter, the product of integrating linguistic and non-linguistic information. The only substantive difference between the way the [contextualist] sees the process of identifying the proposition expressed and the way someone postulating aphonic elements in syntax sees it is that the latter is just *insisting* that the search for and integration of contextual information in the interpretation process is triggered syntactically.[34]

Yet as Neale notes, there is no argument to show that contextual contributions *must* be triggered syntactically. Furthermore, as stressed by Cappelen and Lepore 2005, if CSAs provide one's sole evidence for which expressions deserve a context-sensitive lexical analysis, then it

---

[34] An *aphonic* element is a syntactic item which lacks phonetic properties. See also Bach 2007: §III.5

appears one will be led inescapably to the position that *all* (or perhaps almost all) expressions are context-sensitive, for it seems that one can generate a CSA for absolutely any expression in our language.[35] There is thus, they contend, a very slippery slope from the move to treat, say, 'tall' or 'flat' as context-sensitive (where this treatment is motivated solely by CSAs) to the position where 'red' and 'man' and 'thirteen' are also context-sensitive. Yet, if indexicalism ends up (as it does for Stanley 2002, and for Rothschild and Segal 2009) claiming that context-sensitivity is endemic in natural language (e.g. claiming that all noun phrases have a meaning which is fixed only within a context of utterance) then it once again becomes extremely hard to see what the motivation could be for the brute demand that all context-sensitivity be entirely syntactically managed. Rather than redefining all expressions as syntactically context-sensitive, why not move to an account of natural language semantics which allows context to contribute to content in a richer, more systemic way?

So, the thought is, viewed from a relatively abstract vantage point where we see how indexicalism relates to minimalism on one side and contextualism on the other, it looks as if the ground it seeks to occupy is slippery. If we take CSAs seriously enough to shift us from minimalism then it becomes obscure why we should hang on to the fundamental principle that lexico-syntactic structure fully fixes semantic content, but without some way to ground this principle, indexicalism comes to look like a purely stipulative stopping-off point en route to contextualism. The moral, I think, is that if we are prepared to take CSAs seriously then there is little reason to think that we will find our feet again until we hit contextualism.

(4.2) Contextualism

Yet just as they disapprove of moves to enrich syntax to accommodate CSAs, so advocates of minimalism and occasionalism also agree that contextualism is not the way to go. The problem is the one already

---

[35] This is the argument, which runs throughout Cappelen and Lepore 2005, that what they term 'moderate contextualism' (the view that some expressions not standardly analysed as context-sensitive are in fact context-sensitive) is destined to collapse into what they term radical contextualism (the view that all expressions are in fact context-sensitive). This argument will be looked at in more detail in relation to incompleteness arguments in Chapter 3, §3.1.

noted in the introduction of occasionalism: for any putative sharpening, *s*, of a proposition, *p*, that sharpening will itself be open to divergent interpretations. Thus *s* itself will stand in need of a contextual sharpening, but this appears to launch us into a vicious regress. Considering his example of Odile's utterance of 'There is milk in the fridge', Travis 1989: 23 writes:

> In deciding that Odile spoke truly of the refrigerator, we solved one problem, or a few, about how to sort things into those containing milk and those not. But in principle there may always be more. In fact, we can easily think of countless more...On the evidence [a contextually determined understanding] Q will not be a [speaker/S]-insensitive property either. Nor will we make further progress towards expunging S-use sensitivity by repeating the move and speaking of some property attributed on occasion in speaking of Q.[36]

According to the contextualist there is determinate, context-insensitive content to be had, their objection is just that the content provided via the lexico-syntactic constituents of the sentence alone isn't it. Yet minimalists and occasionalists agree that, if you are swayed by the phenomenon thrown up by CSAs at all, then this is a reason to think that no (or perhaps almost no) content offered in a context-independent manner will ever reach the standard of a complete proposition. For instance, the contextualist will want to claim that, though a sentence like 'the apple is red' expresses an incomplete or inappropriate content if we look just to the lexico-syntactic constituents of the sentence, there is a complete and appropriate proposition to be had (perhaps at the level of thought). The task then is to get from the former to the latter.

However, the pressure here concerns how we specify that putatively complete and appropriate content: if it is spelt out by refining terms or adding content (so that this token of the sentence conveys, say, that *the apple is red on its skin*) then, as noted above, this additional content no less than the former stands in need of contextual precisification. On the other hand, if one holds that we need only expand the content so far and no further (e.g. so that no further precisification of 'on its skin' is needed) this can only be because a contextual understanding of the added content is presumed. Yet this second move is tantamount

---

[36] This line of argument is echoed directly in some pro-minimalist writings, for instance Borg 2004a: 241.

to adopting a Travis-style occasionalism for added or expanded material and, it would seem, occasionalism at one remove is still occasionalism. If our aim is to stop the content a sentence expresses from being shifty then it doesn't seem possible to achieve this just by expanding the propositional content in some context-invariant way. Minimalists take this as a reason to resist the sway of CSAs, occasionalists take it as a reason to reject the standard view of content, but both positions agree that accepting CSAs at face value *and* thinking that context-sensitivity can subsequently be excised by enriching propositional content is inherently unstable.

Furthermore, we might wonder about the ability of an approach like contextualism to draw a boundary between semantic content and purely pragmatic, speaker-meant content. That is to say, how might the theory ensure that the (possibly incomplete) logical form or propositional fragment which it takes to be recoverable from the lexico-syntactic form of the sentence alone gets enriched or filled out up to the point of semantic content but no further? (This concern is raised in Stanley 2002.) For instance, take the sentence 'I've had lunch' uttered in response to the question 'Shall we go to the café?' For this utterance, what makes it the case that the explicature (Sperber and Wilson's 1986 term)—i.e. the pragmatically enriched literal content of the utterance—is:

> i. I've had lunch recently.

rather than:

> ii. I've had lunch recently enough to make going to a café to eat currently unappealing.

Or again, if one utters 'there is a petrol station around the corner' in response to an inquiry from a car driver, does one, from the contextualist point of view, literally express:

> i. there is a petrol station relatively close around the corner.

or:

> ii. there is an open petrol station relatively close around the corner.

or any one of a number of other possible, contextually salient completions? Obviously how we interpret the explicature (i.e. whether we take it to be of the form of (i) or (ii) or some other alternative) will affect what we take a speaker to be literally committed to by her utterance. For instance, one might be tempted to treat the additional information in (ii) as something implied rather than directly asserted by the speaker, however since both interpretations count, in some sense, as an expansion of the logical form of the original sentence, we clearly need additional reasons to stop the latter expansions from counting as part of the explicature. Some contextualists have suggested that, as well as counting as an expansion of logical form, explicature content must satisfy what they call the 'scope embedding test', whereby elements added to content must fall under logical operators like negation (see Recanati 1993: 269–74). However, it is far from clear that these two conditions—expansion and scope embedding—alone can do the work required.[37] Divorced from the constraint that semantically relevant material be exhausted by what we can find in the syntax of the sentence it is quite unclear that we have the resources to draw the kind of semantics/pragmatics boundary which both minimalists and contextualists want to. Thus it seems once again that contextualism risks getting sucked into a kind of standard use-based approach to meaning (where issues of the semantics/pragmatics divide dissolve, to be replaced with issues about, say, typical versus non-typical kinds of usage) from which it seemed, initially at least, to hold itself apart.

(4.3) Semantic Relativism

Finally then, what of the view that we should add parameters to account for CSAs? Well, again the concern I have is one of stability, for there are murky issues concerning how relativism relates both to minimalism and occasionalism and to the other intermediary positions like indexicalism and contextualism. To start with minimalism, it is important to note that minimalism and relativism *agree* on a central point, namely that sentences are in the business of expressing propositions and that every well-formed, non-indexical sentence is capable of

---

[37] Indeed Carston suggests that there can be no failsafe tests for determining the explicature/implicature divide. Thus while the tests proposed may provide useful heuristics, they do not constitute principles for determining explicatures. She writes (2002: 191): 'I was (and still am) of the view that the communicative principle of relevance itself or, more particularly, the comprehension strategy that follows from it, effects a sorting of pragmatic inferences into contributions to the proposition expressed (explicature) and implicatures.'

expressing a proposition. (It is this factor that leads Schaffer 2011 to place the two positions together under the label of 'minimalism'.) So, according to both minimalism and relativism a sentence like 'Flintoff is ready' expresses a proposition without any contextual enrichment. Since many have taken the existence of minimal propositions to be the fundamental explanatory debt of minimalism, this in itself may make some feel uncomfortable with relativism. Furthermore, since both accounts agree on the existence of minimal propositions, there will need to be clear explanatory advantages in adopting the more complex, context-driven mechanisms of relativism over the more austere model of minimalism.

Of course, however, there are supposed to be just such clear advantages to relativism, for the suggestion is that the approach can handle phenomena which floor minimalism, such as CSAs and the existence of faultless disagreement cases (where two people are held to genuinely disagree but where neither party seems to be at fault, e.g. A's assertion that 'Riding roller coasters is fun' and B's contradictory statement that 'Riding roller coasters is not fun'). Relativism holds out the promise of capturing these kinds of features of our linguistic practices because of the stance it takes on propositions: unlike the classical view of propositions assumed by minimalism, according to the relativist propositions are not true or false as they stand, rather they can be evaluated for truth only against a range of contextual parameters. However, one fundamental question we need to ask of the relativist at this stage is how viable their notion of a proposition actually is: what, we might wonder, is left of the notion of a proposition if it is not something truth-evaluable in its own right?[38] The concern is that, stripped of claims of truth-evaluability, the distinction between the relativist's proposition and the contextualists propositional radical risks shrinking to nothing. So, an initial worry for the ground relativism seeks to occupy is that while initially it may seem

[38] Certainly the content we are left with prior to the provision of parameters looks less than complete in the sense adumbrated in Frege. This would seem to be Evans' 1985: 349 (quoted in Recanati 2008: 44) concern with the relativist framework in general: 'To say that the sentence type 'Socrates is sitting'. . . expresses a complete meaning seems to imply that . . . to know what assertion is being made by an utterance of a tensed sentence all you need to know is which tensed sentence was uttered; you do not need further information to tie the sentence down to a particular time . . . It would follow that such an 'assertion' would not admit of a stable evaluation as correct or incorrect; if we are to speak of correctness or incorrectness at all, we must say that the assertion is correct at some times and not at others'. This point is taken up again in Chapter 3, §2.

too close to minimalism—inheriting what many have taken to be the basic error of minimalism, namely the assumption that all well-formed sentences express propositions—when we look at the relativist's notion of a proposition more closely it seems to blur into the contextualist's notion of a formally determined fragment of meaning, a propositional radical.

This risk of blurring with contextualism and indexicalism also emerges in other ways. For instance, considering the first version of the relativist view (which introduced a plethora of distinct parameters), we need to ask, for any sentence, 'why are just these parameters relevant to an assessment of its truth?' and the answer to this question must surely look (at least in part) to the lexical elements of the sentence (roughly, we need a parameter of redness when a sentence contains the word 'red'). Thus, where we previously had a general form for a circumstance of evaluation, against which all sentences were to be assessed, we now have a picture whereby the form of a circumstance of evaluation will differ from sentence to sentence depending on their syntactic and lexical structure. Yet this idea—that it is the words of our language which are responsible for calling contextual features into play, via their introduction of a contextual parameter— might make us think that, at heart, we are treating these terms as indexicals but merely stipulating that (unlike classic indexicals) in these cases the context-sensitive dimension of the expression falls outside propositional content. This is not to say, of course, that this variety of relativism is impossible but to note that, since it places the burden for triggering added parameters at the lexical/syntactic level, it seems to demand a motivation which reveals it as genuinely superior to mere indexicalism.

One way we might seek to motivate this relativist view in opposition to indexicalism or contextualism is via appeal to the evidence surrounding indirect speech reports. So MacFarlane 2009 notes (following Cappelen and Lepore 2005) that we tend to report claims of knowledge homophonically, even when epistemic standards have shifted. So, if Sam asserts 'I know that p', it seems one can later report this with 'Sam said that he knew that p' even if there has been a shift between utterance and report from a low stakes to a high stakes context. Yet if the indexicalist/contextualist view is right, using 'know' across these kinds of shifts in context will result in different propositions being expressed (since context affects propositional content on these views) and this leaves our practice of homophonic reporting unexplained. Furthermore, accounts which posit a change in propositional content would seem to entail that the following kind of dialogue should be acceptable, when in fact it seems odd (MacFarlane 2009: 239–41):

Sam (in low stakes context):	I know my car is parked out back.
Barry (in high stakes context):	Sam said he knew his car was parked out back.
Janet (in conversation with Barry):	No he didn't!

There is, then, some evidence in favour of the view that context contributes a parameter required for evaluation without thereby infecting semantic content. However, as MacFarlane himself also points out (2007: §4.1), other features of our cross-context linguistic practices seem to be less well captured by these kinds of more moderate versions of the relativist view.

For instance, asked if she knows she has hands, Jill might say that she does, but then when exposed to sceptical arguments she might ultimately claim 'I guess I was wrong, I didn't really know I had hands', or the sceptic and the non-sceptic might debate the issue, with one claiming to know that p while the other rejects this, asserting that the non-sceptic doesn't know that p. Now one might think that the relativist view in general can explain these differences by maintaining that it is one and the same proposition which is asserted in a high or a low stakes context, with what changes being the parameter against which one counts as knowing. Yet if this is the claim then there is little more real disagreement in these cases than on the indexicalist/contextualist picture. For while, on the relativist view, it is one and the same proposition in play in all cases, since our protagonists accept different parametric values for knowing there is no room for genuine disagreement or explanation of retractions. When Jill says 'I guess I was wrong, I didn't know that I had hands' what she is really saying is that, relative to the standards of knowledge in a high stakes context, it is false to say that she knows that she has hands, but that doesn't in any way impugn a claim to knowledge in a low stakes context (thus her claim that 'I was wrong' is unexplained). To capture all the facts about indirect discourse, retraction and disagreement, then, MacFarlane 2007 argues that we need to adopt full-blown assessor-relativism (whereby the truth-value of the content a sentence expresses is relativized not merely to additional features in the context of utterance, but also to features within the context of assessment, so that we lose entirely the notion of absolute truth for linguistic contents), but also to maintain that there are some contexts where if A accepts p and B rejects p, then it cannot be that both A and B are accurate in their judgements.[39] Whether this position is defensible or not, the point to notice here is that, once we start exploring what could motivate the relativist view as against indexicalism/contextualism, it seems that the motivation speaks in favour of the most radical version of the view (i.e. the idea of assessor-relativity); yet we might also ask, with Wright (2008, forthcoming) and others, whether such evidence about our linguistic practices can really be strong enough to motivate a truly radical theory like assessor-relativism.[40]

So, motivating some version of the relativist view as against indexicalism/contextualism may prove more problematic than initially supposed. On the other hand, however, it is also not clear what the added parameter view buys us over a straightforward use-based approach to meaning.[41] For the approach seems to hang on to the shadow of a formal approach even while acknowledging that only within a context can terms be given an understanding or method of application which makes them capable of saying the world to be thus and so.[42] Yet once again the worry is that taking CSAs seriously, in the way that the relativist account councils, ultimately undermines the need for the formal structures in which the proposal then dresses the contribution of context to meaning. What, we might wonder, is the real force of

[39] Schaffer 2011 objects to this proposed reconstrual of what we mean by 'disagreement': 'The truth relativist semantics was advertised as providing the best account of disagreement. It is disheartening to learn that we also need to reconceive what disagreement is, for the semantics to perform as advertised'.

[40] So, for instance, I would agree with Iacona 2008 and others that the very idea of faultless disagreement, which motivates so many relativists, is suspect. As Cappelen and Hawthorne 2009: 132 note, there is not 'anything very compelling about the purported intuition of faultless disagreement. Cases where the sense of no fault runs deep are ones where the sense of disagreement runs shallow'.

[41] This is particularly so since most contemporary versions of relativism stress that they take the bearers of truth-evaluable content to be utterances, not sentences; see, e.g. Recanati 2007. Yet if it is only utterances that are capable of saying the world to be thus and so we seem to be edging extremely close to standard conceptions of use-based semantics.

[42] This point is taken up again below (Chapter 3, §2) with respect to the relativist response to incomplete predicates.

claiming that the sentence 'the apple is red' expresses a determinate proposition, though one which is not truth-evaluable without first specifying a context of use which details the way in which the apple must be to count as red, instead of saying, with Wittgenstein and others, that there is no proposition outside a context of use? And note that the provision of parameters on this approach will be a *thoroughly* pragmatic matter. Whereas the usual parameters of world and time can be provided via a formal consideration of the context of utterance, determining whether we need a parameter which appeals to a community standard of redness for apples, or a standard of redness for Braeburn apples, or a standard of redness for Braeburn apples picked before September and stored in the dark, will be something to be settled only by appeal to rich features of the context of utterance, including speaker intentions and shared knowledge among interlocutors. Thus it is thoroughly pragmatic processes which are doing all the work here, with the formal talk of parameters apparently serving little additional purpose. The point is once again that taking CSAs seriously means putting pragmatic processes firmly in the driving seat, but once they are there then the attempt (by both indexicalism and relativism) to wrestle the contribution of context to content back into the shape familiar from the Kaplan–Perry treatment of indexicality looks ad hoc. Rather if one is genuinely swayed by CSAs then it seems they provide a reason to move right away from the formal framework that sees them as anomalies or problems to be dealt with and towards a view which sees them as illustrative of the very way in which meaning works.

(4.4) Summary

Minimalists and occasionalists seem to be in agreement that the ground between their two opposing accounts is unstable. The most conservative move away from minimalism in the face of CSAs is to increase the amount of indexicality claimed in our language, but if one is swayed by CSAs at all then it seems one should recognize that they reveal a phenomenon very unlike that of standard indexicality. Furthermore, embracing a pervasive claim of indexicality in natural language undermines (or robs of all content) the very idea that the route to semantic content must be dictated by syntactic form. A less conservative route then would be to allow context to contribute to content even where that contribution is not demanded by something in the lexicon or syntax, as does contextualism. However, the worry both minimalism and occasionalism see with this route is that, once one takes seriously the phenomenon thrown up by CSAs, then one has no reason to think that any context-independent specification of propositional content will be free from the possibility of running a CSA. Specifically, one cannot ameliorate the issue by claiming that an utterance of 'The apple is red' expresses the contextually enriched proposition that *the apple is red on the skin* since this proposition, no less than the first one, stands in need of contextual understanding. Thus it seems that if one feels the pull of CSAs then one needs a different picture of the way in which content and context hang together. Furthermore, the suspicion that opening the door to CSAs leads directly to the door of use-based theories is reinforced by noting the difficulty, on the contextualist model, of reconstructing a viable semantics/pragmatics divide. Once the walls around a semantically expressed proposition are made permeable by pragmatic processes like free enrichment the concern is that there will be no way to buttress them to keep out the pragmatic information the contextualist wants to treat as genuinely part of an implicature.

Our final intermediary position does preserve a firm distinction between the proposition semantically expressed and those pragmatically conveyed: the relativist account treats contextual contributions not as part of propositional content but as having a role to play outside this, as forming the parameters against which propositions get assessed for truth. Thus it seems, at least prima facie, that the proposal does provide a genuine alternative to standard formal accounts and standard use-based approaches.[43] However the question now is what this talk of added parameters gets us: why think that 'the apple is red' expresses a proposition, though one which is not truth-evaluable outside of a context which specifies a particular understanding of what it is to be red, rather than thinking that determinacy of content itself is a feature found only within a context of use? What is left, we might wonder, of the idea that sentences express propositions if propositional

---

[43] Though, as we will see, this claim apparently comes under pressure when we consider so-called 'incomplete predicates', see Chapter 3, §2.

content turns out to be the thin, partial, fragmentary creature (standing in need of relativization to a mass of contextually delivered parameters) which relativists envisage? While it is clearly a position which is technically available to us we need to know what work the thin notion of propositional content, and the complex, context-driven mechanisms for truth-evaluating this content, can really do for us. There is thus a great deal of weight to be born by the kind of retraction/disagreement data which has been used to motivate the position thus far—a weight that it is not obvious the data can bear (see Wright 2007, also Williamson 2005). Once again the worry is that it is the notion of pragmatic processes, of language in use, which is absolutely in the driving seat here with the relativist's attempt to dress it up in formal Kaplanian clothes perhaps covering a theorist's modesty but doing little substantive explanatory work. Overall, then, minimalism and occasionalism are in agreement: where we seem to have a well-populated middle ground, in reality the relatively new positions on the spectrum seem unstable. In reality, the only solid ground to be found comes at either end of our spectrum: either we join with minimalists and don't take CSAs seriously as indicative of a semantic phenomenon at all, or we join with occasionalists and take them so seriously that they help to shape our entire approach to semantics.

I'd like to close this chapter by considering one final point of agreement between minimalism and occasionalism. This concerns the kind of content which can be recovered without appeal to a context of utterance. For although Travis takes propositional meaning to be determined only in context this doesn't stop him from holding that we can provide standard lexical entries for expressions. Thus for Travis it is right to say things like 'green' means green, and that 'grunts' speaks of one being a grunter. As he writes 2008: 154:

The meaning of an English expression makes it *for* saying a certain sort of thing in speaking English. The meaning of 'is blue', in making these words speak of being blue, makes it for (e.g.) calling something blue on the understanding there would then be of its being so.

In the same vein Dancy 2004: 196 writes: 'To know the meaning of a term is to know the *sorts of* semantic contribution that the term can make to a larger context, and to have a general understanding of what *sorts of* context are those in which it will make this or that *sort of* contribution'. So words have meanings which make them suitable for assigning properties to objects or for saying things to be a certain way, but these meanings leave open, outside a context of use, what it would be for an object to count as having that property or for things to be as they are said to be. Now it seems that the minimalist could agree with much of this picture, for she holds that word meanings generalize over specific contextualized understandings of them—that the meaning of 'green' leaves open the way in which an object might be green (on its surface, on the inside, etc.) So it seems that both accounts agree that lexical content (and thus the complex content delivered by sentences) plays the role of a determinable, with many different states of affairs being its determinants. This way of conceiving of occasionalism is perhaps born out by Dancy 2004: 194 when he writes: 'The meaning of the term, understood in general, is the range of differences that it can make; its meaning in a given context is to be found somewhere in that range...There is a sense, then, in which the term has the same meaning wherever it appears, though it makes different contributions in different contexts and those different contributions determine what it means there'.

Where minimalism differs from occasionalism then is over the question of whether such determinable content can itself be thought of as genuine, truth-evaluable content. Travis 2008: 159 is adamant that it can't:

[I]f I do not [speak of being a grunter on some particular understanding of being a grunter] then I fail to state any condition under which anything might be true. Being a grunter on no particular understanding of being one is just not a way for [anyone] to be.

It is this commitment to the idea that any content recovered simply on the basis of lexico-syntactic features alone (without any rich appeal to the context of utterance) is destined to fall short of propositional, truth-evaluable content that makes the occasionalist a true opponent of the minimalist. For the minimalist wants to hold, contra Travis, that a sentence like 'Sid grunts' does state a condition for truth, namely it is true iff Sid grunts. Of course there are an indefinite number of more precise ways for this to be true (Sid might grunt all the time, after heavy exercise, when asleep, inaudibly, etc.), but the fact that there are indefinite ways to satisfy the truth condition does not, the minimalist maintains, mean that it is not a genuine truth-condition prior to this kind of precisification (see Sainsbury 2008). The picture endorsed by the minimalist here then is a realist one with respect to properties— there is held to be a fact of the matter about whether or not Sid possesses the property of being a grunter and a statement that he is a grunter is true just in case he does possess this property, even though there may be some contextually salient way of being a grunter which Sid fails to satisfy. This sort of atomistic picture, of words picking out properties independent of contexts of use, is rejected in occasionalism. At heart, then, it seems that the fundamental points of contention between the minimalist and the occasionalist are the issues which use-based theorists have traditionally urged in the face of formalism, namely 'can words, or only speakers, refer?' and 'are sentences, or only utterances, capable of making claims about the world, i.e. of expressing propositions?'[44] These issues will, in one way or another, concern us for the rest of the book.

---

[44] See Williamson 2009: 135 for a recent expression of general scepticism about Wittgensteinian approaches to meaning.

CHAPTER 2

Minimal Semantics and Psychological Evidence

As we have seen, minimalism wants to claim that there are minimal contents (minimal truth-conditions, minimal propositions) attaching to natural language sentences which are (i) truth-evaluable, (ii) entirely dictated by the lexico-syntactic elements of a sentence and (iii) which are maximally free from contextual effects. These minimal contents provide the literal meaning of sentences relativized to contexts of utterance, though, the minimalist acknowledges, they do not usually provide the intuitive contents of speech acts involving those sentences. Minimalists are committed to this last claim because, even if there are such things as minimal contents for sentences, it is clear that these are not the kinds of things which get communicated in normal conversational exchanges. To take an example, the minimalist is going to claim that a sentence like 'That apple is red' just means that *that apple is red*, however what gets communicated by an utterance of this sentence will typically be a pragmatically enriched proposition, like *that apple is red to degree n on most of its skin*. Thus, as noted in the last chapter, the minimalist is committed to drawing a sharp distinction between semantic content and pragmatic content or speaker meaning.

There are then (as noted in the Preface) two main kinds of objection to this minimalist picture:

(i) *Minimal propositions are unnecessary*: they play no explanatory role and thus can be dismissed.

(ii) *Minimal propositions are impossible*: some or all natural language sentences fail to express complete, truth-evaluable propositions on the basis of their lexico-syntactic elements alone.

Chapters 3–6 will focus on objection (ii), as it provides the strongest challenge to minimalism, but in this chapter I want to think about the first challenge, whereby minimal propositions are held to be explanatorily inert. The primary ground for scepticism about the explanatory value of minimal propositions lies, it seems, in consideration of what goes on in the mind of a subject during the process of coming to understand a communicative linguistic act. Specifically, as Recanati and others have stressed, it seems minimal propositions are not the kinds of contents subjects entertain en route to a grasp of communicated content: the hearer who understands 'This steak is raw', when uttered in a restaurant setting, as meaning *this steak is undercooked* need not, it seems, first entertain the minimal proposition that *this steak is raw* (i.e. entirely uncooked). Thus, the thought is, minimal propositions are explanatorily inert in accounts of linguistic comprehension and they should thus be rejected. To assess this challenge I think it will be helpful to start (in §2) by considering the relationship between semantics and psychology more generally. As we will see, the challenge to minimalism here relates to an extant objection to Grice's approach to linguistic meaning and spelling out exactly how the proposed worry relates to each account will be the topic of §3. Then, in §4, I'll suggest how I think a minimalist should respond to the challenge. Finally, in §5, I'll widen the discussion to survey a range of points where a minimalist and her opponent might agree or disagree and I'll highlight which features I'm going to take as central in the rest of the book. Before all this, however, I want to start by returning to the point noted above, namely the minimalists acknowledgement that minimal semantic contents may standardly fail to match our intuitions about speech act contents. What, we might wonder, could possibly entitle a minimalist to be so sanguine about such an apparently revolutionary claim?

(1) Minimalism and what is said

As noted, minimalists are happy to reject the idea that a semantic theory should limn our intuitive judgements of what is said by the utterance of a sentence in a given context. They reject this as an appropriate aim for a semantic theory as they suggest that there is no such thing as a semantically informative notion of what is said by a speaker. A first reason to be sceptical about the idea that our intuitive judgements of what a speaker says in uttering a given sentence are semantically informative is that at least some such judgements clearly concern non-literal or implied content. So, for instance, someone who utters 'It is a lovely day' may well be taken to have said that it is a horrible day (if speaking ironically), but of course that doesn't entail that the sentence uttered ever has this content as part of its literal meaning. So if intuitive judgements of speech act content are to be taken to be semantically informative what will be required is a specialized, technical notion (perhaps 'what is *strictly or literally* said') capable of isolating a sub-set of our intuitive judgements of conveyed speaker meaning. The question then is whether there is any such technical notion available and the minimalist's claim is that either there is not or, to the extent that there is, such a notion is parasitic on something else. If this is right, then either the proposed trip through 'what is literally said' is misconceived or it is otiose (since either we cannot make these kinds of judgements at all or the making of the judgement depends on the exercise of some additional criterion and it is this additional criterion which is doing the real work).

The argument against a semantically relevant sense of what is said has been spelt out at length elsewhere (see Cappelen and Lepore 1997, Borg 2004a: Chapter 2, §2.5). However, to take just one example, suppose that while watching the first Test match between India and England at Lords in 2011, Amarii says, while pointing at Tendulkar, 'That man is a great cricketer'. What would count as a rendition of what Amarii literally says here? There are clearly a plethora of potentially perfectly acceptable indirect speech reports which are available:

(1) A said that that man is a great cricketer.

(2) A said that the man over there is a great cricketer.

(3) A said that Tendulkar is a great cricketer.

(4) A said that the man with the highest number of first class hundreds is a great cricketer.

(5) A said that the man who actually had the greatest number of first class centuries in June 2011 was a great player of the beautiful game.

(6) A said that Tendulkar is the player English bowlers fear the most.

Which of (1–6), and the indefinite number of other potentially acceptable reports, count as capturing our intuitive judgements of what A literally said? While some, like (6), obviously don't and others, like (1), obviously do, the middle-ground here is very murky indeed and the minimalist's claim is that if we do manage to draw a line anywhere here (counting some of this middle-ground as capturing intuitive assessments of literal content and others as failing to) this can only be because we are utilizing a prior principle concerning either what the sentence 'that man is a great cricketer' literally means (relative to this context of utterance) or some lexico-syntactic principle about which words can replace which other words while preserving literality. For instance, it is not clear that we have *any* intuitions firm enough to tell us whether (3) is a literal rendition of the original speech act or is merely an acceptable indirect speech report. Furthermore, it seems that if we do come to a decision here, say assessing (3) as a literal rendition, this decision will be prefaced on an antecedent view about the semantic content of indexicals like 'that man' and names like 'Tendulker', rather than itself helping to establish those semantic analyses. Thus it is an antecedent view about semantics which is doing the work here, rather than the judgements of literal speech act content. For this reason, then, the minimalist embraces the broadly Gricean idea that what a semantic theory should aim to deliver is an account of the meaning of sentences rather than an account of our intuitive judgements of speech act content. (Furthermore, minimalism agrees with Grice's account of sentence meaning as dictated by lexico-syntactic constituents alone and therefore as minimally contextually affected, with both approaches allowing only the contextual processes of disambiguation and reference assignment for indexicals, etc. to be semantically relevant.) As we will see in §5, when we come to look at the various points of disagreement between minimalism and its opponents, this marks a fundamental point of departure between minimalism and an account such as Recanati's (2004, 2010) 'truth-conditional pragmatics', but before we come to this, I want first to consider the objection which emerges out of the fissure which minimalists take to exist between sentence meaning and speech act content.

(2) The relationship between semantics and psychology?

The objection we have to consider here is that because minimal propositions fail to cohere with the content subjects intuitively assign to speech acts they run the risk of being found explanatorily redundant (in the terminology of the Preface, this is a kind of 'argument from above', objecting to minimal contents as they fail to match relatively high-level, consciously available judgements of content). To properly appreciate this worry, and the answer the minimalist is going to want to give to it, I'd like to start by considering the relationship between semantics and psychology. For in addition to the common ground noted above between minimalism and Grice's approach to meaning (where both approaches hive off a notion of sentence meaning and take this to be distinct from the highly context-sensitive notion of speaker meaning), it seems that the two approaches also agree on the general question of the relationship between semantics and psychology. To see this I'd like to sketch very briefly what I take to be the three main options for relating semantics and psychology (these options are not meant to be exhaustive—for instance, some kind of two-way dependency could be envisaged—however I do think they cover the main positions in logical space). As we will see, each of these options can be read in two distinct ways: a metaphysical version and a (weaker) epistemic variety. I'll suggest that both Gricean and minimal semantics share a common metaphysical outlook, but that both accounts then seem to run into problems with the associated epistemic claim. So, our question now is: how might we construe the relationship between semantics and psychology?

(2.1) Independence

(a) *Metaphysical independence.* According to this view there is no constitutive or dependence-based relationship between a correct semantic theory and the states of mind involved in language comprehension in ordinary agents. Constructing a semantic theory is taken to be one kind of enterprise while the construction of a theory of language processing is something quite different. Prima facie, this position may seem less than compelling. After all, if some piece of information, *I*, plays no role whatsoever in an agent's coming to grasp the semantic content of an expression, *E*, we might wonder what could make *I* a genuine semantic fact about *E* at all. The thought behind such a rejection of metaphysical independence is that it is simply implausible to hold that the semantic facts about a human language are ones which no human ever cognises. However, on reflection, I think such immediate scepticism about metaphysical independence is unfounded and that the position could yet turn out to be a plausible option. For we might envisage a semantic theory as constrained to capture knowledge that *would* suffice for understanding, regardless of whether it fits the actual cognitive processing of any language user. It would, it seems, advance our understanding of language to have a theory which could suffice for linguistic understanding, even if we simply lacked any information about whether or not the theory accurately captured the ways in which ordinary speakers came to linguistic understanding. Indeed, this kind of metaphysical independence might be suggested by at least some of the things that Davidson says about the role of a semantic theory, where a truth theory is required to *do duty* as a theory of meaning and to describe knowledge *capable* of underpinning (aspects of our) linguistic competence rather than as making prescriptive claims about the form which that competence actually takes in ordinary subjects.[1]

(b) *Epistemic independence.* According to this view there is held to be no epistemic route from one domain to the other: claims about the correct form for a semantic theory do not entail any predictions about psychological processes or the contents or structure of the mind of typical language users, and

---

[1] Davidson 1984. We should note, however, as Äsa Wikforss pointed out in conversation, that it would probably be a mistake to take metaphysical independence as the official Davidsonian line, given other remarks he makes, such as his requirement that conversational participants construct passing theories of one another (Davidson 1986). A clearer advocate of the independence line then is Soames 2009.

vice versa. A claim of epistemic independence might perhaps be embraced by someone who held that semantic theorizing is solely concerned with conceptual analysis and
that such conceptual analysis need not be answerable to
what language users typically think or do when faced with
a given linguistic prompt. Semantics here would thus not
be required to answer to empirical discoveries in cognitive
science.

(2.2) Psychological facts depend on semantic facts

(a) *Metaphysical dependence*: on this view there is held to be a
constitutive relationship between the contents of the mind
of the language user and the content of a natural language
(and hence the content of a correct semantic theory for
that language), such that the former depends on the latter.
This metaphysical assumption is most famously associated
with the kind of linguistic determinism proposed by Whorf
and endorsed by many others. Thus for the linguistic deter-
minist the kinds of things one can say constrains the kinds
of things one can think. To give the rather hackneyed examples familiar in this area, because Eskimos have so many
more words for snow than do English speakers, Eskimos are
supposed to be able to think more kinds of thoughts about
snow than English speakers. Or again, since some nomadic
tribes lack a complex number vocabulary (for instance, the
language might have words only for one, two and many)
speakers of this language are unable to think complex
thoughts involving number (their language prevents them
from *thinking* 'I've got four sheep', not just from *saying* it). It
seems that linguistic determinism is not a theory much in
favour at the moment (see Pinker 2007 for discussion), but
we should note that the same kind of metaphysical assumptions which lie behind linguistic determinism also lie
behind certain other contemporary approaches which
claim that we think in a natural language (see Carruthers
1996).

(b) *Epistemic dependence*: on this view the route to an account of mental content runs through linguistic content, since thought content is essentially inaccessible and thus cannot provide a direct object of study. Such an epistemic dependence claim might be made in conjunction with (2a) or independent of it. Made without commitment to metaphysical dependence, we have the kind of picture commonly associated with the so-called 'linguistic turn' in philosophy, which sought to place philosophy of language centre stage for the study of the mind (see Dummett 1993, Evans 1982).

(2.3) Semantic facts depend on psychological facts

(a) *Metaphysical dependence.* According to this view, facts about semantic content are determined by facts about the minds of language users. What a semantic theory aims to capture on this view is the knowledge which underpins grasp of linguistic meaning among ordinary language users. It is the mind which is taken to be the primary locus for content, thus words and sentences acquire their meaning via their relationship to mental states.

(b) *Epistemic dependence.* According to this view, the route to a correct semantic theory runs via an account of the contents of the minds of language users (thus a putative semantic theory might be confirmed or disconfirmed by psychological evidence).[2]

Now, it seems that both Grice and minimal semantics sign-up to (3a). For Grice the dependence of the semantic on the psychological is clear, for he aims to explicate semantic content in terms of intentional content—that is to say meaning is ultimately to be understood in terms of speaker intentions.[3] For the minimalist the

---

[2] At its most extreme, a claim of epistemic dependence might amount to what Davies 2006 disparagingly calls 'cognitive scientism'—the view that *all* the relevant facts are to be revealed via experimentation and thus that semantics is nothing over and above the collation and ordering of experimental findings. However it seems that (3b) need not be read in such strong terms.

[3] Though see Avramides 1989 and Garcia-Carpintero 2001 for caveats concerning the usual *reductive* reading of the dependency claim in Grice.

allegiance to (3a) is perhaps less overt, yet still the claim is that a minimalist theory aims to capture that part of our psychological make-up responsible for a subject's competence with linguistic stimuli, thus it would still seem right to characterize the theory as signing up to the dependence of semantics on psychology. So, according to both approaches semantic content depends in some way on mental content, on what is to be found in the minds of language users; but now we might ask 'what about (3b)?' A claim of metaphysical dependence might well be thought to carry a claim of epistemic dependence in its wake, for if semantic content depends on psychological content then, ceteris paribus, we would expect psychological evidence to be relevant to semantic theorizing. Thus, unless we posit some kind of disruptive feature which serves to muddy the path from psychology to semantics, it would seem that psychological facts *ought* to provide good evidence for semantic facts. However, it is with respect to the claim of epistemic dependence in (3b) that both our accounts seem to run into problems. The worry is that neither Gricean semantics nor minimal semantics fit properly with relevant psychological evidence.

(3) The objection: psychological evidence runs counter to the theories

To begin with Gricean semantics: on Grice's model it seems that literal sentence meaning is *prior* to speaker meaning. On hearing an utterance, a subject S is supposed to first grasp the literal meaning of the sentence uttered, then see that this flouts some general principle of good communication, finally this licenses the subject to proceed to infer some more suitable proposition as the one the speaker actually meant to convey. So to take an example, imagine that A says 'There is nothing to eat'. The hearer, B, can then reason as follows:

(i)   The sentence 'There is nothing to eat' literally means *there is nothing to eat*
(ii) The proposition in (i) is trivially false.
(iii) Asserting trivial falsehoods is in contravention of the general maxims of communication.

(iv) I believe that A is a competent speaker and abides by conversational maxims ____

(v) Thus I should infer some more suitable proposition as the
one A means to convey, e.g. I should take A as intending to
communicate that *there is nothing suitable to eat.*

For Grice, then, it seems to be an integral part of his account that
sentence meaning comes first: it is what a hearer must grasp prior to
proceeding to a grasp of speaker meaning. But does this Gricean
account fit with the psychological evidence?

The first point to notice is that it obviously doesn't fit with first-
personal psychological content, for we often arrive at attributions of
speaker meaning without consciously entertaining sentence meaning
and then engaging in the kind of extended inferential reasoning Grice
suggests. However, this realization is not necessarily problematic for
Grice, for his account might still hold as an account of occurent mental content. That is to say, although we don't consciously engage in the
kind of reasoning which Grice suggests, such a process might still provide the unconscious route to a grasp of speaker meaning. So does the
Gricean picture describe the unconscious processes by which we
arrive at speaker meaning?

The answer to this question seems to be 'no', for we sometimes
seem to be in a position to grasp pragmatically enriched speaker
meaning *before* we are in a position to grasp literal sentence meaning. There are at least three kinds of case which are relevant here:
sub-sentential assertion, metaphor comprehension, and scalar
implicatures. Turning to non-sentential assertion first: it is clear
that a significant proportion of the things people say do not (at
least at the surface level) reach the level of complete sentences.
Thus we have exclamations like 'Fire!' or 'Help!', and comments
like 'Nice dress', 'Bear country' and 'From France'. To make the
case that these or similar utterances are genuine cases of non-sentential assertion (i.e. the production of something which falls short
of sentencehood but which nevertheless conveys a complete proposition) we need to be sure that there is no syntactically present
but phonetically unmarked material in the utterances. That is to
say, we need to be sure that the words spoken exhaust the syntactic
content of the utterance, and in at least some cases this doesn't

seem to be the case.[4] Whether or not all instances of apparently sub-sentential assertion can be handled by mechanisms like ellipsis is a much debated point (see Stainton 2006b for extended argument in favour of genuine subsentential assertion and Stanley 2000 and Merchant 2010 for arguments against at least some apparent instances of it) and it is not something we can hope to settle here. Thus the point I want to make is a conditional one: if it turns out that there are such things as genuine non-sentential assertions then they seem to show that Grice's model of how speaker meaning is recovered cannot be correct. For obviously if a speaker does not produce a complete sentence but still succeeds in communicating a complete proposition at the level of speaker meaning, then grasp of that speaker meaning *cannot* itself depend on a prior grasp of propositional sentence meaning. So non-sentential assertion, if a genuine phenomenon, provides a first piece of evidence against the Gricean model.

A second challenge comes from so-called 'direct access' views of metaphor recovery (e.g. Gibbs 2002), where it is held that we are at least sometimes able to recover metaphorical meaning for words and phrases before we are in a position to grasp complete sentence meaning. That is to say, at least sometimes subjects proceed to a metaphorical interpretation of part of a sentence before they have heard the sentence uttered in its entirety. So for instance, where we have talk of 'icy glares' or 'green shoots of recovery' the claim is that we proceed directly to a metaphorical interpretation of the phrases before we hear the whole sentence the phrases are embedded in. Once again, if this is right then it seems to cause problems for Grice's account because it runs counter to the priority claim: hearers are not, contrary to what the Gricean account seems to demand, waiting to process a complete sentence prior to working out speaker meaning.

Finally, this idea that pragmatic effects must, at least sometimes, occur at a local rather than a sentential level also seems to be demonstrated by some experiments concerning the recovery of scalar implicatures.

[4] Common cases where syntactically elided material is allowed include question and answer contexts; for instance, if asked 'Would you like a drink?' and you respond 'No thanks, I wouldn't' your answer is commonly held to contain the syntactically present but unvoiced material *like a drink* which is easily recoverable from the immediate linguistic environment.

A scalar implicature occurs when a speaker opts to use a weaker or stronger item on a given scale and thereby pragmatically conveys that the alternative terms on the scale do not hold. So for instance, though the lexical entry for 'some' is held to be that familiar from first-order logic, namely *some and possibly all*, many utterances of 'some A's are B's' convey the pragmatically enhanced reading that 'some *and not all* A's are B's' (e.g. 'some delegates came to my talk' conveys the enriched reading that some but not all of them did). Or again, 'or' is taken to have a lexical entry matching that for the inclusive-or in logic, namely 'A or B or both', but again many utterances involving 'or' convey a pragmatically enhanced reading, namely the exclusive-or 'A or B and not both' (e.g. 'Main meals come with chips or salad'). For Grice, since such enhanced scalar readings are pragmatically enhanced instances of speaker meaning they should only be available to subjects once they have determined the literal meaning of the complete sentence in which the scalar terms appear. So, recalling the picture above, if I hear you say 'Some delegates came to my talk' I should first work out the literal meaning of this sentence, then I should see that this flouts some principle of good communication (for instance, it is not the most informative thing you could have said), finally I should infer some alternative proposition, e.g. *some but not all the delegates came to your talk*. However, this model seems to be contradicted by experimental

Figure 1. A Storto & Tannenhaus-Style grid for accessing the on-line processing of implicatures.

findings concerning how ordinary subjects process scalar terms. So, in a set of experiments Storto and Tannenhaus tracked the eye movements of subjects when exposed to a grid of pictures and a sentence relating to the pictures which contained a scalar term. To give an example of the kind of test they ran: hearers were exposed to a two-by-three grid like that in Figure 1.

They were then exposed to part of a sentence, for example 'The car or the clock is next to a ...' and their eye-movements were tracked to this point. The result was that by this stage in the sentence the majority of subjects were already focused on the pictures in the column on the left-hand side. What this seems to show is that by this stage in sentence processing subjects were already processing 'or' not in its weaker inclusive sense (one or the other or both) but in its stronger exclusive sense (one or the other but not both). For it is only if 'or' is read exclusively in this sentence fragment that one has enough information to rule out the column on right of the grid, which depicts the same pair of objects and thus would serve to make true an inclusive interpretation of 'the car or the clock is next to a ...'. The findings from these eye-tracking experiments, together with cases of apparent sub-sentential assertion and direct access to metaphorical interpretations, seem to show that on at least some occasions context acts to affect content *before* sentence meaning has been recovered. That is to say, they seem to show that pragmatic effects can occur at a local (word- or phrase-based level) as well as a global (sentence) level.[5] Yet this runs counter to the priority apparently assigned to literal meaning by Grice, thus evidence about the psychological processing of linguistic stimuli seems to run counter to Grice's proposal.

Turning now to minimal semantics, it seems that a similar kind of challenge—stemming from the psychological evidence concerning linguistic understanding—can be made against the theory. Indeed this seems to be the basis of Recanati's objection (2004: 20) to the minimalist approach in terms of what he calls the 'availability principle':

---

[5] See also Sauerland 2004 for an alternative kind of argument against the global Gricean account of pragmatic influence, and Russell 2006 for a response.

What is said must be intuitively accessible to the conversational partici-pants (unless something goes wrong and they do not count as 'normal interpreters').

The availability principle is one which Recanati suggests any feasi-ble theory of semantic content must respect, yet it is a principle which minimalism clearly flouts. For, as noted, even if there are such things as minimal contents they are not the kinds of things which speakers and hearers consciously entertain in most normal conversational exchanges. If I hear you say 'There's nothing to eat' or 'You won't die', the contents I am likely to consciously entertain include *there is nothing to eat in the fridge* or *you won't die from that cut*, they don't include *there is nothing to eat (in some contextually uncon-strained domain)* or *you won't die*. Thus minimal contents are not (usually) what conversational participants consciously entertain on hearing an utterance but also nor are they the things agents (usu-ally) bring to consciousness when reflecting on how assignments of utterance meaning were made. If asked how I got to *there is nothing to eat in the fridge* I'm likely to appeal to facts like your looking in the fridge, but I'm unlikely to appeal to the minimal content the minimalist assigns the uttered sentence. It seems then that minimal contents are simply not available to normal subjects and as such they cannot, Recanati objects, play the role of semantic content. According to Recanati (2004: 20) the availability constraint 'leads us to give up Minimalism. That is the price to pay if we want Availa-bility to be satisfied'.

So, when we turn to look at what is in the minds of subjects when they are engaged in linguistic processing it seems that what we find is not Grice's picture of grasp of literal meaning plus an act of inference to speaker meaning, nor is it the minimalist's minimal propositions. Whether we are appealing to conscious, first-personal content or some less immediate notion of unconscious or occurrent content, the psychological evidence seems to run counter to both theories. Yet this is problematic since, as noted in the previous section, both accounts subscribe to the view that semantic content is metaphysically depend-ent on psychological content. The worry is that, in the absence of a story about why one cannot move from psychological evidence to semantic theorizing, the current evidence shows that both accounts must be rejected.

(4) The response

So, how worried should the Gricean or the minimalist be by the suggestion that their theories fail to fit with relevant psychological evidence? Well, Kent Bach (2006: 25) has argued that the Gricean shouldn't be worried at all, for, as he writes:

> Grice did not intend his account of how implicatures are recognized as a psychological theory nor even as a cognitive model. He intended it as a rational reconstruction. When he illustrated the ingredients involved in recognizing an implicature, he was enumerating the sorts of information that a hearer needs to take into account, at least intuitively, and exhibiting how this information is logically organized. He was not foolishly engaged in psychological speculation about the nature of or even the temporal sequence of the cognitive processes that implements that logic.

Now, on one reading, Bach's response to the challenge of the last section is, I think, the same as the one I want to propose below on behalf of the minimalist; however, I think there is also another reading where it is perhaps a little more problematic. My worry is that talk of 'rational reconstruction' runs the risk of driving too great a wedge between the semantic theory and the psychological theory, for if all one is offering is a way in which speaker meaning *could* be recovered, with no requirement that ordinary speakers *do* recover meaning in this way, then we seem to be sliding away from a picture which treats semantic content as dependent on psychological content and towards an account which treats semantic content and psychological content as more or less independent of each other (i.e. moving towards option (1a) in §1). A rational reconstruction which makes absolutely no psychological speculation runs the risk of providing a theory of meaning which might be alright for Martians but simply doesn't hold true for us.[6]

Perhaps then we could respond to the challenge here not by denuding our theory of all psychological speculation but by widening our understanding of what counts as psychological evidence. The response I want to make on behalf of the minimalist is that we view minimalism as providing a theory of the form and content of the language faculty, where this is taken to be a genuine component of the cognitive make-

---

[6] For a recent example of someone who embraces the rational reconstruction move, and the separation of semantics and psychology, see Soames 2009: 322–4.

up of ordinary agents (so, semantics is at least in part a branch of individual psychology, as Chomsky recommended for syntax). However,
minimalism is not a theory of conscious content, nor even a theory of
the occurent mental states involved in given acts of linguistic processing. Rather what minimalism specifies is the content a competent language user is guaranteed to be able to recover, given adequate lexical
resources *plus* the proviso that attentional resources are not diverted
from processing literal meaning, and agents are guaranteed the possibility of recovering sentence-level content because the theory they have
cognized is one which trades, ultimately, in sentence-level meanings.
The claim is then that, at some level of specification, there are structures in the mind/brain which represent the basic elements of the minimalist theory (word meanings, syntactic rules for constructing
sentences, and semantic rules for determining sentence meanings from
those word meanings and syntactic structures). Furthermore, the deductive processes posited by the theory en route to determination of sentence meaning will have to be mirrored by operations within the mind,
where this is most easily understood as being mirrored in the causal
interactions between brain structures.[7] However even if minimalism is
the right way to characterize the knowledge underpinning our linguistic competence, it doesn't seem that the theory need be committed to
the claim that, in every instance of communicative success, the theory
acts all the way to deliver sentence level content. Sometimes, it seems,
we go part way towards constructing a representation of sentence-level
content but we stop, either because we are distracted or, more often,
because fragments of meaning are all we need to proceed to a guess
about what the speaker is trying to convey. The minimalist is happy to
concede that what we are really interested in in communicative
exchanges is getting at what the speaker intends to communicate and
this is often very different to the literal meaning attaching to the sentences she utters. Thus the minimalist should be happy to allow that

---

[7] Of course there are serious and seriously difficult questions here concerning how we move between
an abstract statement of a semantic theory and an account of psychological processes (let alone talk of
brain structures); see Davies 1987 for an illuminating discussion of this point. However I hope that the
overarching point—that there is no simple move from an assumption about the kind of semantic theory
realized in the mind of a subject to claims about the kinds of processes that a subject must undergo on a
specific occasion of communicative success—can be made without too deep an excursion into these
murky waters.

sometimes hearers simply stop thinking about semantic content before the language faculty has had a chance to deliver sentence-level content (i.e. a hearer should stop semantic processing whenever she has enough evidence to get at whatever the speaker was trying to convey).[8] Yet this doesn't show that the theory realized in the mind of the language user is not one designed to deliver sentence-level content nor that it is one which doesn't trade essentially in complete propositions. All it shows is that the psychological processes realizing the theory are sometimes stopped on the way to delivering sentence-meaning.

So, the claim is that minimal semantics does embrace both (3a) and (3b), although only on a refined reading of the epistemic claim: psychological evidence *is* relevant to semantic theory construction, but not necessarily psychological evidence concerning how a particular utterance is processed. Minimalism is thus a theory which is open, at least in principle, to confirmation or disconfirmation by the psychological evidence, but this must be evidence about what subjects know about their language, not merely evidence about how they come to grasp what speakers are (pragmatically) trying to convey. Even if hearers may sometimes be able to grasp an instance of speaker meaning without calculating the semantic content for the particular sentence uttered, nevertheless, according to minimalism, it is possession of a theory of meaning which ultimately trades in sentence-level contents that explains (at least in part) why subjects are in a position to recover speaker meaning at all.

(5) Disagreements and agreements

The challenge in this chapter has focussed on Recanati's objection to minimalism from his Availability Principle. In a range of seminal pieces,

---

[8] There are, it should be noted, implications of this point for the kind of modularity picture I advocated in Borg 2004a. To put things crudely, it can't be the case that the language faculty remains entirely encapsulated until the point of outputting a sentence-level content. Rather the picture is one where the outputs of the language faculty are available at incremental levels, so that, as it were, other modules or central-processing systems can 'see' the construction of sentence-level meaning stage by stage and can utilize the sub-sentential fragments of meaning which are going into the construction of sentence-meaning. The modularity claim will then be that, although pragmatic and semantic interpretation processes run in parallel (rather than the kind of sequential picture seen in the original rendition of Grice's view above), with pragmatic processes able to operate on sub-sentential clauses before the semantic analysis of the sentence is complete, still no pragmatically enhanced reading is permitted to feed back into the semantics module to effect the semantic analysis of the sentence.

Recanati has argued for an alternative stance to minimalism, which he labels 'truth conditional pragmatics' (TCP). According to TCP, context can come to affect literal content even when such an effect is not required by any lexico-syntactic item in the sentence (that is to say, TCP allows what we called 'free pragmatic effects' in the last chapter). Prima facie, then, it would seem that minimalism and TCP are diametrically opposed. However, on closer inspection, the degree to which these two accounts (and, indeed, any account which objects to minimalism on the basis that the contents it posits fails to match our intuitive judgements of speech act content) are genuine competitors is much less obvious.

First, as Recanati 2010: 12–3 recognizes, since minimalism can be (and indeed is here and in Borg 2004a and Cappelen and Lepore 2005) construed as a theory of sentence meaning *not* as a theory of intuitive utterance content, it is not in fact clear that there is really any substantial disagreement between the two approaches (since the two theories are theories of different things). Recognizing this potential lack of opposition, Recanati 2010: 14 coins his own term, 'I-minimalism' (which, after p. 14, he abbreviates simply to 'minimalism'), for the approach he really seeks to oppose. 'I-minimalism' is Recanati's term for any approach which adheres to the constraints minimalism places on semantic content (i.e. which accepts that there can be no semantically relevant contextual effects without these effects being demanded by some lexico-syntactic item) but which *also* embraces the idea that such semantic contents must limn intuitive judgements of what is said. Clearly there are advocates of I-minimalism—Jason Stanley being the most pre-eminent—but still it seems that the majority of those who self-identify as minimalists are not I-minimalists. So, although Recanati frames the debate in his 2010 as one between TCP and minimalism, it is worth noting that, at least in the terminology of this book, the debate he is having is one between TCP and indexicalism, not one between TCP and minimalism (since minimalism rejects the key assumption of TCP about the job description of semantics).

Second, it seems that there is actually significant common ground between the position advocated here and TCP, as becomes clear if we look at Recanati's own definition of 'free pragmatic effects'. For Recanati himself defines free pragmatic enrichment as enrichment that occurs post-propositionally. Prima facie, it may seem that my use of the term 'free pragmatic effects' (introduced in Chapter 1, §3.3) to refer to pragmatic effects which are not lexico-syntatically demanded differs from Recanati's, defined in terms of post-propositional effects (I'm grateful to an anonymous reader for raising this point). However I don't think this is in fact the case. For it seems that when a pragmatic effect is mandatory (i.e. required to get to a proposition) Recanati holds that it must in fact be traceable to something in the syntax (or, more specifically, something in the 'sub-syntactic base-ment', to borrow a term from Taylor 2001). This is precisely why the need for it occurs on all occasions on which a given term is used, rather than being prompted by contextual features alone. So, for instance, were it to turn out (contra to both Recanati 2004 and Borg 2004a, §4.3) that 'rain' requires contextual specification of a place in order to determine a complete proposition, then it seems that, for Recanati, this need would be articulated within the lexical entry for 'rain' (see Recanati 2004: 8–10, Borg 2006). As he writes (2004: 9) 'If really the contextual provision of a place was mandatory, *hence an instance of saturation*, every token of 'It's raining' would be unevalua-ble unless a place were contextually specified' (my emphasis). On my reading of Recanati, then, he does not in fact allow for syntactically unmarked pre-propositional contextual effects on semantic content. Thus the only time we get free pragmatic enrichment in his frame-work is when a contextual effect is demanded by context alone rather than being lexico-syntatically demanded.

Free pragmatic effects for Recanati, then, are ones which take us from a proposition to a conversationally more appropriate proposi-tion. Non-free or mandatory pragmatic effects, on the other hand, are those which are required in *all* contexts to deliver an acceptable utter-ance content (i.e. to get one from something sub-propositional to something propositional) and these are all held by Recanati to be the result of saturation (the provision of a value for a lexico-syntactically marked variable). So it turns out that for Recanati the move from a sub-propositional content to a complete proposition is *never* the result of a free pragmatic effect, it is *always* the result of saturation; 'free prag-matic effects' then are, just as defined in Chapter 1, those which are not lexico-syntatically required. It seems then that, perhaps contrary to initial appearances, both minimalism and TCP are in agreement that all sentences are capable of yielding complete propositions on the basis of their lexico-syntactic constituents alone. (TCP apparently embraces minimalisms commitment to the truth of propositionalism.) On both accounts free pragmatic effects (effects not demanded by any lexico-syntactic constituents) may take one from a conversationally inappropriate propositional content to a conversationally appropriate one, but such effects are never needed to get one to a proposition in the first place.

The debate between minimalism and Recanati's faction of contextualism then comes down fundamentally to a debate about the task of semantics, but since everyone recognizes that we need one notion of content to account for the systematic, normative, learnable aspects of language, and one notion of content to account for the rich, unsystematic, paradigmatically human stuff that goes on in grasp of speech act content, it is not clear that we really have much of a disagreement here at all.[9] Once the contextualist accepts that every well-formed sentence gives rise to a minimal proposition via saturation alone, proclamations of the demise of formal semantics seem significantly premature (see Borg, 2012).

For the purposes of this book, then, I'm going to take the primary opponents of minimalism to be those (such as Sperber and Wilson, Carston and Travis) who reject the idea that there is a proposition to be recovered for all well-formed sentences on the basis of saturation alone. On this opposing model, if we want to get to a complete proposition we need at least sometimes to admit optional, top-down or free pragmatic effects as semantically relevant. However, although disagreement over the issues of propositionalism and free pragmatic effects will be at the heart of the argument here, it is worth bearing in mind that this does not exhaust the dimensions of agreement and disagreement in this area, for there are a range of further principles theorists might be concerned with and thus there is a complex network of agreement and disagreement among participants to the debate. In closing then I'd like briefly to survey this network (outlined in Figure 2), arguing that, although I'll often talk of 'the opponents of

---

[9] This impression is also borne out by various points in Recanati 2010 which appear to take contextually unenriched, minimal propositions as providing the literal meaning of sentences; see, e.g., Recanati 2010: 51, 92–5, 103, 112, 123–4, 128.

minimalism' in what follows, it would be a mistake to think that there is a single unified camp here, rather than an eclectic and perhaps shifting morass of allegiances.

A first point of division among theorists in this are concerns the principle Cappelen and Lepore 2005 use for defining their notion of minimalism: namely, allegiance to the 'Basic Set Assumption'. According to this principle, the only context-sensitive terms in a language are the intuitively obvious ones, the expressions ordinary speakers would class alongside expressions like 'this' and 'today'. Thus Cappelen and Lepore 2005: 2 take minimalism to be committed to the claim that the class of context-sensitive terms is exhausted by those Kaplan listed plus or minus a bit. While this is not a claim endorsed by many others in the field (for instance, as noted in Chapter 1, my variety of minimalism does not endorse this principle), it might be a claim which finds favour with some. For instance, as we saw in Chapter 1, §4.1 it seems clear that Travis embraces a pretty limited set of expressions as genuine indexicals. There are also some reasons to think that Bach might be fairly sympathetic to this kind of limitation (since he is happy with the idea of semantics yielding sub-propositional fragments of content and thus has no need to seek to enlarge the class of indexical terms beyond the obvious ones).

A second point of contention (which will come to the fore in Chapter 4) concerns the kinds of contextual features a semantic theory can appeal to. Specifically, we might ask whether a semantic theory can appeal to rich, intentional features of a context of utterance such as the mental states of speakers (Bach 1999: 72 labels such features 'wide'), where the assumption is that if the intentional states of speakers are held to be semantically relevant then we must reject claims of modularity for semantic understanding (see Borg 2004b). As Recanati 2010: 2–3 writes:

> if we let what the speaker means be one of the factors on which truth-conditional content depends, that means that *we give up the modularity view*. We accept that pragmatics and semantics *do* mix in fixing truth-conditional content—a quite fundamental concession to the opponent of modularity.

The vast majority of theorists in the area do accept speaker intentions as semantically relevant (though not all agree with Recanati on the repercussions of this move), however my variety of minimalism, as noted in Chapter 1, §1, does not. Wide content is also rejected as semantically relevant by Bach, though (unlike my account) this leads him to accept that any sentence containing a true demonstrative will fail to express a proposition via semantic analysis alone (though note that sentences containing pure indexicals *are* held by Bach to express propositions, since he maintains that no appeal to speaker intentions are required to determine a referent for a pure indexical).

A third crucial axis of debate concerns the semantic relevance of bottom-up pragmatic effects (saturation), where the pragmatic effect is demanded by something in the lexico-syntactic form of a sentence, versus top-down (free) pragmatic effects, where the provision of the contextual information is driven solely by conversational demands. Advocates of top-down or free pragmatic processes may allow either:

(i) Effects which operate over existing lexico-syntactic elements (free enrichment, sense extension, broadening, narrowing).

(ii) Effects which introduce new material (unarticulated constituents—abbreviated below to 'ucs').

We should note that it is possible to blur the distinction between bottom-up and top-down processes by allowing top-down elements in the syntax (what Recanati 2010: 139 calls 'covert optionals'): these are elements which are present in logical form but which are placed there due to solely conversational demands. This would yield a *form* of unarticulated constituent (something relevant to the interpretation of the sentence which is not demanded by the initial lexico-syntactic content alone), but one which does then appear directly in the logical form for the interpreted utterance and would thereby get its value from saturation.[10]

However, leaving covert optionals to one side and holding (i) and (ii) apart, there is then a further question of whether both kinds of free pragmatic processes are admitted or only one. Recanati 2004, 2010 posits both, maintaining that there are genuinely unarticulated constituents. For instance the content in italics in (7) and (8) below mark semantically relevant content which is not delivered by anything in

---

[10] As Recanati notes, this would seem to fit Marti's 2006 variety of indexicalism (she writes 2006: 149 'whether a variable is generated in the syntax is left completely free') and Stern's M-That operator for metaphor (see, e.g., Stern 2006). It is perhaps also the way to think about Chierchia's optional syntactic level strengthening account of scalars.

the lexico-syntactic form of the sentence (UCs) (9), on the other hand, contains material which is delivered by something in the lexico-syntactic form since, according to Recanati, no proposition is expressed without the additional content, thus the requirement for it must be marked somewhere in the lexico-syntactic form:

> (7) 'It's raining' →it's raining *in Chicago.*
>
> (8) 'Amarii danced all night'→Amarii danced all night *at the ball.*
>
> (9) 'Kawasi arrived'→Kawasi arrived *in Hyde Park.*

Recanati argues that the moves in (7) and (8) are moves to incorporate UCs: there are literal propositions expressed by the lexico-syntactic constituents of the sentences alone but not the appropriate ones (the additional material is thus driven by context alone). (9), on the other hand, is supposed to be an instance of saturation, as no proposition is expressed without a place.

That there is no proposition in (9) without the provision of a place is supposed to be shown by an infelicity test (Recanati 2010: 83):

> A: John has arrived.
> B: Where has he arrived?
> A: *I have no idea.

The fact that A's reply is in some way unacceptable is supposed to show us that a location is demanded by A's initial assertion. On the other hand, such location non-specific readings are held to be fine (though perhaps unusual) for (7) and (8) (cf. Recanati's 2007b Weathermen example). Now it seems there are serious questions we can ask about exactly how robust such infelicity tests are in determining when, prior to contextual enrichment, a complete proposition is expressed versus when a sub-propositional content is expressed (this is a question we will return to in Chapter 3). Indeed, Recanati 2010: 117 himself recognizes this concern:

> I concede that, by exerting enough cleverness…it is possible to come up with occurrences of 'finish' or 'notice' for which the argument slot is not filled with a specific value provided by the context, but is existentially bound. Such occurrences are marginal, however, and I think they can be handled by saying that in such cases a *meaning shift* occurs—the words are taken in a special deviant sense.

However even if the infelicity test (or some other one) were ultimately to be vindicated and we could in principle isolate some cases
as the ones we want to treat via semantically relevant top-down effects
rather than via mandatory bottom-up ones, still there is a further question about why we should treat the effects as being handled by UCs
rather than by some kind of meaning modulation.

For instance, an alternative approach to positing UCs in (7) would
be to treat the case via modulation (or free enrichment) of the expression 'rain'. One option would be to take the lexical entry for 'rain' to
be *rain at salient l* and then analyse the general reading as a broadening
of that lexical meaning. Alternatively, one could treat 'rain' as meaning
rain somewhere and then allow this meaning to be pragmatically narrowed to the desired content. Or again, 'dance' on some occasion
might contribute the pragmatically narrowed concept 'dance at the
ball' to the proposition expressed. This kind of move would at least
have the advantage of preserving what Crimmins 1992: 9–10 calls 'the
principle of full articulation', whereby all elements of semantic content
are held to be articulated in the lexico-syntactic form of a linguistic
item, meaning not just *any* additional content can be inserted into the
semantics but only strenghtenings or weakenings of the pre-existing
lexico-syntactically determined content. Although it is unclear what
the constraints on broadening/narrowing of senses are supposed to be,
the possibility of this kind of approach means that it is currently
unclear whether there remains any role for UCs to play on the contextualist model. (We might also note that without UCs contextualism may come to seem more closely aligned to Travis' occasionalism,
with its underspecified lexical meanings, than it perhaps once did.)
Finally, we should note that if all non-standard pragmatic effects were
the result of modulation of senses, then the top-down/bottom-up
distinction would evaporate in one sense: all effects would be bottom-
up in the sense that they would be effects on something pre-existing
in lexico-syntactic form. However the distinction would remain in
another significant respect: marking the difference between an effect
demanded by lexico-syntactic constituents and an effect merely *allowed*
by lexico-syntactic constituents.

We have then, as shown in Figure 2, not a straightforward opposition between minimalism and an opponent. Rather we have a set of
possible points of agreement and disagreement and a range of nuanced

	Travis	Carston	Recanati	Stanley	C&L	Borg	Bach
1) Top-down pragmatic effects on the proposition literally expressed (semantic content)?	✓	✓	✓	x	x	x	x
2) Semantic content is speech act content?	✓	✓	✓	✓	Not exactly	x	x
3) Basic Set Assumption?	?	x	x	x	✓	x	?
4) Wide context is semantically relevant?	✓	✓	✓	✓	✓	x	x
5) Unarticulated pragmatic effects on semantics?	x	✓	✓ (officially)	x	x	x	x
6) Do lexico-syntactic features alone sometimes give rise to propositions?	x	✓	✓	✓	✓	✓	✓
7) Do lexico-syntactic features alone always give rise to propositions?	x	x	✓	✓	Probably	✓	x

Figure 2. Some points of agreement and disagreement in the debate.

positions that thus open up. (We should note that Figure 2 almost certainly doesn't exhaust the dimensions of difference here, though it does, I hope, capture the main points of current contention.) In what follows I'm going to take the most significant point of contention between minimalism and alternative approaches to semantics to revolve around the issue of whether free, top-down, purely optional pragmatic effects are sometimes/usually/always required to get one to a complete proposition expressed. That is to say I will focus on the rejection of propositionalism and the claim that either we must allow that semantics is infested with rich pragmatic processes or we must admit that semantics deals with sub-propositional constituents (where these two options are, it seems, mere terminological variants of each other).

CHAPTER 3

Propositionalism and Some Problem Cases

The conclusion of Chapter 1 was that, when we ask about the possible motivation for adopting a particular stance on the form a semantic theory should take, the positions we can really motivate are (some form of) standard formal semantics (e.g. minimalism) or (some variety of) standard use-theoretic semantics (e.g. occasionalism). However, if these are our only two genuine options it may seem that the battle is over, for there is something of a consensus view in recent literature that a position like minimalism depends on the truth of 'propositionalism' (the idea that every well-formed declarative sentence expresses a complete proposition relative to a context of utterance). Yet, it is argued, propositionalism is obviously false. The primary class of cases appealed to in the literature to demonstrate the falsity of propositionalism are sentences which contain an expression which is not standardly treated as context-sensitive but which nevertheless seems in some way intuitively incomplete prior to contextual enrichment. So, take the sentences 'Flintoff is ready', 'Pietersen has had enough', and perhaps 'It is raining': in each case we seem to be unable to evaluate the sentence for truth or falsity until we learn from the context in which a token sentence is uttered what Flintoff is ready to do, what Pietersen has had enough of, or where it is raining.[1]

---

[1] Whether 'it is raining' is a genuine case of incompleteness or not is a much discussed issue (see Recanati 2007b for an overview). In Borg 2004a I argued that the sentence can give rise to an argument of inappropriateness but not incompleteness (that is to say, there is a proposition the sentence literally expresses, namely, *that it is raining*, but this is not the proposition usually conveyed by an utterance of the sentence).

Sentences like these put pressure on the minimalist to give up one or more of her first three core commitments (as given in Chapter 1, §1.1). For, unchallenged, they seem to show either that, contrary to (i), not every well-formed declarative sentence has a complete proposition as its semantic content, or that, contrary to (ii), there is not an exclusively lexico-syntactic route to semantic content, or that, contrary to (iii), the set of context-sensitive expressions in natural language is not significantly constrained. The aim of this chapter is to see how minimalism might respond to these apparently incomplete cases without giving up on any of her core commitments. One of the key claims I want to make here is that the cases standardly appealed to should not be thought of as a single, homogeneous set. Rather it is possible that very different things may be going on in different cases and thus the minimalist is licensed in proposing a range of different strategies which might be appealed to in different cases (this point is made in Sainsbury 2008). Unless it can be shown that there is a case which resists all of the minimalist's coping strategies, then, this argument against propositionalism fails.

The structure of the chapter is as follows: in §1 I'll introduce the challenge to propositionalism in a little more detail, then in §2 I'll consider how opponents of minimalism might deal with the problem cases (with the suggestion being that they look especially problematic for semantic relativism). Then, in §3, we will turn to the minimalist responses to the problem and I'll sketch what I take to be the range of options open to the minimalist. As noted, the contention will be that there are a wide range of moves open to the minimalist to deal with problem cases and that it is far from clear that there are any cases for which none of the explanatory moves will prove adequate. Thus the rejection of propositionalism on the basis of these kinds of putatively incomplete expressions proves (as yet) ill-founded.

(1) The challenge to propositionalism

As noted at the outset, a key assumption of minimalism is what Bach 2007b has labelled 'propositionalism', which he defines as 'the conservative dogma that every indexical-free sentence expresses a proposition'. However, if minimalism is committed to propositionalism, then many writers recently have assumed that minimalism must be rejected for it is taken to be simply obvious that propositionalism is false. There are a range of potentially problematic cases for pro-postionalism (such as non-declarative moods, metaphor, sentential fragments and conventional implicature) but in recent work the prime candidate for motivating a rejection of propostionalism has been the apparent existence of well-formed sentences which apparently fail to express complete propositions prior to rich contextual input. This fail-ure is witnessed in a 'felt inability' (the phraseology here is due to Taylor 2001: 53) to truth evaluate the sentences as they stand. Thus consider the following examples, where only the material outside the square brackets is verbally or orthographically present:

1. Jill went to a local bar [local to whom?].
2. The café is on the right [relative to what?].
3. Tipper is ready [for what?].
4. Paracetemol is better [than what?].
5. It is raining [where?].
6. Ted is tall [for a what?].
7. The apple is red [in what respect?].
8. There is milk in the fridge [in what form and quantity?].

All of these sentences can and have been used to argue that we can't attribute truth or falsity to the claims (some) sentences express with-out first learning further information, from a specific context of utterance, which answers the sort of questions in square brackets above. For instance, with respect to (3) Gauker 2011 suggests: 'Apart from some facts about the background against which the sentence is uttered, the sentence does not tell us *what* Tipper is ready for. We can-not tell from the sentence uttered and our knowledge of its literal meaning what facts have to hold in order for an utterance of the sen-tence to be true' (see also Bach 1994, 128ff, Taylor 2001, Carston 2002, Recanati 2004, Clapp 2007, MacFarlane 2007a, among many others). Since we don't know, without contextual information, under what conditions the content expressed by these sentences would be true, the conclusion is that what these sentences express on the basis of their lexico-syntactic constituents alone must be semantically incomplete. To reach the level of a proposition we need to appeal to the context of utterance, even though nothing marked in the lexicon or syntax of the sentence requires or compels this appeal, thus propositionalism is wrong. How then might one respond to this kind of argument for semantic incompleteness?

(2) Non-minimalist responses to the problem cases

Although I am primarily concerned with the possible minimalist responses to these kinds of cases, let's begin by noting how competitor accounts might deal with the issue of incompleteness. First, according to the indexicalist, such cases do not show that propositionalism is wrong, what they show is that there is more syntactically marked context-sensitivity in our language than we might initially have envisaged. Our felt inability to truth-evaluate the claims syntactically expressed by sentences like (1–8) outside a context of utterance is warranted, but this is because there are syntactic elements within the sentences which require contextual relativization prior to determining their semantic contribution. So, for instance, an indexicalist might argue that the sentence 'Ted is tall' contains the gradable adjective 'tall' which cohabits with context-sensitive variables at the level of logical form (a proposal in the style of Stanley 2002), or which is an indexical in its own right (a proposal in the spirit of Rothschild and Segal 2009), or which picks out a context-sensitive property (a proposal in the spirit of Hawthorne 2004). In each of these cases, we are right to think that 'Ted is tall' is not truth-evaluable prior to contextual input, but this is simply because 'tall' is a context-sensitive term. The sentences above then are held to be entirely on a par with sentences containing obviously context-sensitive elements like 'This is red' or 'That's mine'. Neither kind of sentence, it is argued, suffices to show that there is something wrong with propositionalism, rather what is shown is simply that sentences with context-sensitive elements require relativization to an appropriate context of utterance prior to determining their semantic content (overtly context-sensitive expressions are the topic of the next chapter).

The contextualist, on the other hand, will argue that the phenomenon of incompleteness does suffice to show that propositionalism is wrong—that, in at least some cases, there cannot be a purely lexico-syntactic route to propositional semantic content. For at least some of the examples in (1–8) the contextualist will claim, given just the lexico-syntactically realized elements of the sentences, we end up with something which is less than fully propositional. To get from these syntactically derived 'propositional radicals' (Bach's term) to a full-blown proposition or a complete thought what we need are top-down pragmatic effects.[2] That is to say, contextual information must be allowed to play a role in the content of the proposition literally expressed even though it is pragmatically not syntactically mandated (i.e. even though the pressure for incorporating such content comes from features of the context of utterance itself and not from syntactic elements within the sentence).

Finally, considering the relativist position on incomplete predicates, the claim will apparently be that the sentences in question are context-sensitive, though not in the sense of expressing different propositions in different contexts, but in the sense of admitting different contextually provided parameters against which the content the sentence expresses can be assessed for truth or falsity. So two utterances of 'Flintoff is ready' are held to express one and the same literal content, though this is a content which requires provision of a contextual parameter prior to truth-evaluation, thus what the sentence expresses may have different truth-values in different contexts. Whether the relativist view coheres with propositionalism or not then is something of a moot point. On the one hand, the advocate of a relativist view for, say, 'ready' might claim that a sentence like 'Flintoff is ready' does express a complete proposition, though one which is not truth-evaluable prior to provision of a contextual parameter for readiness. This would seem to give us the kind of approach to Travis-style cases suggested by Predelli 2005, and the 'radical relativism' sketched, but not endorsed, by Recanati 2008: 44–5. It would also seem to fit with the model of assessor-relativism proposed by MacFarlane 2005. Finally, Kölbel 2008: 27 also outlines a relativist response to Travis-cases apparently along these lines: 'The proposition expressed by the sentence 'The leaves are green.' remains invariant as long as we are talking about the same leaves at the same time. However whether that proposition

---

[2] We should note that this point is not accurate at least as far as Recanati's 2004, 2010 version of contextualism is concerned; see Chapter 2, §5.

counts as true, whether assessing it counts as correct, depends on the specific purpose against which we are evaluating that proposition. We cannot in advance predict for what purposes people may venture to assert the proposition that those leaves are green at that time. Thus again, we need to add a new parameter to the circumstance of evaluation: propositions have their truth-value relative to pairs <w, p> of a possible world w and a purpose p'.

One might worry that on this approach what counts as a proposition is no longer particularly transparent, for we are asked to entertain the possibility of complete propositions which are not, per se, truth-evaluable. More fundamentally, however, the relativist who adopts this move doesn't actually seem to accommodate the driving intuition in incompleteness cases, which precisely was that the sentences in question *fail* to express complete propositions prior to contextual input of some form. Now, the relativist might respond by simply rejecting intuitions of incompleteness as semantically relevant. She might perhaps suggest that the intuitions are not of propositional non-completeness, but of propositional completeness paired with non-truth-evaluability.[3] Ultimately, given the problems with the second relativist strategy to be looked at below, this move may turn out to be the most promising one for the relativist. Note, however, that such a move would lead to relativism inheriting what many have taken to be the most serious explanatory debt of minimalism, namely the claim that there is a minimal proposition to be expressed by a sentence like 'Flintoff is ready' or 'Pietersen has had enough' prior to any rich contextual input. Thus we should be clear that, to this extent at least, the explanatory debts of the two approaches would turn out to be equivalent.

A more natural move by the advocate of relativism, then, would be to claim that what is expressed by 'Flintoff is ready', prior to provision of a contextual parameter for counting as ready, is something which fails to meet the standards of a complete proposition (since, after all, it

---

[3] Note, however, that such a move would leave her at a loss to explain the apparent divergence in judgements between cases which, on this relativist model, are analysed entirely on a par. That is to say, it is unclear how such a position would explain the fact that speakers have intuitions of incompleteness for 'Flintoff is ready' but not for either 'Flintoff is ready to bat' or 'That is a red Braeburn apple grown in the UK in 2009', when in all three cases, according to relativism, we have a content which is truth-evaluable only given the provision of additional contextual parameters.

is not truth-evaluable as it stands). However, while this move might accommodate intuitions about incompleteness, it is clearly incompatible with the arguments used to motivate adding parameters in the first place, which require the content expressed by sentences prior to relativization to parameters to be propositional. So, recall that a major motivation for relativist views was the desire to capture the data surrounding agreement, disagreement and retraction. For instance, concerning a taste predicate like 'fun', most advocates of relativism want it to be the case that when A says 'Riding roller coasters is fun' and B says 'It is not the case that riding roller coasters is fun' they are genuinely disagreeing with each other (albeit in a 'no fault' sense); see Kölbel 2003, Lasersohn 2005. The agreement/disagreement data is supposed to be captured by claiming that the sentence 'riding roller coasters is fun' expresses the same proposition in the mouths of both speakers (e.g. it doesn't express the relativized content that *riding rollercoasters is fun for the speaker*) but that assessment of this proposition is relative to a standard of taste which may differ across interlocutors. However, if what is expressed by (at least some) sentences prior to provision of appropriate parameters is something less than fully propositional it is not obvious that such agreement/disagreement data can be captured (at least for those sentences), for it is at least prima facie compelling to think that what we can agree or disagree about must be propositional.[4]

Furthermore, as Recanati 2008: 58–9 points out (see also McGrath's 2007 review of Kölbel 2002), when people agree or disagree over sentences like 'Flintoff is ready' or 'it is raining' it is implausible to think that what they are agreeing or disagreeing about is some context-insensitive content:

There are plenty of cases in which we must distinguish between the *lekton* [the content retrieved by syntactic processing alone] and the complete content, but in which there can be no genuine (dis)agreement about the *lekton*. Thus I call you on the phone, and commenting upon my situation I say 'It

---

[4] See Cappelen and Hawthorne 2009 for a defence of the view that agreement/disagreement requires propositional content. We might also wonder why, if semantic relativism admits of propositional radicals in these cases, it finds them an anathema in other cases. Wright 2008: 169 expresses what I take to be a related worry about the status of relativized propositions, arguing that they are not capable of being genuinely representational.

is raining'. If you say 'No, it isn't', meaning that there is no rain in *your* situation, there is misunderstanding rather than genuine disagreement.

To capture agreement/disagreement data in these cases, then, it seems that we need to allow that what people are debating is the content arrived at by allowing the contextually determined parameters to play a role (what Recanati terms 'the Austinian proposition'): if the speaker on the phone means *it is raining where I am* then it is this contextually enriched proposition which must be rejected if one wants to disagree with her. It is then the proposition supplied by indexicalism not that supplied by relativism which forms the subject of agreement or disagreement. Now Recanati 2008: 59–61 argues that this does not mean relativism has no explanation of our behaviour in these cases. In brief, his explanation is as follows: 'we can maintain that agreement or disagreement is about complete contents...Alleged 'faultless disagreement' cases...are no exception. In such cases, the disagreement is about the Austinian proposition consisting of the *lekton* together with the standards of the community. The speaker says that the painting is beautiful (for the community), and the audience denies that it is beautiful (for the community).' If this is right, however, the boundaries between indexicalist/contextualist approaches, which allow contextual information to contribute to the proposition expressed, and this kind of relativist approach seem to be significantly blurred. Recall that the indexicalist will claim that (due to the presence of, say, a hidden indexical) the sentence 'that painting is beautiful' expresses a propositional content such as *that painting is beautiful according to some contextually determined standard*, while the contextualist will claim that (due to the availability of free enrichment) this is the first proposition to be recovered for any utterance of this sentence (i.e. it gives the 'explicature' in Sperber and Wilson's terminology). Recanati's relativist then seems to *agree* with these views that the first proposition to be recovered, and about which we agree/disagree, does indeed include these standards as part of its content; but if this is the case, then the status of relativism as a distinct position seems seriously undermined.

Of course, an advocate of the relativist view for, say, taste predicates need not advocate the approach across the board for all predicates. Thus in response to concerns about incompleteness an advocate of the relativist position for some expressions might concede that in these cases we should opt for an indexicalist or contextualist treatment. However, if the relativist view doesn't in fact suffice to handle cases like (1–8) above this might be thought to add to the questions raised about the true explanatory value of the approach voiced in the last chapter, especially since incompleteness cases apparently display the same kind of behaviour that was taken to motivate relativism in other areas.

To summarize then: indexicalism rejects the claim that incomplete expressions show propositionalism false, rather they show the need to treat more expressions than the obvious ones as indexicals. Contextualism does take the existence of incomplete expressions to show propositionalism to be false, revealing instead the need for free pragmatic enrichment. Finally, it is somewhat unclear whether relativism takes incomplete expressions to show propositionalism false or not, with neither answer seeming to fit entirely comfortably with the overall relativist approach.

(3) Minimalist responses to the problem cases

In the remainder of this chapter, then, I want to examine possible minimalist responses to incompleteness. As we will see below, I think there are a number of avenues a minimalist might pursue here: first, she might hold that the intuitions emerge from some overlooked overt indexicality (§3.2), second, she might argue that intuitions of incompleteness and context-sensitivity really emerge from an overlooked ambiguity (§3.3), third she might argue that they emerge from some overlooked covert syntactic structure, where this covert structure might be either context-insensitive (§3.4) or context-sensitive (§3.5). Finally, the minimalist might simply reject at least some arguments of incompleteness out of hand (§3.6). Before we examine these options, however, I want to start by considering a very important argument surrounding both CSAs and incompleteness, namely the slippery slope argument of Cappelen and Lepore 2005. Exploring this argument will, I think, help to clarify what is really at issue in arguments about incompleteness and, following on from this, help to clarify the range of possible minimalist solutions.

(3.1) The slippery slope from incompleteness to contextualism?

According to Cappelen and Lepore, if we treat some expression *e* as context-sensitive on the basis of intuitions of incompleteness for sentences containing it, we are destined to end up treating all expressions as context-sensitive, for the kinds of questions which evoke feelings of incompleteness for *e* can be raised for any expression whatsoever (see also Borg 2004a, Chapter 4, §4.5.1). For instance, if one feels that 'Steel isn't strong enough' is semantically incomplete because one needs to know, from the context of utterance, what steel is not strong enough *for* prior to truth evaluation, then one must also hold that the sentence 'Steel isn't strong enough to support the roof' is semantically incomplete. For, as Cappelen and Lepore 2005: 63 stress, the latter sentence, no less than the former, leaves open further questions about the conditions under which it will be true; e.g. how long must the support last (a few seconds, many years?), what temperature range is relevant to the claim, how much steel is envisaged, and so on and so forth. Just as the first sentence, and the others in (1–8), leave open further questions about the precise conditions under which they will be true, so do any precisifications of those sentences. Thus if we judge one sentence incomplete, it seems we must deem all sentences semantically incomplete. Cappelen and Lepore frame this slippery slope as a descent into contextualism, for they define what they call 'moderate contextualism' (MC) as the view that at least *some* expressions not standardly treated as context-sensitive are in fact context-sensitive, while they define 'radical contextualism' (RC) as the view that *all* expressions in natural language are context-sensitive. So admitting one expression as context-sensitive on the basis of incompleteness amounts, for them, to adopting moderate contextualism and their argument is that it will lead inevitably to adopting radical contextualism. As they write 2005: 59: 'If Incompleteness Arguments... suffice to show that MC is true (i.e. if they suffice to show that an expression e not in the Basic Set [of intuitively obvious context-sensitive expressions] is still context-sensitive), it follows that RC is true'.

Now this way of framing the slippery slope—as a slide from moderate to radical contextualism—is not one I would want to embrace, for as stressed in Chapter 1 and in Borg 2007, I would prefer to define contextualism by the denial of an exclusively lexico-syntactic route to semantic content (i.e. by the possibility of free pragmatic enrichment). Given this understanding of contextualism, the argument that accepting one expression as context-sensitive on the basis of incompleteness will lead us directly to contextualism doesn't go through, for even if it turned out that all expressions were covertly context-sensitive (i.e. if some kind of radical indexicalism were true) this wouldn't, in itself, suffice to show that there were free pragmatic effects (indeed, if all expressions were indexicals this would seem likely to make any appeal to free pragmatic enrichment otiose). However, although I'd reject the direct move to contextualism envisaged by Cappelen and Lepore, it does seem to me that there is a less direct move from an acceptance of an incompleteness argument to what I would count as genuine contextualism. This descent into contextualism occurs, I think, because if one accepts that an intuition of incompleteness is relevant to determining the literal meaning of the sentence in question, one thereby undermines, or empties of all content, the requirement that all contextual effects on semantic content be syntactically triggered. That is to say, if it is these intuitions which are doing the work in motivating a context-sensitive analysis, then it is unclear why one would then think that the accommodation of these intuitions must go via the syntactic route; why not simply allow that semantic content is sensitive to this requirement and meets it via free pragmatic enrichment? The worry (which was discussed initially in Chapter 1, §4.1) is that, if it is essentially the intuitions about meaning thrown up by incompleteness or by context shifting arguments which are motivating us here, then the appeal to syntax becomes an entirely idle wheel (see also Szabo 2006). As Neale 2007 stresses, if the aim of semantics is to capture these kinds of intuitions, and given that we lack any independent argument to show that there must be an exclusively lexico-syntactic route to semantic content, the more parsimonious route would be simply to allow that pragmatic information can have a direct effect on semantic content. Content is enriched because our grasp of the communicative situation tells us that this is so, there is no need to add the (now unmotivated) requirement to find some hidden syntactic correlate for the contextual contribution.

Furthermore, since the resolution of putative incompleteness puts pragmatic processes firmly in the driving seat as far as the recovery of semantic content is concerned (since it is pragmatic, context-driven processes which determine what syntactic constituents a sentence contains and what values these syntactic elements take), the explanation of how one comes to grasp semantic content on the radical indexicalist model seems down on all fours with the model offered by the advocate of free pragmatic enrichment. Recovery of the proposition expressed by a sentence will go via a rich appreciation of the context in which sentences are uttered (i.e. it will require knowledge of what the speaker was intending to convey, what objects, properties and events were salient, etc). Again, then, the idea that there is a formal, syntax-driven route to meaning seems to have been entirely emptied of content. It is the pragmatic processes which are doing all the work, with the radical indexicalist's insistence on a syntactic marker in all cases being an apparently quite unnecessary appendage. So, the thought is, if intuitions of incompleteness alone provide arguments for hidden-indexicality, they also provide arguments for free pragmatic enrichment and indeed are more plausibly captured in this latter way. If this is right, then there is in fact an argument, albeit a less direct one than that envisaged by Cappelen and Lepore, from a claim of indexicality for one expression on the basis of intuitions of incompleteness to a claim of contextualism (where this position is defined by the possibility of free pragmatic enrichment).

Note, however, that the argument I envisage here for the descent into contextualism does not make use of the claim (stressed in Cappelen and Lepore 2005) that if one holds one expression *e* to be context-sensitive on the basis of incompleteness intuitions then one must hold all expressions context-sensitive (rather it makes use of the claim that if intuitions of incompleteness are what we want to accommodate then the proposed trip through the syntax en route to the semantics is unwarranted). This in itself may be a good thing, because, although I've endorsed the slippery slope in question myself (see Borg 2004a: §4.5.1), it is not absolutely certain that it does go through. For, although Cappelen and Lepore are certainly right that we can generate the same kinds of questions for a proposition like *that Flintoff is ready to bowl* which can be levelled at the proposition *that Flintoff is ready*, nevertheless an opponent might still contend that people simply feel uncomfortable with assigning propositional status in the latter case in a way that they do not in the former. If this is right, then what it shows is that, while the intuition of incompleteness might be expressed or elicited via questions about the conditions under which the alleged proposition will be true or false, the intuition does not *reduce* to the ability to ask such questions.[5] This seems to be the position of Bach when he responds to Cappelen and Lepore as follows:

[A]lthough further such questions can always be asked, the issue is whether an answer is needed to yield a proposition. Once a proposition is determined, further questions may still need to be answered, but only in order to determine what the speaker means in uttering the sentence...[Cappelen and Lepore's] central criticism is that I haven't provided a 'principled' basis, a 'criterion', for deciding whether or not a given sentence manages to express a proposition, something capable of being true or false. They're right. Such questions have to be settled on a case-by-case basis and what they're asking for is a general criterion. However the lack of a general criterion doesn't show that the distinction is bogus. After all, there is no criterion, no principled basis, for distinguishing men who are bald from men who aren't. Would [Cappelen and Lepore] argue, regarding men with at least one hair on their heads, that either they're all bald or that none are?[6]

---

[5] This would be to deny MacFarlane's 2007a: 242 rendition of the problem of incompleteness (as one which is *rooted* in the conditions under which a putative proposition is true) and to hold instead that intuitions of incompleteness, though often voiced in terms of such concerns, should really be viewed as a brute phenomenon: for some sentences but not others subjects have the intuition that what they express prior to contextual enrichment fails to reach the standard of something truth-evaluable but is rather incomplete as it stands.

[6] Bach 'Minimalism for dummies', http://userwww.sfsu.edu/~kbach/replytoC&L.pdf. Now the worry of course is that if the fact that a sentence fails to express a proposition isn't marked by some testable property of the content the sentence expresses (like whether or not it leaves questions open) then we are left with nothing more than brute intuitions and, furthermore, it is clear that not everyone's intuitions go the way Bach wants. So for instance, Cappelen and Lepore don't intuit that any of the examples (1–8) are incomplete, while according to Bach's intuitions (3) and (4) are incomplete but (5–8) are certainly not, yet Travis's intuition is of incompleteness in all these cases (and indeed, in every case), and it seems that, since Stanley holds that every common noun is syntactically context sensitive, he too ought to have the intuition that all of (1–8), and indeed subject/predicate sentences in general are incomplete prior to contextual enrichment. Thus while Bach's complaint that no general condition needs to be offered (because we can settle the issue of propositionality/lack of propositionality on a case-by-case basis) might be warranted in principle, it does leave him open to the charge that, while we can expect our intuitions about vague properties, like baldness, to be fairly uniform, it is not obvious at all that our intuitions of incompleteness display a similar degree of agreement. In what follows, however, I will assume, with Bach and contra this point, that there is some sub-set of sentences (including ones like 'Flintoff is ready' and 'Steel is strong enough') for which ordinary speakers tend to have strong, unshiftable intuitions of incompleteness.

If this is right then perhaps the slippery slope from a claim of incompleteness for one expression to a claim of incompleteness for all can in fact be avoided, for there remains something special about the paradigm cases of incompleteness and this, it is suggested, is something which an adequate theory ought to respect. That is to say, ordinary speakers react differently to the sentences 'Flintoff is ready' and 'Flintoff is ready to bowl', and they tend to feel uncomfortable with the claim that *Flintoff is ready* expresses something truth evaluable in a way that they do not feel uncomfortable with a claim of truth-evaluability for *Flintoff is ready to bowl*.

So, where does all this leave us? Well, on the one hand it leaves us embracing the outward form of Cappelen and Lepore's slippery slope argument: I do think that treating one expression *e* (not standardly treated as context-sensitive) as an indexical just on the basis of incompleteness arguments does take the first step on a slippery slope to contextualism (as I would define the position, i.e. via the possibility of free pragmatic enrichment). Not, however, because if we treat one expression as an indexical for this reason we must treat all as indexicals, but rather because (as argued in Chapter 1, §4.1) allowing this kind of reasoning to affect our syntactic analysis actually undermines any reason we might have for thinking that syntactically represented elements fully dictate semantic content. If we are going to accept that intuitions of incompleteness tell us about semantic content then we should simply allow that they tell us about semantic content directly (i.e. via free pragmatic enrichment)—the extra trip through hidden syntax is unmotivated. So accepting an incompleteness argument for *e* does, I think, launch a descent into contextualism, but not for the reasons Cappelen and Lepore give. Thus, on the other hand, I remain agnostic about Cappelen and Lepore's actual slippery slope argument. For although they are clearly right that the openness to further questions often taken to be indicative of incompleteness applies equally well to all sentences, it may still be that incompleteness is not *equivalent* to the ability to ask such questions. I think this remains something of a moot point, but I would like to leave open the possibility that there are some sentences (perhaps 'x is ready', 'x has had enough' or sentences with gradable adjectives) for which subjects have genuine intuitions of incompleteness, when they do not have such intuitions for fuller versions of those sentences. With these points in mind, then, let's turn to the minimalist's options in the face of putative incompleteness.

(3.2) Treat some problem cases as involving standardly indexical terms

To many people familiar with the debate in this area, the idea that minimalism could accommodate some cases of putative incompleteness by analysing them as containing overlooked indexicality will sound like apostasy, for isn't minimalism simply *defined* as the claim that there are no context-sensitive terms beyond the obvious ones? However, as should be obvious by now, that is not how I think the position should be understood. Contrary to the approach of Cappelen and Lepore 2005, minimalism here is not defined by the assumption that there are no context-sensitive terms beyond those intuitively and immediately recognized as such by ordinary speakers. Rather the position is characterized as the inheritor of the formal semantics model of a purely lexico-syntactic route to semantic content and the limitation on context-sensitivity (which minimalism certainly does sign up to) is held to emerge in the course of motivating, and giving substance to, this claim. So, the worry which I raised in Chapter 1, §3, was that if we allow semantic intuitions about context shifting arguments (CSAs) to play the primary role in decisions about an expression's status as syntactically context-sensitive or not, then it is no longer clear what could motivate the idea that the route to semantics is entirely syntactically marked. For if it is these kinds of semantic intuitions about what a speaker succeeds in conveying which are our primary concern then it seems we have no reason to insist on a syntactic marker for context-sensitivity rather than allowing our semantics to capture our semantic intuitions directly by permitting free pragmatic enrichment. The point I wanted to stress above was that the same goes for intuitions of incompleteness: if we are prepared to take intuitions concerning incompleteness seriously as indicative of a sentence's semantic status then this entails putting pragmatic processes in the driving seat in a way which makes it quite unclear why we should hold on to the idea that context can only affect content when syntactically mandated. If we are going to allow that an intuition that, say, 'Flintoff is ready' is incomplete reveals something fundamental about the semantic status of that sentence then we have no reason to think that what it tells us is that 'ready' is an indexical, rather than telling us simply that the sentence stands in need of (non-syntactically triggered) contextual input. That is to say, we no longer have any reason to hang on to the idea that the route to semantic content is exclusively paved with syntactic footholds.

The claim of §3.1 then was that a minimalist cannot allow that an expression is context-sensitive simply on the basis of intuitions about incompleteness without risking a slide into contextualism. Note, however, that this still leaves room for the possibility that the minimalist can explain some putative cases of incompleteness in terms of indexicality, so long as there are *independent* grounds for a context-sensitive analysis. So, while Cappelen and Lepore define minimalism by the claim that there are no context-sensitive terms beyond the obvious ones, I'd (at least partially) define minimalism by the (admittedly not very catchy slogan) 'no context-sensitivity without clear lexico-syntactic evidence of context-sensitivity'. Minimalism (as I conceived it in Borg 2004a and as I conceive it here) is a reaction to the tendency in some quarters to wheel in context-sensitivity (whether lexico-syntactically triggered or as a result of free-enrichment) as a panacea for all our apparent semantic ills: can't get your account of belief reports right? Put in a hidden indexical. Concerned about CSAs? Make all sentences massively context-sensitive. Perplexed by the behaviour of epistemic terms? 'Knows' must be an indexical. It is this sort of manoeuvre that I take minimalism to recoil in horror at. Yet a rejection of any kind of quick and easy move to context-sensitivity was never, at least as I saw it, tantamount to saying that the only context-sensitive expressions are those people unreflectively spot as context-sensitive. I think a minimalist can afford to be relaxed about the idea that, for all she knows, it might turn out that, say, gradable adjectives are context-sensitive. The evidence in this case currently looks somewhat weak, I think, and one point the minimalist is keen to make is that the behaviour of expressions like 'tall' (or 'knows', etc) which has generally prompted theorists to provide a context-sensitive analysis (CSAs and incompleteness) can be explained *without* this move to context-sensitivity (see the proposals below in §§3.3 and 3.4). But the point I want to stress here is that it is, I believe, perfectly cogent to construe minimalism not as a theory that states that we have a complete and final account of the lexicon of our language which reveals just *these* expressions (demonstrating some discrete list) to be context-sensitive (the model of minimalism found in Cappelen and Lepore 2005), but rather to see it as more of a mission-statement.

Minimalism for me is the view that there can be no lexico-syntactic context-sensitivity without clear, independent evidence of that context-sensitivity, i.e. without clear behavioural evidence (say, about the way the expression combines with other expressions) and this will be the kind of evidence to be delivered by those working in linguistics departments and dealing with modifier interactions, cross-linguistic evidence, etc, rather those thinking up complex possible contexts of utterance in philosophy departments. The turn to context-sensitivity cannot, according to the minimalist, be the immediate recourse of someone who is concerned that the content a sentence appears to deliver fails to fit our intuitions about what a speaker who utters that sentence says or about how the content of a speech act is assessed over time, etc. From this point of view, the debates about CSAs and incompleteness turn out to be red herrings: for claims about lexico-syntactic form what matters is syntactic evidence, not the sort of semantic intuitions conjured up in these cases. So if we could produce independent evidence of context-sensitivity then it might still be possible for at least some of the cases used to demonstrate incompleteness to be explained via an appeal to overlooked context-sensitivity, without this amounting to taking a first step on the slippery slope to contextualism. On this approach, Stanley's binding argument (see Stanley 2002 and elsewhere) is certainly a step in the direction of the right kind of evidence for these kinds of claims, though it is clear questions can be asked about how robust this particular piece of evidence is (see Chapter 1, §4.1).

That there might be more overt indexicality than can be found on Kaplan's original list is perhaps most clearly demonstrated by those expressions which, despite not making Kaplan's list, nevertheless seem essentially perspectival. Thus in the case of expressions like 'local' or 'left' it seems much more plausible that intuitions about word meaning itself (independent of any CSA construction or claim of incompleteness) suggest treating those words as genuinely context-sensitive. That is to say, there are reasons to think that, on reflection, ordinary subjects *do* respond to words like 'local' and 'left' in just the same way that they respond to 'this' and 'that', treating them as having a lexical meaning

which is genuinely context-sensitive.[7] Indeed, we might note that
Cappelen and Lepore 2005: 1 actually include these expressions, albeit
tentatively, on their list of the 'Basic Set of Context Sensitive Expressions'
under the banner of 'contextuals': 'which include common nouns like
"enemy," "outsider," "foreigner," "alien," "immigrant," "friend," and
"native" as well as common adjectives like "foreign," "local," "domes-
tic," "national," "imported," and "exported"'. Thus at least some putative examples of incompleteness might really be examples of standard
context-sensitivity (parallel to 'this is mine'). I'll return to the question
of just how far an appeal to standard indexicality might be allowed to
go for the minimalist in §3.5.

(3.3) Treat some problem cases as involving ambiguity

On this approach, any felt inability to truth-evaluate prior to contextual input actually emerges from a need to disambiguate which of two
or more homophonic expressions is in play. So, for instance, one of the
cases raised by Travis which seems most problematic from a minimalist
point of view revolves around colour terms: in Travis' 2008: 111 infa-
mous example, we are asked to consider how can Pia say something
intuitively true with her utterance of 'The leaves are green' when
talking about painted leaves to a painter looking for something coloured green for his composition, but say something false with the very
same sentence picking out the very same painted leaves when talking
to a botanist looking for green leaves for an experiment on photosyn-
thesis. The apparent difference in truth-value across these shifts in
conversational context seem clearly to demonstrate that colour terms
are incomplete without reference to contextually determined ways in
which objects are said to satisfy the property in question.

However, it seems that the minimalist might begin to make some
headway with this problem by adopting Kennedy and McNally's 2010
ambiguity approach to colour terms. On this approach, 'green' may
either pick out a property of manifest colour (a gradable term, divided

---

[7] If this is right it would accommodate Cappelen and Hawthorne's 2009: 39 feeling that 'there are
some contractions where [minimalism] is particularly unpalatable—it is difficult to see how "Nicola
turned left" can express the same truth-condition in a way that abstracts from the perspective that is
operative for the speaker'.

into COLOUR QUANTITY and COLOUR QUALITY uses) or a classificatory colour property, where the object is claimed to have some property related to the colour, e.g. an underlying biological make-up, serving as a signal, etc. This second expression is an absolute, non-gradable term. The evidence for a genuine ambiguity here comes from facts about the very different kinds of modifiers the two uses allow. For instance, uses of colour terms to pick out manifest colour allow modifiers like 'very' or 'mostly', while classificatory uses prohibit such modifiers—the apple on the tree can be said to be 'quite red' but the traffic light signal can only, non-metaphorically, be said to be red or not red (though one can certainly say, e.g. 'the traffic light was almost red', what this indicates is the time interval before the light became red, not the degree of redness it possessed at the time of utterance). If this kind of ambiguity analysis is shown to be warranted then at least part of the explanation in the Pia case is that she does not produce two sentences of the same type in the two different contexts. Rather in the first she uses a term picking out manifest colour, while in the second she uses a different term to pick out classificatory colour; the confusion arises because these two different terms are homonymous. What Kennedy and McNally's work shows is that there are a range of often subtle linguistic facts which may get compressed in putatively problematic cases and which need to be fully drawn out and investigated before these kinds of cases can be taken to require a move to free pragmatic effects.

Finally, we should also note that the move to posit some form of overlooked ambiguity is only one of the things that might emerge from a more careful consideration of specific cases. For instance, it might emerge that at least some problem cases are well handled by appealing to the presuppositional information associated with a term. So, for instance, while it might be a fact that subjects judge 'Flintoff is ready' as problematic in contexts where there is no salient thing for which he is ready, this might reflect not the context-sensitivity of 'ready' and its incompleteness without contextual completion but rather a sensitivity to the presuppositional information associated with the term. In this way intuitions about sentences like 'Flintoff is ready', where the proposed reading is that he is ready *simpliciter*, are traced to the inaccessibility of the proposed reading (since it flouts presuppositional information) rather than judgements about genuine well-formedness (thanks to Chris Kennedy for this point).

(3.4) Treat some problem cases as involving hidden
       (context-insensitive) syntax

One possible move the minimalist might make in the face of putative cases of incompleteness is to claim that there *is* a substantive difference between 'Flintoff is ready' and 'Flintoff is ready to bowl', however the difference is *not* that the latter does, while the former does not, express a proposition. Rather it is that the latter does, while the former does not, explicitly mark at the surface level all the argument places required by the verb. On this approach, the claim would be that an expression like 'ready' is lexically marked as a transitive expression, it means *x is ready for something*. Thus when only one argument place is filled at the surface level, the existence of the other remains, marked (by an existentially bound variable) in what Taylor 2001 refers to as the 'sub-syntactic basement'.[8] The explanation for our intuitions of incompleteness in the case of 'Flintoff is ready' (and *mutatis mutandis* the lack of such an intuition in 'Flintoff is ready to bowl') is that we are aware of the need (supplied by the lexical structure of 'ready' itself) for two arguments, which is in tension with the phonetic delivery of only one argument. On this approach, then, 'ready' always expresses a content marking two argument places *even* when it appears concatenated with only one argument at the surface level, as in 'Flintoff is ready'.

The proposal to hand is not equivalent to adopting an indexicalist position on 'ready', for 'ready' on this model makes *exactly* the same contribution to any proposition literally expressed by a sentence in which it appears. So, in a context where what is salient is being ready to join the fire service, 'Jill is ready' literally expresses the proposition that *Jill is ready for something* not that *Jill is ready to join the fire service,* and in a context where taking an exam is salient 'Jill is ready' still means simply that *Jill is ready for something.* There is no hidden context-sensitivity here, there is only a hidden argument place, putatively delivered via the transitive nature of 'ready' (in Schaffer's 2011 terms, the proposal is a form of variabilism not indexicalism. The question of the compatibility of variabilism and minimalism will be returned to in Chapter 6). Furthermore, it seems that there is some evidence that what we

---

[8] Exactly what this proposal might amount to will be examined in more depth in Chapter 5 when discussing what I will term 'organizational lexical semantics'.

want in these cases is simply an existential claim like 'ready for something', rather than a specific, contextually determined variable, for it seems that a speaker can always rescind from the contextually salient value in these cases. Thus, consider a situation in which what is contextually salient is the question of whether Flintoff can continue bowling and where a speaker, S, says 'Flintoff will continue'. Clearly the audience will take the speaker to be asserting that *Flintoff will continue bowling*. However, if Flintoff is then led limping from the field, it seems clear that S could seek to vindicate herself by continuing her utterance with 'not bowling, of course, but being depressingly prone to injury'. Now such a speaker will no doubt be guilty of flouting all sorts of Gricean rules of good communication, but she doesn't seem to literally contradict herself (as would be the case had her initial utterance literally expressed *Flintoff will continue bowling*).[9]

Taking intuitions of incompleteness in certain paradigm cases in the way suggested above was a move I first proposed in Borg 2004a: 225–231. However it is not a proposal which has gained wide credence, so, we might ask, what is wrong with the idea of treating 'A is ready' as expressing the proposition that *there is something for which A is ready*?

Recently, Chris Gauker 2011 has objected that the proposed equivalence fails since 'x is ready' and 'x is ready for something' display different entailment relations. So compare the following two inferences:

> *Ready Up:*
>   *Tipper is ready.*
>   Tipper is ready for something.
> *Ready Down:*
>   *Tipper is ready for something.*
>   Tipper is ready.

Gauker suggests that Ready Up is clearly valid and notes that this is captured by treating 'ready' as having the lexical entry '__ ready __'. However, he objects that Ready Down is invalid, yet, on the proposal

---

[9] Of course, the minimalist cannot claim that this sort of evidence about speech acts yields the sole support for any proposed semantic analysis, but it does at least demonstrate that there is a more general, context-free content to which speakers can appeal in these cases. I'll return to the question of what (in lieu of intuitions about speech act content) might warrant the positing of additional argument places below, with respect to an objection from Jay Atlas.

to hand, Ready Down comes out just as valid as Ready Up. However, in response to this objection, I think the minimalist might query Gauker's intuition of invalidity here. Personally, I find it hard to hear anything at all wrong with Ready Down, specifically I can't think of a context in which it could be true that Tipper is ready for something and yet not true that Tipper is ready. Of course, there are plenty of contexts in which Tipper is ready for something but is not ready for some contextually salient thing, but the minimalist claim precisely is that the semantic content of 'Tipper is ready' is *not* that Tipper is ready to do some contextually salient thing. This latter content has the status of a pragmatic speaker-meant proposition only and it thus does not affect the validity of arguments like the one above. Furthermore, if there genuinely is any felt discomfort with *Ready Down* (a discomfort which is not felt, say, with Gauker's comparison argument 'George is looking for something therefore George is looking') this could be attributed to the fact that we move from a premise in which argument places are explicitly marked at the surface level to a conclusion where they are tacitly marked as demanded by the lexical entry of the expressions involved alone. This move from an explicit to a merely tacit presence might strike our ears as odd and I would suggest that, if we have any problem with Ready Down at all, it is at most that it generates a sense of oddness not of straightforward invalidity.

However, Gauker also has an argument to show that *Ready Down* cannot be treated, as I've suggested, as valid. He writes:

Suppose for a reductio that *Ready Down* is valid. Then, by the same token, we should say that the following argument is valid:

Negative Ready Down:
There is something that Tipper is not ready for.
Therefore, Tipper is not ready.

We could have an incomplete predicate—'unready'—that meant the same as 'not ready'. Then if *Ready Down* is valid, then by the same token, the argument having the premise 'There is something that Tipper is unready for' and the conclusion 'Tipper is unready' should be valid. But if that argument is valid, then so is *Negative Ready Down*. But if *Negative Ready Down* is valid, then 'Tipper is not ready' cannot mean 'Tipper is not ready for anything', because the premise of *Negative Ready Down*, 'There is something that Tipper is not ready for', does not imply 'Tipper is not ready for anything'. But if 'Tipper is not ready' does not mean 'Tipper is not ready for anything', then the minimalist cannot account for the fact that *Ready Bottom* ['Tipper is ready and Tipper is not ready'] is a contradiction.

There are two points I'd like to make here. First, I think there is something potentially untoward in the move from *Negative Ready Down* to the introduction of the predicate 'unready'. Note that, for the minimalist, *Negative Ready Down* contains both a quantifier and a negation, in both the premise and the conclusion. Thus in both cases there are different scope readings to be considered.[10] Both the premise and the conclusion, on the current minimalist proposal, can be read either as '∃x ¬ready <tipper, x>' or as '¬∃x ready <tipper, x>', and this difference in scope readings reveals that *Negative Ready Down* is not in fact valid—it is possible for the premise to be true (i.e. when it is read as '∃x ¬ready <tipper, x>') and the conclusion to be false (i.e. when it is read as '¬∃x ready <tipper, x>'). This point may be disguised by the introduction of a predicate like 'unready' which stipulates the narrow scope reading for the negation and which thus does result in a valid argument. So, I think it is consistent for the minimalist to maintain the *Ready Down* is valid while at the same time claiming that *Negative Ready Down* is invalid.

Second, and more fundamentally, Gauker objects that the minimalist who allows for a narrow scope reading of the negation in this way cannot account for the fact that the sentence 'Tipper is ready and Tipper is not ready' is a contradiction, i.e. the minimalist will have to allow that it is true in some context. Yet, just as with *Ready Down*, this seems to me something the minimalist who opts for hidden argument places might in fact be willing to admit. For if the sentence is equivalent to 'Tipper is ready for something and Tipper is not ready for something', as the current proposal has it, then there will clearly be contexts in which this is true. *Ready Bottom* can't be treated as a straightforward contradiction by the minimalist: there are contexts in which it is false (namely those where the second variable is bound by the first quantifier, claiming that '∃x (ready<tipper, x> & ¬ready <tipper, x>') and contexts in which it may be true (namely those where '∃x ready <tipper, x> & ∃y ¬ready <tipper, y>'). So, although I'd reject Gauker's claim that treating *Ready Down* as valid entails treating

---

[10] Atlas (forthcoming) in objecting to the move to posit an existentially quantified variable in these cases also correctly points out that Borg 2004a wrongly ignores the issue of scope for the negation.

Negative Ready Down as valid, I'd also reject the claim that *Ready Bottom* is a contradiction. Unreflectively, *Ready Bottom* may strike as a straightforward contradiction (because it's surface form is that of 'p and ¬p') but because of the more complex syntactic form allocated to the sentence on this proposal this initial impression is held to be incorrect. Yet isn't Gauker right to think that *Ready Bottom must* be treated as a contradiction, that this point is non-negotiable? Well, I don't really think so: although the initial reaction of ordinary speakers to a sentence of this form must carry significant weight, it seems that this immediate reaction can be undermined with a degree of reflection and that a little bit of prompting ('is there any way in which this sentence might be true?') would elicit reactions compatible with the analysis suggested here. So while Gauker is I think quite right to point out that, on the minimalist proposal of this section, *Ready Down* is valid and that this may allow *Ready Bottom* to be treated as non-contradictory, it seems to me that neither of these claims constitutes a reductio of the position.

Mark Sainsbury, though he is happy enough with minimal truth-conditions for sentences like 'Sid grunts' or 'That's red', is not happy with them in cases like 'Pietersen has had enough' and 'Flintoff is ready':[11]

[The former] cases contrast sharply, I believe, with other Contextualist examples. 'Jill is ready' is not equivalent to the near-trivial 'Jill is ready for something or other,' and 'This girder is strong enough' is not equivalent to the near trivial 'This girder is strong enough for something or other'. We should not let the fact that there are specific ways to grunt undermine our confidence in the full correctness (barring considerations related to tense) of the claim that 'Sid grunts' is true iff Sid grunts. By contrast, 'ready' and

---

[11] Sainsbury 2008 also objects to the way I presented my view in Borg 2004a, pointing out correctly that the actual axioms I gave, where I relativized incomplete predicates to the context of utterance (e.g. treating 'ready' as meaning 'ready to do something in the context of utterance'), were wrong. Obviously, an utterance of 'Jill is ready' might be true not if Jill is ready to do something in the context of utterance but if she is ready to do something in some other context. The relativization in the original formation was introduced to account for the presence of tense in the example (and to leave room for other examples which contained overt indexicality, like 'She is ready'). However, Sainsbury is quite right that the axioms don't work as they stand. Instead then I need to ensure that overt indexicals don't impact on the completion of 'ready'. So perhaps the correct way to accommodate tense in these cases is along the following lines (suggested by Sainsbury, pc):

If a speaker in uttering 'Jane is ready' refers (with the tense) to time t, then the utterance is true iff Jane is ready for something at t.

'enough' may well demand a treatment which reveals their content as context-sensitive.

As something of an aside, we might note here that, if independent evidence (i.e. evidence not reliant on our semantic intuitions concerning particular utterances, of the kind appealed to in CSAs or incompleteness) were to be presented for the context-sensitivity of 'ready' and 'enough' then, as noted above, I think the minimalist *could* accept a context-sensitive analysis for them. For as I argued earlier (contrary to Cappelen and Lepore 2005), I think minimalism can accept the possibility of extending the class of syntactically context-sensitive expressions should genuine evidence of context-sensitivity come to light (though, personally, for 'ready' et al., it seems extremely unlikely to me that such evidence will be forthcoming).

However, let's leave this point to one side, and proceed on the assumption that there are no independent tests which suffice to show 'ready' is context-sensitive. Why is Sainsbury so clear that 'ready' doesn't have an unspecific meaning (to be spelt out simply as *is ready* or via the more complicated underlying form ⌜∃x ∃y ready <x,y>⌝)? His objection seems to be that there are tests for unspecific meanings (of the kind he allows to be assigned to 'Sid grunts' and 'That's red') which are failed by paradigm cases of putative incompleteness. So, considering the sentence 'John runs', he writes: 'Context may make some more specific way of running salient, but in doing so, the semantics are not touched. The test is that one can coherently deny that John runs in a salient way, without this being either a retraction or a contradiction'. Or again, for 'That's red', a speaker who says 'That's red, though not in the salient respect' doesn't apparently contradict themselves or necessarily retract the initial part of their statement. Sainsbury also suggests a second test: 'A test [of unspecific meanings] is this: if we can add something equivalent to 'in some way or other' without making a significant difference, the verb is semantically neutral concerning the way it is to be satisfied'. However, as far as these two tests are concerned, it is far from obvious that we get a difference of behaviour for an expression like 'ready' (understood either simply as 'ready' or as 'ready for something') and other expressions, like 'runs'. For instance, considering the first test, in a context where signing a contract is salient, a speaker who says 'Jill is ready, though only to talk about things and not yet to sign' seems to me (as noted above) to be open to charges of Gricean communicative failings rather than a charge of straightforward inconsistency (as would be the case if 'ready' meant *ready to do the salient thing*). Neither does the second test provide clear evidence that 'ready' does not have an unspecific meaning. Sainsbury suggests that the default reading of 'Sid grunts' is that he grunts *in some way or other* (where this interpolation doesn't make a significant difference), but it is hard to see why one couldn't simply claim that the default reading of 'Jill is ready' is that she is ready *in some way or other* (where it seems to beg the question to claim, without further argument, that this interpolation does make a significant difference). At best then I think Sainsbury's tests are neutral with regard to the claim that 'ready', like 'grunts', has an unspecific meaning (at worst—for opponents of minimalism—I'd say that they actually encourage this reading of 'ready').

Finally, Jay Atlas has offered a range of objections to this minimalist position (eg., see Atlas forthcoming) which we need to consider. Some of his objections relate to the minimalist framework in general (for instance, he is unhappy with the move by minimalism to treat so many utterances as non-literal, i.e. allowing that what the speaker communicates diverges from the semantic content assigned to the sentence produced) and as such are addressed by the motivation and defence of minimalism offered throughout this book. Others, however, are directed specifically at the current proposal for paradigm examples of incompleteness. His central objection is that the motivation for positing bound variables in these cases can only come from a consideration of what people actually express when they utter the sentences in question, but that this kind of consideration is one that has already been ruled out of bounds for determining semantic content by the minimalist (since she holds that judgements about what a speaker conveys when uttering a sentence are not semantically relevant, i.e. that 'what is said' is a pragmatic notion). Thus, considering the sentence 'It's raining', he writes:

If one thought that a semantic theory should theorize about the recursively generated sentence-strings of a language, with attention to their syntactic features, how in the world did Borg get her intuition that the sentence 'It's

raining' permits recovery of an existential quantifier quantifying over locations from its lexical content and its syntactical structure?[12]

He continues:

The difficulty that Borg faces is that she wants a sentence-semantics to be
propositional, truth-conditional, logically formish. And she is a victim of a
prejudice shared with Cappelen and Lepore: the proposition (that must be)
expressed by 'It's raining' is the 'least common denominator' of or an 'abstrac-
tion' from all the speech-act contents of uttering grammatical sentences
beginning with 'It's raining...' And, surely, there have to be locations referred
to, directly or indirectly, in the contents of those speech acts!...Borg believes
that John Searle and Recanati are contextualists because they confuse verification-conditions with truth-conditions...Now it turns out that Borg is an
existential-quantificationalist because she confuses verification-conditions
with truth-conditions.

A first, minor, point to note is that I don't think I did (in Borg
2004a or anywhere else as far as I can recall) claim that the semantic
analysis of 'It's raining' is *it's raining at l*. On the contrary, in fact,
I argued that (2004a: 218; see also the pragmatic explanation of the
added locational element in 2004, §4.6), although one's initial
impression might be that the sentence is not truth-evaluable without a location,

as Recanati and others have stressed, there seem to be situations which show
that this initial impression is mistaken, that is, which show that a sentence
like 'It's raining' can determine a complete proposition without the provision of a contextually specified location... [Thus] the problem is not that *no*
proposition is recovered on the basis of formal features alone, but that this
very general proposition is rarely the one expressed by the speaker who
utters 'it is raining'.

Also, unlike Cappelen and Lepore, I've never suggested that minimal
contents should be 'the least common denominator' across different
utterances of a sentence. Indeed, I explicitly reject this claim in Borg
2007, arguing instead that minimal propositions are often not asserted
by a speaker at all. Atlas is, however, quite right to point out that the
nature of minimalism rules appeals to what is intuitively said by a

[12] Atlas forthcoming.

speaker out of court in the process of justifying any proposed semantic analysis. So, let's rephrase what I take to be Atlas' main challenge with reference to examples where I have suggested that there might be a covert existential quantification, e.g. cases like 'ready'. His question then becomes, I take it, in the absence of an appeal to what speakers usually express by uttering 'Jill is ready', what could possibly motivate the view that 'is ready' means 'is ready for something', i.e. what could possibly license the appeal to an expanded logical form?

A first answer to this question is that I don't believe minimalism must eschew all appeals to speaker intuitions or standard use. As I've tried to make clear elsewhere (Borg 2005), even a formal semanticist must accept that linguistic meaning emerges in some way as a result of what speakers do with (and think about) their words. A semantic theory which delivers sentence level contents will only stand a chance of being correct if it has the right lexical entries for the expressions it treats, but it is hard to see where we will get accounts of lexical meaning from except via appeal to what people can tell us about the meanings of their words and a study of the conditions under which they use or retract them. Notice however that intuitions about lexical content hold at the type level (what does the word 'ready' mean?) not at the level of one-off utterance meaning (what did this speaker mean when she said that 'Jill is ready'?) It is the latter kind of appeal to intuitions, at least as supposedly semantically relevant, that minimalism regards as unacceptable (and I've argued that she should regard them as unacceptable since admitting them as semantically relevant would be to immerse a putatively formal theory in the broiling waters of pragmatics, effectively destroying the divide between formal and use-based accounts). Secondly, the correctness or otherwise of positing an additional argument place in the logical form here would be open to exactly the same kinds of verification as any other putative unvoiced syntactic element is open to (e.g. evidence to do with distribution and binding used to motivate the presence of a phonetically null subject in agentless passives like 'The boat sank') and we might hope that these kinds of tests could eventually show such an analysis right or wrong (thus revealing, for any given expression, whether a minimalist should pursue the response to intuitions of incompleteness given in the last section or the one pursued in this section).

Finally, it was not the intuitions about what speakers typically or always express which led to the proposal that 'Flintoff is ready' be analysed as *Flintoff is ready for something*, rather it was a desire to take seriously the intuition that, as it stands, 'Flintoff is ready' is incomplete (by treating our intuitions of incompleteness as revelatory of the essentially transitive nature of 'ready' rather than as revealing the context-sensitivity of the expression). Now, as seen with Cappelen and Lepore's position on this example, it is possible for the minimalist to simply deny that the intuition exists (or, better, to deny that it can exist only for 'Flintoff is ready' and not for 'Flintoff is ready to eat pasta', etc.) However, it seemed to me in Borg 2004a and it still seems to me now that there is also another route she could take, which is to accept that an intuition of incompleteness is had by ordinary speakers faced with, say, 'Flintoff is ready', but not for them when faced with, say, 'Flintoff is ready to bowl', but then to argue that the force of the intuition has nothing to do with semantic differences between the sentences (specifically, it does not show that the latter does, while the former does not, express a proposition). Instead, then, the intuitive difference can be taken to emerge from the phonetic differences between the two sentences (i.e. the fact that the latter sentence fills all the argument places 'ready' requires with phonetically realized material, while the former fails to do this).[13]

[13] Lenny Clapp has objected that this proposal entails that we should find intuitions of incompleteness pretty much whenever we have a discrepancy between surface form and logical form, such that the former omits material to be found at the latter, yet such intuitions are not the norm. For instance, we don't, as Clapp points out, have an intuition of incompleteness for B's utterance in the following case:

A: I want some milk.
B: Me too.

Notice, however, that the same point seems to hold for 'ready':

A: Shall we go to the cinema now?
B: I'm ready.

It seems then that ordinary cases of ellipsis do not give rise to incompleteness intuitions: we don't have an intuition of incompleteness in cases where the value of the unvocalized material is easily recovered from the surrounding discourse. It is only when considering 'I'm ready' or 'Steel is strong enough', etc. out of context, where the divergence between what is contributed to the logical form by the lexical information associated with an expression and what is realized in the phonetic form of a sentence containing that expression is particularly stark, that we feel any discomfort with these kinds of cases. To get intuitions of incompleteness, then, we need not only a discrepancy between surface form and logical form, we also need it to be the case that the content of any phonetically omitted structure is provided solely by the lexical information associated with the terms in a sentence, rather than being recovered from the surrounding linguistic context. I'll return to this point in Chapter 6.

Nothing in the arguments canvassed so far seem to demonstrate to me that this move is necessarily mistaken.[14,15]

(3.5) Treat some problem cases as involving hidden (context-sensitive) syntax

In §3.2 I suggested that the minimalist might remain sanguine about the idea that there are more indexicals in our language than can be found on Kaplan's original list. The point stressed there was that, from the minimalist's perspective, it was not so much a question of 'how many indexicals are there?' as 'what kind of evidence can be found for treating expression *e* as an indexical?' For, from the minimalist point of view, the only appropriate evidence for a claim of lexico-syntactic context sensitivity was lexico-syntactic evidence (robust type level intuitions about word meaning or syntactic evidence, e.g. about the

---

[14] We might note that Stanley 2000: 231 rejects in passing the view that 'tall' might be held to mean 'tall for some comparison class', arguing that the putative literal meaning is not available to speakers and thus fails a condition for semantic content. He writes: 'Suppose then that I showed a speaker a picture of a tiny dwarfish man, surrounded by normal sized men. Pointing at the dwarfish man, I uttered "That man is tall". On the envisaged theory, the semantic content of my sentence, relative to this context, is a true proposition...But this semantic content is utterly inaccessible to the speaker...there is no possibility of a sensible discourse along the following lines:

    A: (*pointing to the dwarfish man*) That person is not tall.
    B: That's absurd; everyone and everything is tall except for the smallest thing."

However it is hard to know how much weight one can rest on Stanley's point here. For instance the following response by B seems perfectly okay to me:

    B: Well, he would be tall for a five-year-old, but I think he is much more than five.

That is to say, it seems fine to point out that while he isn't tall for the obvious comparison class he is tall for some other class, but this would seem to show a sensitivity to a more liberal content for 'tall' than the one Stanley envisages. What makes this case particularly odd to my ears is that Stanley goes on to claim (2000: 232) that the following discourse is fine:

    A: Every bottle is in the fridge.
    B: Well, your fridge couldn't possibly be that large!

Yet, to my ears at least, both cases seem entirely on a par, involving a semantically competent but presumably uncooperative interlocutor.

[15] We might also note, as pointed out by Nathan Salmon (pc), that if applied to gradable adjectives, this kind of move might seem to offer a solution to sorities puzzles. If 'bald' were understood to mean *bald with respect to some standard* it might well be the case that removing just one hair from someone with n hairs on their head could move them from not-bald according to some standard to bald according to that standard. However, this might also seem to be worrying, revealing that the move to incorporate existentially marked argument places overgenerates in precisely the way that contextualist solutions do, allowing us always simply to dissolve what appear to be genuine problems. As Williamson 2005: 294–5 notes in opposition to contextualism: 'Contextualism supplies a perfectly general strategy for resolving any apparent disagreements whatsoever. Since some disagreements are genuine, we should not always follow that strategy'. An advocate of existentially marked argument places needs then to be very careful that the move doesn't become a universal panacea, which is to say that evidence for unpronounced argument places (in terms of intuitions about lexical meaning and syntactic evidence) needs to be very carefully considered.

combinatorial properties of the expression), rather than high-level intuitions about the intuitive speech act content of utterances containing the expression. So, the claim was, indexicality might remain a property we could discover an expression to have even if it was not obviously classified in this way by ordinary speakers. An upshot of this general claim about indexicality is that, if we think there can be overlooked overt indexicality, it would seem that there can be no reason for then disallowing the possibility of covert context-sensitivity, i.e. the idea that a sentence might contain syntactically represented but phonetically unpronounced elements whose semantic contribution was dependent on features of the context of utterance. Perhaps, for instance, modal claims might introduce a hidden relativization to near-possible worlds, where determining which worlds these are is something which requires adversion to the context of utterance. Still, the claim is, so long as non-speech act evidence can be accumulated for such an analysis, this kind of approach could still fit within the general minimalist framework. Thus again, while context-sensitivity per se might standardly be held to be the nemesis of semantic minimalism, on my understanding of the position it is only improperly motivated indexicality (i.e. indexicality required merely to get our account of semantic content to limn our intuitions about speech act content) which is problematic.

Be this as it may, however, there are obviously going to remain many cases which are used to demonstrate incompleteness and for which it seems no appeal to context-sensitivity is ever going to be licensed by looking at our accounts of lexical content nor at the syntactic behaviour of an expression. So what is the minimalist to say in these remaining cases?

(3.6) Treat some problem cases as arising from misplaced intuitions

According to Cappelen and Lepore 2005: 116:

An utterance of 'A is ready' expresses the proposition *that A is ready* and it is true just in case A is ready.

That there is a complete proposition to be recovered from a sentence like 'Flintoff is ready' (prior to pragmatic enrichment) might, they allow, seem initially surprising, but it shouldn't be. Recall that the worry with the putative proposition *that Flintoff is ready* is supposed to be that we can't specify the conditions under which it would be true.

The putative truth-condition Cappelen and Lepore offer doesn't tell us, for instance, whether the sentence is true if Flintoff is ready to bowl but not bat, or ready to walk out of the press conference but not ready to go to the party, etc (see MacFarlane 2007a: 242). However, as Cappelen and Lepore point out, in this respect 'Flintoff is ready' is no different to any other sentence for which claims of incompleteness seem much less compelling.

For instance, if we take the sentence 'Flintoff is ready to bowl' to express the proposition *that Flintoff is ready to bowl* we can still ask: is this proposition true in a world where he is ready to bowl at Smith but not at Tendulker, or ready to bowl a bouncer but not a googly, or ready to bowl a cricket ball but not a bowling ball? Given that putatively complete propositions (like *Flintoff is ready to bowl*), then, do not serve to settle all the questions one might ask about the conditions under which they are true, the fact that putatively 'incomplete' propositions also don't do this shouldn't be held against them. So, *unless* one is willing to concede that no sentence expresses a complete proposition outside a context of utterance (as, say, is Travis), then one cannot hold that 'Flintoff is ready' fails to express a proposition purely on the grounds that it leaves open a range of questions about the more fine-grained description of the situation which makes the sentence true. Furthermore, as Cappelen and Lepore point out, we do know something about the conditions under which *that Flintoff is ready* will be true—it will be true if he is ready to bowl, or ready to bat, or ready to eat pasta, etc. Which is just to say that it will be true just in case there is something which Flintoff is ready to do.

So, on this last defence of propositionalism, intuitions of incompleteness are judged simply to be confused. Though an intuition of incompleteness *might* pick up on some other property of a proposition (for instance, an intuition of incompleteness for 'A is ready' might be a confused response to the fact that the proposition semantically expressed by this sentence is almost trivially true, holding in almost any world where A exists, or it might reveal a sensitivity to the pre-suppositional content carried by 'ready'), still our intuitions do not indicate anything peculiar about the metaphysical status of the proposition *that A is ready* (and of course, the same goes for *that A has had enough, that A is tall,* etc.) Now this is a defence of minimalism for which I have much sympathy (see Borg 2004a, §4.5.1). After all, it is not as though we have a clear criterion of proposition-hood waiting in the wings and by whose lights *that Flintoff is ready* is ruled clearly sub-propositional while *that Flintoff is ready to bowl* is ruled clearly propositional. Rather, by the pretty murky conditions we have for propositional status (that a content should be a thinkable, a sayable, and, what I have taken here to be crucial, that it be truth-evaluable) it seems to me that the former content clearly does count as propositional. After all, while the proposition *that Flintoff is ready* will be satisfied by almost every situation in which Flintoff is to be found, still we do know in principle what it would take for this proposition to be false—it would simply have to be that there is nothing for which Flintoff is ready.

Now some theorists have objected that this claim must be mistaken for there are clear reasons to think that such minimal propositions are not really propositions at all. Thus we find MacFarlane 2007a: 242, when discussing Cappelen and Lepore's claim that 'Chiara is tall' expresses a proposition (rather than a propositional fragment), writing:

What Cappelen and Lepore mean, presumably, is that [the proposition that *Chiara is (just plain) tall*] has a truth-value at every circumstance of evaluation…I believe that most philosophers' worries about minimal propositions are rooted in puzzlement over the question this claim naturally provokes: At which circumstances of evaluation is the proposition that Chiara is (just plain) tall true? Here I'm using the technical term 'circumstance of evaluation' the way David Kaplan taught us to use it in *Demonstratives* (1989). A circumstance of evaluation includes all the parameters to which propositional truth must be relativized for semantic purposes. Though Kaplan himself included times in his circumstances of evaluation (and contemplated other parameters as well), the current orthodoxy is that circumstances of evaluation are just possible worlds. In this setting, our question becomes: at which possible worlds is the minimal proposition that Chiara is (just plain) tall true?

The objection to minimal contents then is that they are simply too thin, too minimal to count as genuine propositions since they do not serve to determine a set of worlds within which they are satisfied (see also Clapp 2007). Recanati 2004: 92–3 appears to have a somewhat similar challenge in mind with respect to truth-conditional versions of minimalism when he writes:

The central idea of truth-conditional semantics (as opposed to mere 'translational semantics') is the idea that, via truth, we connect words and the world. If we know the truth-conditions of a sentence, we know *which state of affairs must hold for the sentence to be true*; and that means that *we are able to specify that state of affairs*. T-sentences display knowledge of truth-conditions in that sense only if the right-hand-side of the biconditional is *used*, that is, only if the necessary and sufficient condition which it states is transparent to the utterer of the T-sentence. If I say '*Oscar cuts the sun* is true iff Oscar cuts the sun', without knowing what it is to 'cut the sun', then the T-sentence I utter no more counts as displaying knowledge of truth-conditions than if I utter it without knowing who Oscar is (i.e. if I use the name 'Oscar' deferentially, in such a way that the right hand side is not really *used*, but involves some kind of mention).

The suggestion here seems to be that genuine semantic content should guarantee that a subject who grasps that content *knows how a world satisfying that content will be* (in some substantial, not merely disquotational sense), yet minimal contents fail to provide such a guarantee.

However, at this juncture, it seems to me that a minimalist should ask her opponent exactly what condition on genuine semantic (propositional or truth-conditional) content minimal content is supposed to fail to meet. There are, I think, three possible candidates: first, perhaps a genuine proposition, p, must guarantee that, for every possible world, w, someone who grasps p is capable of telling whether or not w satisfies p (*mutatis mutandis* for truth-conditions). So, for instance, grasp of the semantic content expressed by the sentence 'The cat is on the mat' must suffice to allow us to decide whether the sentence is true or false in a world where the cat is floating a few centimetres above the mat (see Searle 1980). However, the problem with this criterion is that it seems far too strong. For instance, if we are worried by the presence of the preposition 'on' it might be suggested that it should be given a contextually enriched, pragmatic sharpening. Though it is a little unclear exactly how this might go, one suggestion would be that (leaving aside the issue of incomplete definite descriptions) the enriched proposition should be something like *the cat is on the mat in the normal sense of being on associated with cats and mats*. Now (even allowing that there are such things as 'normal senses' here) there is a problem of grain, for it is not obvious that such senses should attach at the level of cats and mats or to something more fine-grained. The normal way in which a cat sits on a mat might not be identical to the normal way in which a Manx cat sits on a doormat (specifically, while the former might specify tail location, the latter clearly won't). However, leaving this problem to one side, it still seems that the original worry can resurface for this contextually enriched proposition, for we can still ask is the proposition that *that cat is on that mat in the normal sense of being on associated with cats and mats* true in a world where the cat has most of three legs on the mat but most of one leg off it?

Perhaps then we should opt for something which makes the context-sensitivity of the proposition more evident, say *the cat is on the mat in the contextually salient sense of on*. However, even here it seems open to question whether the requirement to provide a determinate answer in all possible worlds is satisfied. For instance, imagine that you are looking for the cat and I assert 'The cat is on the mat', where this means that *the cat is on the mat in the contextually relevant sense*. Even having supplied a context it's not clear exactly when my utterance is true or false, for instance imagine the cat is wholly on the mat but the mat has been moved slightly to the left. Is what I say true, or is it false since it seems that the contextually relevant sense of 'on' here should specify something about the cat's location? And assuming that we want to say the utterance is true in this case, we can then ask how far to the left can the mat shift and what I say remain true: is my utterance still true if the cat is on the mat in a different room, a different house? Intuitions vary here, but the point is simply that appealing to 'contextually relevant senses' doesn't seem to help for there is no reason to think that the addition of a contextually relevant sense will result in a proposition which immediately tells us, for all possible worlds, whether or not the proposition is true or false at that world. For, given any contextually salient sense, it seems we can always gerrymander a situation where the answer is initially unclear, just as we could for the original minimal proposition. The problem we are homing in on here is, I think, that it is only maximally specific contents which would be capable of collapsing knowledge and verification (i.e. ensuring that if one knows a truth condition one can, without further information, verify whether it is satisfied in every possible world) but there is no reason to think that the literal meanings of sentences are given by maximally specific propositions.

A second, somewhat weaker version of the link between grasp of semantic content and the ability to sort worlds would be to claim that a genuine proposition, p, must equip someone who grasps it with the ability to tell for some large number of possible worlds whether or not p is satisfied in those worlds. However there are two points here: first, this is a condition which minimal propositions seem to meet. For instance, take the sentence 'Some apple is red' as having the minimal content *Some apple is red*. Such a content will sort worlds into those where some apple is red in some way (worlds which satisfy the truth-conditions of the sentence) and worlds where every apple is not red in any respect (so which fail to satisfy the truth-conditions), and one might imagine that we have a pretty large number of possible worlds on each side here. Of course, it is also true to say that a contextually enriched content, such as *that apple is red to degree n on most of its skin* would yield a more fine-grained sorting of worlds—it would get less worlds satisfying and more worlds failing to satisfy the content—but it is hard to see why this difference in number should be taken to ground a distinction between the semantic and the non-semantic. Indeed, and this brings us to the second point, one might worry about the very idea of grounding a difference in kind, i.e. propositional versus non-propositional, on a difference of degree, i.e. the number of worlds it enables a subject to sort, since we would need strong independent reasons to draw a line anywhere on the degree axis and assume that it cleaves the semantic from the non-semantic. It seems to me then that neither of our first two proposals are feasible.

Perhaps instead, then, the proper condition on proposition-level semantic content is not one concerned with what it *tells* the subject (i.e. not one about the sort of world-sorting abilities it endows on someone who grasps it), perhaps instead the proper condition is concerned simply with whether or not it sorts worlds appropriately, regardless of whether or not a subject has the ability to track this sorting in every case (this is apparently the force of MacFarlane's worry above). On this approach then a proposition p must suffice to determine, for every possible world, whether p is true or not in that world. As it stands, this condition is too strong (for instance, there are issues with worlds where objects fail to exist, worlds where fundamental laws are very different to those of this world, and perhaps with vagueness). However the basic idea—that propositions or truth-conditions must determine how the world must be in order to satisfy them—is one that a minimalist should embrace. For minimal truth-conditions do sort worlds effectively even though a subject who grasps a minimal truth-condition may have to do more work to *tell* which worlds are sorted in which way (this point will become pressing in the next chapter, concerning sentences containing genuine indexicals). The picture here bears affinities to Williamson's 2000 stance on vague predicates. As Williamson infamously holds there is a firm cut-off point for the correct application of vague predicates like 'bald', even though where this cut-off point lies is something which is epistemically closed to us. Similarly, then, the current stance holds that there is a fact of the matter about whether or not, say, the sentence 'That cat is on that mat', relative to a context c, is true or false, but the approach also allows that this fact of the matter may be unknown to an agent who both fully comprehends the literal meaning of the sentence and is in a position to assess the relevant state of affairs in the world. On both accounts, then, there is held to be a fact of the matter about whether the sentence is true or false of a given state of affairs, though it is allowed that the agent may be unable to ascertain whether the sentence is true or false of the given situation. The difference between the two approaches, then, lies in the extent of this epistemic opacity: for Williamson the truth or falsity of a sentence containing a vague term in a borderline case is essentially and permanently hidden from us (there is a fact of the matter about whether or not Bloggs, a borderline case of baldness, is bald but it is a fact we will never know). On the current approach to semantic content though, the thought is that an agent could in principle at least discover what the fact of the matter is, even in borderline cases, by further investigating the meaning of the expressions involved (e.g. setting out to discover whether the English word 'on' denotes a property true of cats and mats when cats have only three out of four legs resting on the mat, where this investigation would involve probing, among other things, ordinary speakers usage of the term). So, according to the minimalist, a sentence like 'the cat is on the mat' expresses a complete proposition on the basis of lexico-syntactic constituents alone and this proposition is what a subject needs to grasp to understand the literal meaning of the sentence, yet grasp of such a proposition may not, in and of itself, allow a subject to immediately tell for all possible worlds whether they are worlds which satisfy or fail to satisfy the propositional content (even though there is a fact of the matter to be discovered here).

The claim is then that conditions based on what grasp of a proposition or truth-condition ought to allow a subject to do (e.g. sort all worlds, sort most worlds, etc) will be ones which minimal content runs the risk of failing to meet. However the minimalist can afford, I think, to accept this, since she antecedently insists on a minimal conception of what possession of a semantic theory alone will allow one to do.[16] On the other hand, it seems that any plausible condition based on what a proposition or truth-condition *itself* should do will be one which a minimal theory of content will be able to meet. Thus the objection that minimal propositions are not genuine propositions can, I think, be rejected.

(3.7) Conclusion

To conclude then: the overall argument of this section has been that intuitions of incompleteness which apparently emerge around some well-formed sentences are not sufficient to show that those sentences fail to express propositions. Thus incompleteness intuitions do not show propositionalism wrong, and thus they do not show that minimalism must be rejected. First, we should note that in at least some cases the move to a context-sensitive explanation of their apparent incompleteness remains open. For instance, for expressions like 'right', 'left', 'local' and 'nearby', where speakers' lexical intuitions suggest an essentially perspectival lexical entry, it would be perfectly consistent with minimalism that they be treated as genuine, syntactically marked context-sensitive terms. Second, we need to pay attention to the subtle and often complex linguistic facts here, which may reveal richer and more nuanced structures within a natural language than a superficial take on our language captures. So, for instance, we may discover more ambiguity, or a greater role for presuppositional information, or richer lexical entries, within putatively problematic cases than initially supposed (§3.3 and §3.5). As Kennedy and McNally 2010: 97 note:

---

[16] After all, the minimalist credo states that knowledge of semantic content, on its own, is a paltry thing, something that only once embedded in the complex network of cognitive faculties realized within an ordinary human mind becomes truly worth knowing. This point is stressed in Borg 2004a.

Once context-dependency is identified in meaning, it's a fast and slippery slope to the conclusion that everything is indexical. However, easy-to-overlook linguistic data from expressions like degree modifiers show that humans do limit the semantic space of possibilities and grammaticize those limits to a certain degree. Such observations underscore the relevance of the results of linguistic research for debates such as those raised by the Travis facts.

Finally, in at least some cases, the minimalist is simply going to deny that the putatively problematic cases are really problematic at all. In this way she will deny her opponents claim that there is anything fundamentally wrong with the minimal contents minimalism posits for the sentences concerned (§3.6). Overall, then, as suggested by Sainsbury 2008, the minimalist cannot give a universal answer to cases which purport to show propositionalism fails, but taking them on a case-by-case basis it becomes plausible to believe that the minimalist can in fact deal with them. Armed with the full gamut of explanatory strategies available, minimalism can dissolve all the problem cases without recourse to free, purely contextually driven, pragmatic effects on genuinely semantic content.

However, even if this is right, it may in fact bring little comfort to the minimalist, for it seems now that a different objection hooves into view. For if it turns out that the recovery of the propositions expressed by at least some sentences (for instance, those containing demonstratives or contextuals like 'nearby' and 'local') relies on an appeal to rich, intensional aspects of a context of utterance (like the intentions of the current speaker) then it seems that the minimalist's credentials still remain fraudulent. That is to say, despite the claim to be offering a formally respectable theory capable of delivering the propositional content of each and every well-formed sentence, if it turns out that she is still smuggling in an appeal to the intentions of the speaker (in order to account for genuine cases of context-sensitivity) then it still seems that the minimalist project to deliver an account of propositional semantic content free from the dark magic of pragmatics is doomed.[17] This, then, is the challenge from apparently intention-sensitive terms and it is the topic of the next chapter.

---

[17] Recanati 2004: 57 objects that appealing to speaker intentions within a formal semantic theory is a form of cheating: 'We pretend that we can manage with a limited, narrow notion of context...while in fact we can only determine the speaker's intended referent (hence the semantic referent, which depends upon the speaker's intended referent) by resorting to pragmatic interpretation'. See also Borg 2007, §3.iv.

CHAPTER 4

Intention-Sensitive Expressions

The problem to be addressed in this chapter concerns the apparent clash between, on the one hand, our strong intuition that speaker intentions are, in at least some cases, relevant to reference determination and, on the other, the stated aim of this essay to defend an approach to semantic theorizing which seems destined to treat current speaker intentions as irrelevant in determining semantic content. Exactly why minimal semantics has a problem with semantically relevant speaker intentions is something I will examine further in §1. Once the problem is laid out, however, it will be clear that there are three possible avenues for the theorist to pursue: first, she might deny the assumption that speaker intentions are actually relevant for reference determination (the proposal to be explored in §2). Second, she might deny the claim that minimal semantics has a problem with referential intentions (the proposal to be looked at in §3). Third, she might try to hold apart issues of reference determination and issues of semantic content (the topic of §4). As we will see, the first two putative solutions both face apparently serious (and related) problems. Hence I will suggest that it is the final move to hold apart issues of reference determination and issues of semantic content which provides the best solution for the minimalist to pursue. By adopting this position, I will argue, she can deflect the concern that grasping the semantic content of a well-formed sentence which contains a context-sensitive expression requires appeal to rich, intensional aspects of a context of utterance and in this way minimalism can retain its claim to be free of pragmatic magic.

(1) The problem of semantically relevant intentions

It is a well-rehearsed point in the literature that context-sensitive expressions seem to cause problems for formal approaches to semantics—they are, in Davidson's words, 'a very large fly in the ointment'.[1] Part of the problem that they cause (although not exactly the one Davidson himself was worried by) concerns the apparent role of the current speaker's intentions in determining semantic content for at least some of these terms. (In what follows I will concentrate on demonstratives as these provide the strongest intuitive cases for expressions whose semantic contribution is fixed by a speaker's intentions. However we should be aware that the class of putatively intention-sensitive terms ranges much wider than this, including at least indexicals, see Predelli 1998a, 1998b, and names, see Kripke 1980.) The worry, as we will see below, is most acute at the more extreme (minimal) end of formal semantics, however, it should be clear from the outset why speaker intentions are in principle disruptive to any variety of formal semantics. The worry can be seen as a kind of clash of perspectives: formal semantics aims to establish parallels between natural languages and the languages of logic, giving an account of literal linguistic meaning which runs directly from the formal, codifiable properties of a language. It aims to capture sentence meaning (which holds regardless of the motivation behind someone's utterance of a given sentence) entirely as a function of syntactic form and lexical meaning. However, if the general aim of a semantic theory is to capture the repeatable and the codifiable, then clearly the presence in natural language of a class of expressions whose semantic contribution is determined by nebulous and highly context-relative features like the intentions of the current speaker is problematic. An expression whose semantic contribution is determined by what the current speaker is thinking sits uncomfortably within an approach which treats semantic content as essentially immune to the vicissitudes or peculiarities of specific speakers. Thus, from the outset, it looks as if allowing current speaker intentions to be semantically relevant runs counter to the ethos of formal semantics and risks sliding the position towards the territory occupied by use-based approaches to meaning (by opening the door to meanings which are settled via an appeal to what the speaker intends to do with her words).

---

[1] Davidson 1967: 33. He goes on 'Both logicians and those critical of formal methods here seem largely . . . agreed that formal semantics and logic are incompetent to deal with the disturbances caused by demonstratives'.

Furthermore this a priori tension between the nature and aims of formal semantic theorizing and the nature of speaker intentions crystallizes into an apparently very powerful objection given more rigorous versions of the formal semantics programme. For, as I construed it in Chapter 1, minimal semantics holds that the path to meaning is paved exclusively with deductive, computational processes.[2] For the minimalist, meaning runs along purely syntactic rails and the move from syntax to semantics is one which can be rendered explicit in formal terms (e.g. via the canonical derivation of truth-conditions).[3] Yet within this kind of framework any appeal to speaker intentions seems illicit. For reasoning about speaker intentions seems clearly non-deductive: to work out what someone is thinking it seems we need to engage in rich, content-driven inference to the best explanation—the kind of reasoning the minimalist eschews en route to recovery of semantic content. This is a point I've argued for elsewhere (Borg 2004b), but the central idea is that, in attributing mental states, anything one knows is in principle relevant, though in practice one consults only a tiny subset of everything one knows. This open-endedness in principle combined with constraints in practice seems to show that the reasoning behind attributing mental states is not merely a function of structure but is sensitive to the content of the beliefs involved.

The problem for the minimalist may then be stated as follows:

(P1)   The semantic contribution made to sentences by at least some expressions depends on the states of mind of the speaker who produces those expressions.

(P2)   Reasoning about another's states of mind requires making an inference to the best explanation.

(P3)   According to minimalism, the only reasoning processes involved en route to recovery of semantic content are deductive, computationally tractable processes.

(C)   Minimalism cannot give an account of the semantic contribution made by at least some expressions.

---

[2] As noted in Chapters 1 and 2, not all minimalists feel the pull of a purely computational route to content, see Cappelen and Lepore 2005 and Borg 2007 for discussion.

[3] One reason a minimalist might be keen to hold on to the idea of an entirely formal, syntactic route to semantic content stems from the theory's connection with modular accounts of the mind; this argument is to the fore in Borg 2004a, Chapter 2.

However, laid out in this way, it is clear that there are at least three possible moves the minimalist might make in response to the argument. Perhaps the most obvious move is to reject (P1): despite initial appearances to the contrary, it might be a mistake to think that speaker intentions are relevant to reference fixing for demonstratives or other expressions. This idea, which I will term 'conventionalism' about reference, will be explored in §2. On the other hand, a minimalist might think to resist (P2). Although, as sketched above, it *looks* as if assignment of speaker intentions is not a formally tractable process, perhaps this is a mistake. One reason for thinking this comes from recent work in cognitive science where it has been claimed that there is a particularly intimate relationship between certain mental states (including referential intentions) and the behaviour which manifests them. Thus, in §3, I'll examine some of this work and see how it might solve the minimalist's problem. Finally, the minimalist might maintain that the argument is not actually valid, that is to say, she might accept all of (P1)-(P3) but deny that they jointly entail (C). This suggestion will be explored in §4.

(2) Rejecting (P1): conventionalism about reference

Although it seems initially plausible to think that speaker intentions are responsible for determining the reference for demonstrative expressions this assumption can be denied. Instead it may be held that there are conventional rules of use for context-sensitive terms which determine the referent for a token expression *without* appeal to speaker intentions. The conventional rules for demonstratives might, it seems, look either to demonstrations (pointing gestures, etc.), or to demonstrations along with other contextual cues, as the features which play this role. For instance, when Kaplan first introduced his distinction between pure indexicals and true demonstratives he suggested that demonstratives required an additional feature from the context of utterance in order to secure a reference, namely a demonstration. Without a demonstration a demonstrative, unlike an indexical, is taken to be semantically incomplete. It is this additional demonstration, rather than any associated intention, which (at least for the early Kaplan) determines the reference for a token demonstrative.[4] Clearly, were it to turn out that demonstrations were responsible for reference fixing and, in addition, that demonstrations themselves could be individuated in non-mentalistic terms (a point we will return to below), then the problem laid out in the previous section would simply evaporate, since it would turn out that there were no such things as semantically relevant speaker intentions (at least from the perspective of reference determination for demonstratives).

One immediate worry with this sort of move, however, is the fact that at least some demonstratives seem perfectly able to function *without* an attached demonstration. For instance, Kaplan himself gives the example of facing a line of soldiers when one of them faints dramatically. This serves to make possible an act of demonstrative reference to that soldier without anyone having to gesture at him in any way.[5] Or again, we seem to be able to pick out abstract objects or objects outside our immediate perceptual environment (e.g. through what is called 'deferred reference', such as pointing at a painting but referring to its painter), though such referents don't seem to be available to be the subject of pointing gestures, etc. Furthermore, even if (a non-intentional account of) demonstrations could help as far as demonstratives are concerned, such an explanation wouldn't easily extend to other expressions, such as indexicals, where no demonstration is required. Yet, as noted at the start of this chapter, there may be reasons to think that speaker intentions are relevant in determining the semantic content of these expressions as well.

An obvious response to these sorts of worries would be to widen our appeal from a focus on physical gestures to include any relevant features (either in the context of utterance or beyond).[6] The suggestion would thus be that although pointings and head gestures, etc. may help to determine a reference, they need not provide the whole story here. Instead we might take the conventional rules of use for demonstratives

[4] Kaplan 1977. Others have also found the idea that demonstrations fix reference appealing; see McGinn 1981 and Reimer 1991. Kaplan 1989 rejects his earlier view, instead taking demonstrations to be mere externalizations of the criterial 'directing intentions' of the speaker.

[5] This is Kaplan's notion of 'an opportune demonstration', 1977: 490, n.9.

[6] Wettstein 1981: 78–9 stresses that significant cues can go beyond those provided by the context of utterance (though of course this claim depends on how broadly or narrowly one is prepared to individuate a context of utterance).

to look to demonstrations *together with* other contextual cues.[7] The kinds of features a conventionalist might appeal to include: salience, prior reference in discourse, relevance, charity, demonstrations, and location in a series.[8] If it is right that reference is fixed by these sorts of features and not by speaker intentions, then it seems that the argument of §1 collapses: it doesn't matter that minimalism can't accommodate speaker intentions at the semantic level since no semantic level appeal to speaker intentions is necessary.

Furthermore, it seems that there are some good reasons to embrace some form of conventionalism here. One such reason (stressed by Corazza et al.) comes from Donnellan-style concerns about the need to avoid 'Humpty-Dumpty-ism' in language, whereby words are allowed to mean whatever a speaker wants them to mean.[9] Clearly, this is an unacceptable proposal for context-insensitive words: 'red' means red even if I now use it intending to refer to the colour blue. Yet it seems that such liberalism would be equally mistaken for context-sensitive words. For instance, imagine a context in which a group of speakers are standing around admiring a red Porsche. If a member of this group now says 'That is my favourite car', intending to say that her favourite car is the white Jaguar parked round the corner, it seems plausible to think that she nevertheless semantically refers to the Porsche in front of her, regardless of her unpublicized intention. After all, any competent hearer in this context will take the speaker to have referred to the Porsche not to the Jaguar, and any later attempt by the speaker to claim that this is not what she said is very likely to fall on deaf ears. In this kind of case, it seems that speaker intentions are trumped by considerations of what competent hearers can in fact recover, which in turn are determined by objective conventions

---

[7] This position originates (as far as I know) with Wettstein 1981, where he calls it 'a contextual account of indexical reference'; I've avoided using the label 'contextualism' given the way this term is used in the rest of this essay. The position is also advocated by Corazza, Fish and Gorvett 2002, and Gorvett 2005, who stress the conventional rules associated with uses of context-sensitive terms, allowing different kinds of uses to be covered by different conventions (so that a use of 'now' as part of an answer phone message refers to the time the utterance is heard, whereas the use of 'now' on a postcard refers to the time of inscription); however they do not spell out the possible content of these rules in very much detail. Finally, the position is also endorsed in Gauker 2008.

[8] This list is from Gauker 2008. Wettstein 1981: 79 also stresses that cues may include what the addressee knows about the speaker's interests, desires and history; whether this then constitutes a genuinely conventional account of demonstrative reference is thus not obvious (see n.14).

[9] Wettstein 1981 makes the similar point that, while conventionalism creates the space for a divergence between speaker reference and semantic reference, intentionalism seems to collapse these two notions.

concerning how reference is fixed for context-sensitive terms. Demonstratives, it seems, can only be used to refer to what a competent speaker can recover, not simply to whatever a speaker has in mind. These kinds of cases thus lead Corazza, Fish and Gorvett 2002: 17 to suggest that:

> We do not...have to appeal to the speaker and/or audience's individuative intentions to account for the reference of indexical expressions. All we need to appeal to are conventionally given contextual parameters.

If this is right then it gives us our first minimalist solution to the problem posed by demonstratives and other apparently intention-sensitive terms.

However, on reflection, it is not so clear that the allegation of Humpty-Dumpty-ism really does hold against the intentionalist. For although it may seem right that speaker intentions unconstrained cannot underpin communicative acts of reference, it remains open to the intentionalist to constrain the set of intentions she is interested in in some way (for instance, requiring referential intentions to be communicative intentions).[10] Alternatively, an intentionalist might accept that a speaker who uses a demonstrative in a way which cannot be recovered by her audience (e.g. using 'that' with the intention of referring to an object when she knows that there are no contextual cues available to help her audience ascertain this intention) is guaranteed to fail in any communicative endeavour she has. However, the intentionalist may take this as a failing at the level of communication which leaves the level of meaning untouched: though she employs a linguistic expression whose meaning is beyond the grasp of her audience (and thus she fails in Gricean respects as a cooperative speaker), nevertheless this doesn't stop the expression having the literal meaning that it does.[11]

---

[10] See Bach 1992a. Corazza et al. 2002: 16–17 respond briefly to this point, arguing that it makes appeal to intentions subservient to appeals concerning public communication and thus that it is conventional features which do the real work on such an account. However it is not obvious that this response suffices to show intentions are not criterial in reference determination: an appeal to public communication might be necessary to explain the nature of referential intentions but this need have no bearing on the metaphysical claim that it is speaker intentions which fix reference.

[11] This is the route proposed by Predelli 2002; the sort of approach Predelli recommends also bears affinities to the approach in Lassiter 2008 to Humpty Dumpty cases in general. With certain provisos about what is required for grasping the meaning of a demonstrative (see §3), Predelli's move would mesh nicely with the general minimalist viewpoint. Galen Strawson has also pointed out (pc) that in some contexts we seem forced to accept the idea that demonstratives refer to whatever the speaker has in mind, since the range of possible referents are all within the mind of the speaker—consider someone who, gazing into space, remarks ruminatively, 'Ah yes, *that* one'.

So, the motivation for conventionalism may be thought somewhat suspect. Furthermore, the account itself faces an apparently serious objection, for it seems that the very notions it appeals to to replace speaker intentions themselves require intentional input. For instance, what makes a given physical movement a pointing at a dog (rather than a pointing at a dog's collar, or colour, or place, etc) is not merely features of the movement's physical orientation but is a matter of what the agent *intended* to pick out with her gesture. Conventionalism thus seems to postpone, rather than genuinely eliminate, the appeal to speaker intentions in issues of reference determination. As Recanati 2004: 57 writes:

It is generally assumed...that the demonstrative refers to the object which happens to be demonstrated or which happens to be the most salient, in the context to hand. But the notions of 'demonstration' and 'salience' are pragmatic notions in disguise...Ultimately, a demonstrative refers to what the speaker who uses it refers to by using it.[12]

Unless the notion of 'demonstration' is understood in entirely physical terms it cannot help en route to a non-intentional explanation of reference determination, yet understood in such a purely physical way it seems clear that demonstrations underdetermine reference assignments.[13]

However, this was an objection which Wettstein 1981: 81–2 noted but by which he was unmoved:

The indeterminacy of pointing... does not necessitate [such] an appeal to referential intentions... [T]he gesture, considered in isolation, is indeterminate. It is a sufficient indication, however, in the presence of additional cues, for example, the fact that the predicate indicates that the speaker intends to talk about a person and there is no other person in the range of the pointing.

Yet, as the above quote from Recanati illustrates, the problem of indeterminacy is one which can be levelled not only at demonstra-

---

[12] See also Kaplan 1978: 396; Bach 1992a.

[13] One might think to avoid this worry by adopting the kind of Fregean theory of demonstrations which Kaplan advocates in *Demonstratives*. On this approach demonstrations are taken to be equivalent to some form of definite description. Yet this doesn't seem to take us much further since, for any physical gesture, there will be a myriad of possible descriptions to choose among and the only candidate, as far as I can see, for privileging one such description over and above the others is some kind of appeal to speaker intentions. Thus once again we have shifted rather than removed the appeal to intentions.

tions but also at most of the other elements to which the conventionalist seeks to appeal (indeed, perhaps all the elements bar the linguistic meaning of standing expressions).[14] Take, for instance, Gauker's (2008: 365) criterion of 'location in a series', so that an utterance of 'that' might be supposed to refer to the next object in a sequence. Still it seems a speaker's state of mind must have a role to play as any object figures in an indefinite number of different sequences (e.g. objects to the left of the speaker, objects furthest from the Eiffel Tower on trajectory x/y, etc) and it would seem that which sequence is relevant is something which can only be settled via an appeal to the intentional states of the speaker. Or again, consider the appeal to salience here (an appeal Wettstein also tentatively endorses, see 1981: n.31): it simply seems wrong to think that what is salient in a context can always be settled without appeal to intentional states. Although there may be some cases, like Kaplan's fainting soldier, where an object commands universal attention, it is far more common for what counts as being salient in a context to depend on an agent and their intentional framework; what is salient in a given physically described scene will differ according to whether we are trained bird spotters, flower enthusiasts, or entomologists.[15] But if it is the interests of the speaker and hearer which determine what is salient, then salience can play no role in a reductive, non-intentional account of reference fixing. Finally, even in Wettstein's example above the assumption that gesture plus predicate can get us to the referent seems mistaken, for it doesn't take into account instances of deferred reference. In a conversation about employers, pointing at a person, x, and saying 'That person has done a lot for race relations' might succeed in securing not x but x's employer, y, as

---

[14] Note also that Wettstein's own account (1981: 79) allows that the knowledge of speaker interests and desires may count as one of the relevant cues. Thus although his account may eschew direct appeal to referential intentions, it does not seem to provide the kind of 'non-mental' approach promised by other conventionalist accounts. Thus it is not obvious that Wettstein-style conventionalism would provide a way to avoid the Frame Problem.

[15] Gauker 2008: 364 defines his appeal to salience as follows: 'The referent of a bare demonstrative should be something that the hearer can easily spot by looking around. There need not be one such object, and it need not be the thing that most grabs the hearer's attention. It should just be something that the hearer can visually locate without having to move too far from his or her present location'. Even leaving aside the use of bare demonstratives in acts of deferred reference (where there is no requirement that the referent be visually accessible) and the issue of apparently salient though non-visual stimuli (sounds, smells, perhaps abstract objects) this appeal to salience seems problematic since, as noted above, what is easily spotted in a context is in part a matter of what's in the agent's mind.

the referent, even though x is the only person in the range of the pointing. (We might also note, as Galen Strawson, pc, pointed out, that on at least some occasions the predicates used are so general as to be of very little help in reference identification, e.g. consider an utterance of 'That's good').

This realization that the elements a conventionalist appeals to must themselves be rendered in intentional (mental) terms in order to get us as far as reference determination is clearly just one incarnation of Quine's general complaint that reference is behaviourally indeterminate—given only directly observable, physical facts an interpreter will be unable to settle on a unique interpretation for a referential expression. Despite conventionalist claims to the contrary, it seems that meaning is not made manifest in overt behaviour alone. Furthermore, the move to replace speaker intentions with purely objective features of a context of utterance seems to undermine the very *raison d'être* of demonstratives. The whole point of these expressions seems to be to allow the speaker an unparalleled degree of freedom in securing linguistic reference to items in the world. Demonstratives can be used, via deferred reference, to pick out a person via the book they wrote or via the book they are holding or via the book they last read. They can be used to refer to a person via their elbow, or via the seat they will occupy, or via the crimes they have committed. Pointing at a painting might make salient the painter or the person who hung it, pointing at a TV image of a face might facilitate an act of reference to the person whose face it is or to the cameraman who shot it. There seems to be no end to the kinds of relationships which can underpin acts of deferred reference. Yet this creativity and novelty seems to seriously undermine the idea that we can list, in the conventional rules of use for demonstratives, a set of (non-intentional) factors which will always make the right predictions about reference. Indeed, even if we could somehow develop an exhaustive list of all the ways in which deferred reference might come about, even then it would seem that only an appeal to speaker intentions could determine which of these multifarious relations between demonstrated object and actual referent was at stake in any given deferred use of 'that'.[16]

---

[16] See Borg 2002 for further discussion of deferred demonstratives. Predelli 2002: 313–14 makes the same objection to Corazza et al. that, since they allow a single kind of use of a context-sensitive term to be potentially governed by multiple different conventions, an appeal to speaker intentions would seem to be necessary to determine which convention is operative on a specific occasion.

Thus it seems that the straightforward move to eliminate speaker intentions from questions of reference determination is problematic. Not only does it run counter to our strong intuition that speaker intentions *are* relevant in determining the referent for an utterance of a context sensitive term, on closer inspection the threat of circularity looms large, since the notions appealed to to replace intentions (demonstrations or those collected under conventional rules of use) themselves seem to smuggle in an intentional appeal. Furthermore, if we try to excise all intentional content from our conventional features then it seems that we are left facing the Quinean charge that no amount of physical behaviour can alone dictate a unique referential explanation. Thus it seems to me that the rejection of (P1) fails and that the minimalist must find another way of avoiding the unpleasant (at least for her) conclusion that her theory is inadequate as an account of semantic content in natural language.

(3) Rejecting (P2): non-inferentialism

The second move to avoid the problem of semantically relevant intentions is to query the argument that current speaker intentions are problematic from the perspective of a formal semantic theory. Although it seems that rich, abductive reasoning is required to access the intentions of others, perhaps this is wrong, at least for the kind of referential intentions relevant to interpreting demonstrative utterances. Thus one way to resist the problem of §1 would be to shrink the perceived gap between features which are obviously directly accessible in a context of utterance and the apparently hidden, inferentially recovered intentional states of the speaker in that context. In this way referential intentions might become accessible without the need for rich inferential work on behalf of the hearer. Such a position is perhaps most famously associated with Wittgenstein 1953, but it also finds a clear statement in the work of McDowell, who writes (1978: 304):

[W]hat warrants the assertion that another person is in pain, on one of the relevant occasions, is the detectable obtaining of the circumstance of that person's being in pain: an instance of a kind of circumstance—another person's being in pain—that is available to our awareness, in its own right and not merely through behavioural proxies.

This kind of move amounts to what I'll term 'non-inferentialism': openness to the states of others exhausts our methods for assigning (certain) mental states to them. Thus there is no inferential step to be taken between seeing A behaving in manner p and assigning to A the mental state m associated with p—we simply *see* another's mental state in their behaviour.[17] This idea—of direct, non-inferential access to (certain) mental states—has also surfaced in recent work on mindreading both within the simulation theory approach and the opposing theory-theory approach. In the former, the appeal to non-inferentialism is bound up with the idea that so-called 'mirror neurons' provide the neurological underpinnings of mindreading. In the latter, the idea is that intentional attribution directly via behaviour (what is sometimes called 'bodyreading') forms a precursor to a full-blown theory of mind. Since both these accounts explicitly hold out the promise of non-inferential access to a speaker's referential intentions (and thus a route for the minimalist to avoid the problem of §1) I'd like briefly to examine each proposal now.

(3.1) Simulation theory and the mirror neuron hypothesis

According to simulation theory we assign mental states to others via an empathetic process of 'putting ourselves in the other person's shoes': we use our own intentional mechanisms in a process of 'pretend' reasoning utilizing the beliefs and desires we think the other person is likely to have. We then assign the result of this intentional processing to the other person. Importantly, this 'as if' reasoning does not result in action, as it would if it were a genuine, first-personal use of the same mechanisms: when I use my own reasoning systems to conclude that you will roll up into a ball because you believe you are being attacked by a bear, this does not entail that I roll up into a ball as well. In its original incarnation, simulation theory is what we might (following Gallagher 2006: 4) call an 'explicit' theory: we are supposed to be simulating the other person at some relatively high-level,

---

[17] Claiming that we can (at least sometimes) see another person's mental state does not, in itself, entail that there is absolutely no inferential work to be done, for it is commonly accepted that vision itself involves sophisticated sub-personal processes. The claim is rather that, on the current picture, the only kind of inference involved in accessing others' mental states is tacit, deductive inference, there is no personal-level, abductive inference required.

conscious stage of mental activity. Now it doesn't seem as if explicit simulation offers much in the way of succour to the minimalist. Remember that what the minimalist needs is an account of the recovery of referential intentions which does not appeal to abductive, inference to the best explanation reasoning, and the suggestion was that the way to achieve this was to see referential intentions as directly realized in behaviour. Yet if we now allow that grasp of referential intentions is not the direct result of witnessing behaviour but is instead the result of bringing a full-blown, explicit simulation process to bear then we once again seem back with an indirect, richly inferential account of intentional attribution. As Gallagher 2001: 93 notes, ultimately explicit simulation theory shares the same theoretical slant on mindreading proposed by alternative theory-theory approaches:

Both theory theory and simulation theory conceive of communicative interaction between two people as a process that takes place between two Cartesian minds. It assumes that one's understanding involves a retreat into a realm of *theoria* or *simulacra*, into a set of internal mental operations that come to be expressed (externalized) in speech, gesture, and interaction. If, in contrast, we think of communicative interaction as being accomplished in the very action of communication, in the speech, gesture or interaction itself, then the idea that the understanding of another person involves an attempt to theorize about an unseen belief, or to mind-read, is problematic.

What Gallagher is pointing towards here is the fact that both simulation theory and theory theory (in their usual forms) preserve the gap between behaviour and mental states, and thus both seem committed to the idea that the recovery of mental states must be an inferential process based on, but not exhausted by, manifest behaviour. However, it seems that simulation theory could be construed in a different way.

In contrast to explicit simulation theories, implicit versions take simulation to occur at a sub-personal level and to be a relatively direct or automatic response to the behaviour manifested by another agent. This kind of implicit version of simulation is often tied to the discovery of so-called 'mirror neurons' in human (and monkey) brains. Mirror neurons (MNs) are neurons which fire in two distinct conditions:

(i) The production of a specific motor action (e.g. grasping with fingers) by an agent.

(ii) The observation of a conspecific performing the motor action in (i).[18]

In (ii) MN activity is somehow 'taken off-line' and does not result in the motor behaviour witnessed in (i). This discovery that our brains are, to some extent at least, doing the same thing when an agent ϕ's and when an agent witnesses someone else ϕ-ing has been taken to lend support to the simulation theory of mindreading. Thus Gallese and Goldman 1998: 497 write:

> Let us interpret internally generated activation in MNs as constituting a plan to execute a certain action, for example, the action of holding a certain object, grasping it or manipulating it. When the same MNs are externally activated—by observing a target agent execute the same action—MN activation still constitutes a plan to execute this action. But in the latter case the subject of MN activity knows (visually) that the observed target is concurrently performing this very action. So we assume that he 'tags' the plan in question as belonging to the target.

We might term this idea that MN activity constitutes plan formation the 'MN hypothesis'. Our question then is: 'does simulation theory together with the MN hypothesis provide the minimalist with a way out of the problem raised for her in §1?'

Recall that the challenge in §1 turned on the idea that the recovery of referential intentions was not a syntax-driven process: that is to say, it relied on more than the formal properties of representations. Thus it seemed that a formal semantic theory, concerned to offer a purely formal, syntactic route to semantic content, could not accommodate demonstrative expressions since the semantic contribution of these expressions is fixed via a speaker's referential intentions. However it seems that on the picture to hand assigning at least some mental states to others is not in fact the result of rich, abductive reasoning on the part of the hearer, since it is not the result of reasoning at all. Assigning

---

[18] Here the range of 'conspecific' is somewhat vague: MNs fire when a monkey witnesses another monkey perform the action in question but also when they see humans perform the same act. MNs do not fire when the subject sees very different entities, like machines, perform the same physically described action. There is also some evidence that what an organism counts as performance of the action by a conspecific is relatively fluid, with one experiment from the Rizzolatti lab showing that when an action is performed using an intermediary object (e.g. an experimenter opening a peanut using tweezers) this initially causes no MN firing, but that after repeated exposure to the action, appropriate MN firing can be induced (discussed in Arbib et al. 2005: 243).

mental states to others is here an automatic, direct result of witnessing their behaviour (behaviour which triggers MN activity in my mind commensurate with formation of a specific plan of action). This circumvents the challenge to minimalism: a formal theory can admit such speaker intentions as semantically relevant because an agent comes to grasp those intentions not through some complicated reasoning based on assumptions about what are the relevant elements of the hearer's entire belief set but instead simply through the speaker's behaviour causing a hearer to assign a particular intentional state to her.

(3.2) Theory-theory and bodyreading

Non-inferentialism also comes to the fore in certain versions of theory-theory approaches to mindreading, according to which we come to understand the actions of others by subsuming them under very general psychological laws. Stating these laws has proved somewhat problematic for theory-theory approaches, but we might assume that they have something like the following form:

> If A wants x and believes that doing y is a way of bringing x about then, ceteris paribus, A will do y.

Theory-theory approaches are often motivated by consideration of empirical data which seems to show that it is only around the age of four that infants acquire adult-like skills in mindreading.[19] Specifically, it is only around this age that they come to recognize that others may hold beliefs which are false or which differ from the way the child herself believes the world to be. One way to explain this surprising fact is by positing a discrete psychological theory (a theory of mind) which children either learn or become able to access properly at this stage of development.[20] Furthermore, this way of understanding our mindreading abilities seems to offer a useful way to understand certain kinds of cognitive impairment, such as autism (see Baron-Cohen 1995). However, there is other experimental data which seems

---

[19] Though we should note that these experimental findings currently look less robust, for the development of non-verbal versions of false belief tests seem to show that children pass the test much earlier than was previously thought. See Carpenter et al. 2002 for discussion.

[20] For theory of mind as an innate, modular endowment see Leslie 1987, for theory of mind as learnt see Gopnik 1988.

problematic on a theory theory approach since it seems clear that pre-linguistic infants (i.e. significantly under the age of four) do engage in at least some kinds of mindreading. That is to say, they view others as intentional agents and are able to recognize and track the referential intentions of their caregivers. Indeed, this latter skill seems crucial as a precursor to language development, since grasping the meaning of an object word requires latching on to the right relationship between linguistic symbol and external object, something which is presumably made possible only by recognizing a caregiver's intentions when they introduce a new word (this point is stressed in Bloom 2000).

The need to accommodate these sorts of more primitive mindreading skills has led some advocates of the theory-theory approach to postu-late a sort of 'stage 1 theory of mind', which serves as a precursor to acquisition of a full-blown theory and which is closely tied to the tracking of behaviour. For instance, Baron-Cohen posits non-inferentially derived intention-attributions which the child arrives at through the use of two innate mechanisms: first, what he terms the 'intentionality detector' (ID) which allows the recognition of an action as intentional behaviour and, second, the monitoring of the caregivers direction of gaze utilizing what he calls the 'eye direction detector' (EDD). Baron-Cohen 1995: 32–3 suggests that:

ID is a perceptual device that interprets motion stimuli in terms of the primitive volitional mental states of goal and desire. I see these as primitive mental states in that they are the basic ones that are needed in order to be able to make sense of the universal movements of all animals: approach and avoidance.

ID is triggered whenever there is perceptual input of motion appro-priate to an agent, thus it may overgenerate intentional attributions (leading to an initial assignment of goals and desires to robots, displays of moving dots, etc.), but it captures the idea that 'goal detection is hard-wired into our species, goals being perceived by a certain kind of motion perception' (Baron-Cohen 1995: 34).

ID and EDD, together with a later developing capacity which Baron-Cohen terms the 'shared attention mechanism' (SAM), under-pin an early (9–14 months) ability to understand the intentions of others *prior to* the development of a full-blown theory of mind. Full-blown theory of mind is required for the attribution to others of divergent or false beliefs, but the claim is that ID, EDD and SAM suffice for the kinds of mindreading infants engage in prior to passing false belief tests. Specifically, they suffice for attributing referential intentions to others: ID together with EDD allows the infant to attribute states like 'having the goal to pick out/refer to x'.[21] Clearly, then, an appeal to this kind of 'bodyreading' as the route to recovery of referential intentions circumvents the problem raised in §1: referential intentions need not be recovered via rich inferential processes since they are simply seen in behaviour. Thus they can play a role within a formal semantic theory in precisely the same way that any visually accessible feature of a context of utterance might. Bodyreading, then, yields another putative solution to the problem intention-sensitive expressions seem to cause for formal semantics.

So, adopting non-inferentialism (from within either a simulation theory or a theory-theory approach) could help to avoid the problem for minimalism raised in §1. Unfortunately, however, it is far from clear that either move is in fact feasible. The worry for both accounts is once again essentially the concern of Quinean indeterminacy—the thought that no amount of behavioural evidence can ever get us to a unique referential interpretation. To see this let us briefly revisit each of the proposals.

Can an advocate of minimalism avoid the putative problem with demonstratives by claiming (following simulation theory and the MN hypothesis) that reference is determined by speaker intentions but that recovery of these intentions by a hearer is an automatic process triggered directly by speaker behaviour? Well, unfortunately, it seems not. The problem is that MN activity seems to occur at the wrong level of description to help the minimalist. MNs are triggered by witnessing

---

[21] Baron-Cohen 1995: 49. Gallagher 2001: 90, commenting on Baron-Cohen's proposals, adds that '[t] here are many more intention-signalling behaviors that infants and young children are capable of perceiving. In addition to the eyes, it is likely that various movements of the head, the mouth, the hands, and more general body movements are perceived as meaningful or goal-directed...In effect, this kind of perception-based understanding is a form of body-reading rather than mind-reading. In seeing the actions and expressive movements of the other person one already sees their meaning; no inference to a hidden set of mental states (beliefs, desires, etc.) is necessary'. For Gallagher, such bodyreading does not form a precursor to the standard use of a full-blown theory of mind for attributing intentions in adults, instead it constitutes our normal, default method of assignment at both infant and adult stages. We do not standardly theorize about the mental states of those we interact with but see the intentional states of others in their actions: 'in most intersubjective situations we have a direct, pragmatic understanding of another person's intentions because their intentions are explicitly expressed in their embodied actions. For the most part this understanding does not require us to postulate some belief or desire that is hidden away in the other person's mind, since what we might reflectively or abstractly call their belief or desire is directly expressed in their behavior', 2001: 86.

certain behaviour but (in a point already familiar from §2) it seems that such physical gestures underdetermine the precise intention which leads to their performance. That is to say, both an intention to have a drink and an intention to examine a cup design might lead an agent, A, to grasp a cup using a precision grasp with fingers. Yet the pattern of MN activation in a conspecific, B, who witnesses A's action will be the same in either case. Thus to the extent that MN activation can be seen as plan formation at all it offers too coarse-grained a picture: MN activation might help in coming to see a precision grip as an intentional action (as opposed to one caused by factors external to the agent) but it seems it cannot help in, say, coming to see a grasp as a grasp-to-drink rather than a grasp-to-look. Similarly, MN activity might help a hearer H in coming to see S's raising of her arm with index finger extended as an intentional action per se, but it doesn't seem to help in determining a unique referential intention (i.e. the intention to refer to a dog rather than the dog's collar) since the behaviour witnessed (and hence the pattern of MN stimulation caused) will be the same in either case. Yet it is clear that it is the more fine-grained intentional attributions which are needed to determine the reference for a demonstrative utterance. Thus since further inferential work is still required on behalf of the hearer prior to grasp of the intentions responsible for reference determination, it does not seem that the MN hypothesis can solve the problem of intention-sensitive expressions for the minimalist.

Now, advocates of the MN hypothesis might reject this claim, arguing instead that MNs are genuinely able to capture the why, not merely the what, of an action (to borrow the terminology of Iacoboni et al. 2005). Recently, for instance, Sinigaglia 2008 (in response to my 2007b) has pointed out that mirror neurons are sensitive not merely to physically described bodily motions but rather react differentially according to the kind of act which is performed, the affordance of the object acted upon and the hierarchy of movements within which the act is embedded. He writes (2008: 75):

MNs code the action to be executed in terms of its own motor goal-relatedness. This goal-relatedness identifies a motor act as such, characterizing it as an act with its own *motor aboutness*, directed to a given object (with a certain *shape*, a certain *size*, etc.) in a specific way (for instance grasping, holding, manipulating, etc.), rather than just 'bare bones behavior', or a mere sequence of bodily movements.

Such motor goal-relatedness is then held to be a kind of intention-recognition. Two experiments seem especially important in this regard: in one, the 'reverse pliers' experiment of Umiltà et al. 2008, it is observed that the very same pattern of neurons fire both when an agent acts with/witnesses action with an ordinary pair of pliers (e.g. picking up a nut and transferring it to the mouth) and when acting/observing the same action performed with a pair of reverse pliers (which require the opposite physical actions to be carried out to complete the overall action). These findings are held to reinforce earlier ones (Rizzolatti et al. 1988 and Rizzolatti et al. 2000) which show that one and the same physical gesture can be coded for by different neural patterns depending on the larger sequence of goal-directed action within which it was embedded (so the flexing of a finger is coded for by different neural patterns depending on whether it is part of a movement to pick up food to eat or to place elsewhere). Secondly, a recent experiment by Cattaneo et al. 2008 seems to show that we respond differentially, at a MN level, to similar actions performed with different intentions as soon as the action is initiated (so that we recognize a grasp to eat as opposed to a grasp to place as early as the reaching stage). In these experiments, then, we seem to have patterns of MN firing which are both capable of responding differentially to an agent's intention, regardless of the sequence of motor acts used to realize that intention (so that one pattern of MNs fire in recognition of a subject's intention to pick up a nut and eat it, regardless of the specific physical gestures involved in picking up the object) and which are capable of recognizing intentions prior to the completion of an act, so can serve a role in predicting and explaining the behaviour of others.

Now, if these results turn out to be robust then they might indeed show an interesting role for MNs in attributions of intention to others (though we might also note that both sets of results are very recent and there remain, I think, questions to be asked about the methodology involved, e.g. the size of samples involved). However, it remains to be seen whether this explanatory role can be extended to the recognition of referential intentions (the point of focus in our current discussion). The problem is that referential intentions seem connected to behaviour in such an attenuated way that it simply seems unlikely that a system designed to respond to the actions of others could be solely responsible for capturing them. For while, say, grasping-to-eat and grasping-to-place must pay off in behavioural differences at some point in the sequence of motor actions, the same doesn't hold for referential intentions. As noted above, one and the same pointing gesture might constitute an intention to refer to a dog or a dog's collar or a dog's colour and there need be no manifestation of this distinction in any of the gross motor acts made by the speaker. 'Motor aboutness' of the kind Sinigaglia posits for actions viewed under the MN framework, then, still doesn't seem to capture the kind of aboutness we need for attribution of referential intentions. Prima facie, recognition of an action (e.g. pointing gesture) as performed with the intention to refer to a specific object or property still requires the kind of high-level intentional explanation which Sinigaglia himself expects to resist explanation at the level of MNs. Of course, this is an empirical claim and as such it is open to empirical refutation; perhaps it will ultimately turn out that MNs do provide the basis for our attribution of referential intentions to others, however at present there is no experimental evidence to support this claim and little reason to be optimistic about it.

Alternatively, then, can non-inferentialism in the form of Baron-Cohen, Gallagher, and other's 'bodyreading', provide the minimalist with a solution to the challenge posed in §1? Again, it seems not. For even if we treat bodyreading as sensitive to all external evidence (including the literal meaning of any context-insensitive expressions in the speaker's utterance, etc) still it seems either that referential intentions are not fully expressed in this behaviour (with some additional act of inference still required) or that individuating the behaviour itself requires rich, inferential reasoning. Pointing at a girl and saying 'That's my favourite' might involve an act of reference to the girl's dress, her haircut or her car, and nothing in the speaker's bodily behaviour need change across these changes in reference. Furthermore, even if we allowed in the wider features of the context (like the topic of conversation) this doesn't seem to help since it is always open to the speaker to intend to change the direction of conversation. As Baldwin and Baird state (following Searle):

[T]he surface flow of motion people produce in most, if not all, cases is consistent with a multitude of different intentions. Thus when observing others in action, we rely on other sources of information—knowledge about human behavior in general, specific knowledge about the particular individual involved, knowledge about the situation—to help to disambiguate which among the many candidate intentions is relevant in any given case... The upshot is that discerning intentions is a complex enterprise; it is knowledge driven as well as rooted in structure detection.[22]

As noted above, the argument that intentions are not fully realized in behaviour echoes well-worn Quinean concerns about indeterminacy. Such concerns have, however, been recognized by some advocates of primitive, behaviourally realized intentions, such as Arbib et al. 2005. They write 2005: 247:

Our approach integrates perception, the building of action, and the meaning of words, despite the fact that many studies of language acquisition assume that gestures entail ambiguity of reference... These authors rely on Quine's classic essay (1960) in which he discussed the ambiguity of reference entailed in, say, speaking about and pointing to, a rabbit. But caregivers tend to focus attention with precision. They do not simply say an unfamiliar word (such as Quine's *gavagai*) while pointing. Instead, caregivers may rub a rabbit's fur while saying, 'fur'; trace the topography of its ears while saying, 'ear', stroke the entire rabbit or rotate the whole animal when saying 'rabbit', etc... Successful teaching entails marking the correspondence between what is said and what is happening.

However, I think many philosophers will suspect that this underestimates the strength of the Quinean challenge: a tabula rasa child (of the kind Arbib et al. envisage) faced with a caregiver tracing the topography of a rabbit's ear while saying 'ear' is no more warranted in taking the meaning of the term to be *ear* than taking it to be *temporal slice of rabbit-ear* or *rabbit-eared shape*. (We might also think that the picture of caregiver/infant interaction given by Arbib et al. is correct only for explicit instances of teaching, yet children's word acquisition clearly outstrips the instances of explicit learning to which they are exposed.)

---

[22] Baldwin and Baird 2001: 175–6. The idea that bodyreading is sufficient for coming to assign referential intentions might seem more plausible in infants than it does in adults. After all the referential intentions which are directed at infants are primarily fairly simple ones: caregivers tend to refer to middle-sized concrete objects in the immediate perceptual horizon of both parties, they are less likely to utilize deferred reference or to refer to abstract objects (though note Gleitman's 1990: 19 well-taken point that 'caretaker speech is not a running commentary on scenes and events in view'). Perhaps, armed with an additional assumption on behalf of the hearer that the speaker is likely to be talking about 'middle sized dry goods' the idea that physical gestures can take us all the way to intention could be workable. However, note that this move still requires some background knowledge on behalf of the infant and that it is clearly not an additional assumption an adult hearer would, in general, be entitled to make, thus it doesn't seem to take us very far in the way of an overall explanation of reference.

Once again, it seems that only with the addition of some background beliefs (say, in the infant case, general beliefs about what speakers tend to be interested in together with, in the adult case, more specific beliefs about this particular speaker's interests) and an act of abductive inference on the basis of these background beliefs and the speaker's current performance can we hope to ascertain referential intentions.[23]

We might also note, as does Hurley 2006: 222–3, that the move to treat intention recognition as so closely aligned to behaviour tracking may threaten to obscure the genuine difference between the two abilities:

Psychologists ask: what is the functional difference between genuine mind-reading and smart behavior reading (Whiten 1996)? Many of the social problems animals face can be solved merely in terms of behavior-circumstance correlations and corresponding behavioural predictions, without the need to postulate mediating mental states. And after all, it might be said, all we ever 'really observe' is behaviour in environments: we infer mental states from this. However, mind-readers do not merely keep track of the behavior of other agents, but also understand other agents in terms of their mental states. Mind-readers can attribute intentions to others even when their actions do not carry out their intentions; they can attribute beliefs to others even when those beliefs are false.

So, it seems that both putative moves to shrink the gap between the behavioural and the intentional via some form of non-inferentialism fail. Despite the attraction of the idea that agents 'just see' the mental states of others in their behaviour, it seems that such a move is problematic, at least so far as referential intentions are concerned. So both premise 1 (the idea that referential intentions are criterial in deter-

---

[23] The concern with non-inferentialism in general here is, I think, that while it might perhaps be plausible to think that we can simply see another's pain it seems far less plausible to think that we can simply see another's referential intention. Anecdotally, I might note that my three-year-old son had a habit of pointing at displays of toys and asserting, in a discourse initial position, 'I want that one'. When pressed to make his referential intentions clearer he tended merely to assert more vocally 'I want that one, THAT ONE'. Clearly, he thought I should be able to perceive his intention but this doesn't seem to me like a situation where there is an objective feature of the context I simply fail to see. Rather the situation seems better characterized as one where I lack enough background information (is he in a *Scooby Doo* or *Phineas and Ferb* mood?) to infer, from his bodily actions, what his intention was. But this is just to recognize that the route to referential intentions is inferential. Of course, the non-inferentialist might object that in this kind of case my son didn't fulfil the criteria for referring to one of the toys on display, but again this makes pressing the question of the criteria for referential intentions and the point of the arguments above was to suggest that no such purely behavioural specifications of criteria are available, since behavioural markers are common across multiple distinct intentions.

mining reference) and premise 2 (the idea that recovery of speaker intentions goes via rich, non-computational reasoning processes) seem warranted. So, if the minimalist needs to accept (P1) and (P2), and since (P3) is simply a statement of one of minimalism's core commitments, it seems that her last option here is to deny the validity of the argument—to show that, perhaps contrary to initial impressions, it is possible to hold all three premises without this entailing the conclusion.

(4) Rejecting the argument: distinguishing reference fixing, reference identification, and semantic content

Minimalism, as introduced in Chapter 1, aims to deliver a formally respectable account of semantic content. That is to say, it wants it to be the case that the processes involved in recovering the semantic content of any well-formed sentence are deductive, computational processes—processes which look to the formal properties of representations and not to their content. What minimalism wants then is an account of the semantic content of a sentence which is genuinely free from the need to peer into the mind of the speaker of that sentence, which doesn't at any point smuggle in an appeal to the dark magic of pragmatics. As we have seen, however, this desire clashes with the need to treat speaker intentions as semantically relevant (since they appear to be responsible for reference fixing for demonstratives), for recovery of speaker intentions is the apotheosis of dark pragmatic magic.[24] Yet it seems that the minimalist who wants to avoid this problem might query the requirement that minimalism treat *all aspects* of semantic content as formally tractable. For it seems that what she is committed to is the claim that semantic content itself is formally tractable and this might leave aspects relevant to the fixing or identification of that content out of the picture. Just as a formal theory will tell you what the sentence 'London buses are red' means, though it won't tell you why 'red' means *red* and not *blue*, so it will tell you what an utterance of the

---

[24] Though note that Stokke 2009, like Cappelen and Lepore 2005, holds there is no problem in incorporating such pragmatic features directly into a formal, Kaplanian semantics.

sentence 'That is red' means, even though it won't tell you why this token of 'that' refers to object x and not object y.[25]

With this distinction in place, then, a minimalist might allow that what makes a token utterance of 'that is F' refer to A rather than B is the speaker's intention to refer to A rather than B. However, she can still maintain that the semantic content of this token of 'that' is exhausted by the object A, so that what the hearer must grasp to understand the utterance is the singular proposition *that A is F*, where no mention is made of the speaker's intentions within the content of this proposition.[26] Finally, however, she might also hold that a speaker can entertain this content *even if* she is in no position to non-linguistically identify A; that is to say, if she is capable of thinking of A only as *the actual object referred to by the speaker with this token of 'that'*. What a hearer needs to do to grasp the semantic content of this demonstrative utterance, then, is to introduce a syntactically generated singular concept which has object A as its content, though this content may be presented under a more complex rigidified description (that is to say, even at the level of thought we need to distinguish content and character). That A is the referent of this utterance is settled by features beyond the reach of semantics and, furthermore, to put this semantic content to use (i.e. to use it to inform one's dealings with the world) the hearer normally needs to go on to non-linguistically identify A, but the point remains that as far as linguistic meaning or semantic content is concerned such issues of substantive object-identification are irrelevant.

Thus a minimal semantic theory might deliver a truth-conditional analysis of the semantic content of 'This is red' along the following lines (taken from Higginbotham 1994: 92–3):

[25] We might capture this claim in terms of Kaplan's framework for demonstratives by noting the difference between elements which fill the contextual parameters in a given context and the ways in which those elements are decided. Gauker 2008: 361 makes this point very clearly: 'In addressing the relation of speaker intention to context, we have to distinguish between the *content* of a context and the *determinants* of that content... One view would be that various speaker intentions constitute *components* of the context... The other view would be that speaker intentions enter the picture only as what *determines* all or part of the content of the context for an utterance. For example, we might say that the context for an utterance of a sentence containing the demonstrative "that" contains the specification that the referent of "that" is a certain computer. But then when we go on to ask what makes it the case that the context specifies that referent for the demonstrative the answer might be that that is what the speaker intends to refer to'. Gauker himself, however, rejects this proposal, see below, though the general approach he discusses here, and which I'll embrace in what follows, is endorsed by Predelli 2005.
[26] As Predelli 2005: 44 writes: 'The intuitively correct interpretation... may easily be obtained... if the index taken into consideration by the system contains co-ordinates intended by the speaker as semantically relevant, even if distinct from the obvious items within the context of utterance/inscription'.

(1) If the speaker of 'this is red' refers with the utterance of 'this' therein to x and to nothing else, then this sentence, as uttered in this context, is true if and only if x is red.

Someone who grasps an instance of this schema might conceive of the relevant contextual parameter as 'the actual object referred to by the speaker of u' and this doesn't guarantee that they can further identify which object satisfies this description. Nevertheless a minimalist can claim that an instance of (1) exhausts the semantic content of the sentence as uttered on this occasion and that this content is graspable without non-linguistic identification of the referent.[27] If this view of the kind of knowledge semantic theorizing provides is accepted it yields our third and final putative solution to the challenge to minimalism from intention-sensitive terms: speaker intentions *do* play a part in fixing a reference for a demonstrative *and* they are recoverable only via rich, abductive means, but features relevant to reference fixing (like features relevant to non-linguistic reference identification) are no part of semantics proper.

According to this final move, it is right to think of demonstrative utterances as expressing singular propositions (which require singular thoughts to entertain), but a hearer is held to be able to entertain such a proposition even if she can think of the referent of 'that' only under the rigidified, token-reflexive description 'the actual object referred to by the speaker using that token of 'that'', or, equivalently, 'dthat (the referent of the speaker's token of 'that')'.[28] One consequence of this is

---

[27] As a reader noted, there are clear parallels between this sort of proposal and Perry's 2001 idea of 'reflexive' contents. Indeed when I first mooted the current proposal (Borg 2004a: 189–93) I explicitly drew on Perry's account. However it is important to note a crucial difference between Perry's reflexive contents and the contents proposed here: for the description in the current case serves as a *reference-fixer*, not as part of the sentence's propositional content itself. The content of the thought entertained on grasping an utterance of 'That is F' is supposed, on the current model, to remain exactly as it is on any other directly referential account (that is to say, it is exhausted by an object and a property). Though the description *the actual object referred to by the speaker of u* fixes the referent it does *not* figure at the level of content. That it is the object itself, rather than any description of it, which provides the propositional contribution of the term is, I take it, supported by the kind of modal arguments for the existence of directly referential terms provided by Kaplan and others. It is also, I think, supported by concerns about a potential divergence of behaviour between a simple term like 'that' and the complex description which is taken to give its meaning.

[28] See Borg 2004a, Ch.3 for further discussion of this point. It might be objected at this point that no such definite description could constitute the meaning rule for demonstratives, since it seems possible for a hearer to understand utterances of demonstratives *even if* they do not possess the relevant concepts for the definite description given above. However, I would follow Garcia-Carpintero's (1998: 561) caution about how we understand the relationship between any such rule and an agent's conscious understanding:

that we will have to allow that a hearer is capable of grasping a singular proposition, or having a singular thought, even when she does not know (in any substantial, non-linguistic sense) *which* object she is thinking about. Now, clearly, if we envisage semantic knowledge as forming part of a wider framework of knowledge (i.e. as part of a broader cognitive system like a whole mind) then we can allow that in many situations hearers *will* be in a position to non-linguistically identify the objects speakers are referring to, since information beyond the purely semantic may be brought into play. However, even if this kind of case is the norm, still on the account to hand it will be *possible* that a hearer grasps the semantic content of an utterance of 'That is F' without being able to non-linguistically identify the referent of this token of 'that', and this will be thought problematic by many.

One worry may be that, on the current picture, we must allow that sometimes a hearer may think she is entertaining a singular thought when in fact she is not since there is no object satisfying the description 'the actual object referred to by the speaker with her token of "that"' (say, because the speaker was hallucinating). However this kind of failure of first-person access to the contents of one's mind is a general feature of any kind of externalism about semantic content, thus it doesn't seem to provide a specific challenge to this minimalist approach to context-sensitive terms.[29] Yet there may still seem to be something intuitively untoward about allowing singular thoughts when the agent is not able to non-linguistically identify the referent.[30] This is a major point and, though we will return to it (under the guise of a debate about the requirements for truly world-involving content) in the next chapter, a full exploration of the nature of singular thought and the conditions such thoughts must meet is beyond the scope of the current

---

'Indexical expressions... could only be claimed to be "synonymous" with descriptions such as "the actual male demonstrated at the occasion of the production of **he**"; but the fact that ordinary competent speakers both are ignorant of the presupposed technical sense of "actual" and of the two-dimensional account of modality...makes clear that a non-straightforward sense of "synonymy" is to be understood. In this non-straightforward sense, an expression can be counted as synonymous with another when the former makes *theoretically explicit* the way in which a competent speaker *tacitly* conceives of the truth-conditional import of the latter'.

[29] Furthermore there is, even in the case of reference failure, a level of thought which can explain the agent's delusion of content, namely the (on this occasion unsatisfied) descriptive character 'the actual object to which the speaker referred with this utterance of "that"'. See Borg 2004a, Ch.3.

[30] See Russell 1911, Evans 1982, Soames 2002 for just some of the many theorists who have found this sort of idea unpalatable. See Jeshion 2002 and elsewhere for someone who finds the idea unproblematic.

enterprise.[31] However I would like to stress that, as far as I can see, the grounds for limiting singular thought to occasions where an agent can non-linguistically identify the referent seem *extremely* shaky. First, there seems to be no substantive, principled notion of non-linguistic identification which could do the work required here (i.e. serve to delineate semantically referential expressions from the non-referential). Once we recognize that demonstratives can be used not just to refer to concrete objects in a shared experiential environment, but also to refer to abstract objects or concepts, and to objects (abstract or otherwise) in some way related to those in the experiential environment (say, referring to a person by the seat she will occupy tomorrow), the idea of drawing a line at some point in this usage via some vague notion of non-linguistic identification seems entirely arbitrary. Secondly, such an idea is not borne out by the behaviour of demonstrative expressions themselves, which all behave as if they belong to a single semantic category of referring terms.[32] Of course, if we allow that the semantic content of a demonstrative can be grasped without this entailing non-linguistic identification of the referent then we will be left with a fairly thin notion of semantic content here. It will not be the case that semantic knowledge, divorced from other kinds of knowledge we have, guarantees an ability to get around the world or interact in appropriate ways with objects. Yet instead of being an objection to the minimalist proposal this seems more like a statement of a credo, for minimalists are already committed to the idea that semantic content is minimal in nature and that it alone cannot be responsible for doing all the work that theorists have sometimes laid at the door of semantics (this was one of the key themes of Borg 2004a).

One final objection we should consider here comes from Gauker 2008 who, despite clearly articulating the distinction between reference fixing and semantic content, nevertheless argues that speaker intentions cannot be relevant to fixing semantic content for demonstratives.

---

[31] See Hawthorne and Manley 2012 for an extended argument that there are no acquaintance-type constraints on singular thoughts.

[32] This point is explored in depth in Borg 2002, focusing on complex demonstratives. Carston 2008 cites what we might call 'Nunberg cases' (see Nunberg 1993 and elsewhere), where an indexical gives rise to a descriptive reading, as showing that some syntactically singular expressions give rise to general, descriptive propositions at the semantic level. However, Borg 2002 argues in passing for a pragmatic rendition of Nunberg cases, while Stokke 2010 argues extensively, and to my mind convincingly, for the pragmatic route.

According to his argument, recovery of speaker intentions relies on grasp of linguistic meaning: one needs to know what someone is saying in order to know what they are thinking. So, on pain of circularity, it cannot be the case that grasp of speaker intentions is necessary in order to grasp linguistic meaning. He writes 2008: 363 that:

My objection to [the theory that speaker intentions determine reference] is that it renders the referent of demonstratives inaccessible to hearers. In order to identify the referent of a demonstrative the hearer will have to figure out what the speaker intended to refer to. But apart from an independent interpretation of the speaker's words, hearers will typically be in no position to do that.

Two points are relevant here: first, as just noted, according to the minimalist non-linguistic identification of a referent is not a constitutive feature of a grasp of referential semantic content. So on this account, the fact that a referent may sometimes be inaccessible to a hearer (from a non-linguistic point of view) is irrelevant. So, it seems Gauker's challenge does not hold against the thin minimalist notion of singular content advocated here. On the other hand, however, it is also not clear that Gauker's general objection—that if we allow speaker intentions to be semantically relevant then there is, as it were, no way for a subject to 'break into the intensional circle'—really holds. For a (non-minimalist) advocate of the semantic role of speaker intentions in this case might argue that, although grasp of current speaker intentions is necessary for grasping the meaning of some expression(s) in the current context of utterance (e.g. the speaker's token of 'that'), there are plenty of other expressions which do not share this feature (i.e. any expression with a 'standing' meaning).[33] Furthermore, knowledge of these meanings, together with all the other information hearers have concerning typical speakers (i.e. what an agent will typically find salient in a context, etc) and this speaker in particular (i.e. what she is interested in, etc) will allow the hearer to work out to what the speaker intended to refer. This, of course, will be an informal, content-driven process of inference to the best explanation (thus it is not the kind of thing our formal theory can be directly concerned with) but the thought is that this rich inferential reasoning does suffice, at least

---

[33] Such a response would, of course, depend on an independent rejection of an extreme indexicalist view, where all or most natural language expressions are taken to be context sensitive.

in many cases, to place the speaker's intentions, and following this, the speaker's intended referent, within the epistemic reach of the hearer.[34]

(5) Conclusion

Intention-sensitive terms cause a prima facie problem for all varieties of formal semantics. Furthermore they appear fundamentally disruptive to any variety of formal semantics which seeks a purely formal, computationally tractable route to semantic content (i.e. one which is genuinely free from the dark magic of pragmatics), as does semantic minimalism (at least as conceived of in this essay). In response to this challenge I've suggested there are three routes the minimalist might pursue: first, she may deny that demonstratives et al. are in fact sensitive to current speaker intentions; second, she might claim that referential intentions are manifest in behaviour and so are available to play a semantic role in exactly the same way as any other contextual element; third, she might seek to hold apart reference fixing/identification and semantic content. If any of these moves is found plausible then we can show how formal semantics, and minimalism in particular, avoids the putative problem of intention-sensitive expressions. However, I also argued that the first two of these moves face serious objections, stemming from Quinean concerns about the indeterminacy of reference. For both the move to reject (P1) and the move to reject (P2) seek to relocate the work of reference fixing from some 'hidden' mental state of the speaker to features which are externally manifested in the context of utterance (either by *replacing* the appeal to intentions with an appeal to publicly observable features or by treating the appeal to intentions as *equivalent* to an appeal to publicly observable features). However, to the extent that an appeal to publicly observable features of a context of utterance can get us to the intentional level at all, it seems that it can take us only as far as a quite

---

[34] Note that this is not to claim (along with those who reject (P2)) that referential intentions are fully manifest in behaviour. Grasp of referential intentions remains, on this picture, a richly inferential process based on, but not limited to or exhausted by, agent behaviour. The point is rather that though this kind of inferential procedure plays a part in reference determination it need not fall within the remit of semantics.

general notion of intentional attribution, namely a hearer's identification of an action, x, as an intentional action (i.e. as self-motivated, not directly caused by factors external to the agent) and, perhaps, to some recognition of the goal of an act. Yet it is clearly a much more fine-grained notion which is required for reference determination and this is something which is not fully presented in the behaviour of an agent at any point.

Thus, I suggest that it is the last move, which imposes a rigid distinction between reference fixing/reference identification on the one hand and semantic content per se on the other, which provides the most attractive proposal for the minimalist. This is a proposal I have put forward before (Borg 2004a, Chapter 3) and the aim of this chapter has been to show that it remains the most plausible line for the minimalist to pursue, even in the light of other possible moves which would fit with the overarching minimalist cause. Such a move entails adopting a quite minimal view of semantic content, whereby grasp of the semantic content of a token demonstrative does not entail that a hearer is able to non-linguistically identify the referent. Yet, since there are independent reasons to be sceptical about epistemically loaded notions of singular content and since the 'thin' nature of semantic content is an essential part of the minimalist manifesto, this outcome should, I think, simply be embraced. However, if this view of singular content is adopted by the minimalist (as I think it should be) it may seem that trouble looms further down the road, for we risk raising once again the spectre of a failure of propositionalism.

The worry this time around is as follows: although the view of singular content advocated in this chapter has been couched in terms of object-involving, wide content we might wonder why this should be the case. Since the minimal notion of content we end up with is so thin, so paltry, we might wonder why we shouldn't give it up altogether, holding instead that semantic concerns are limited to questions of character. Perhaps as far as literal meaning is concerned, we should take the content of a sentence like 'That is mine' to remain invariant across all token utterances of the sentence, with semantics being agnostic about the identity of a referent and indeed whether or not a referent is secured at all. In this way it would only be at the level of pragmatics—language in use—that the world rushes in and provides full-blown object-involving content. However, if the semantics of demonstratives yields only a descriptive character, not a full-blown content for these expressions, then the semantic content of sentences containing these expressions will fail to reach the level of a proposition. Appeal to lexico-syntactic features will yield only a propositional radical—something with a gap in waiting for contextual completion. Furthermore, as we will see in the following chapters, there is a very real threat that this idea generalizes, so that not only for directly referential expressions should we understand their semantic contribution as an underspecified descriptive intension rather than as a worldly extension, it may also turn out that this is how we should understand the meaning of natural language terms quite generally. Thus, for instance, we might think of the meaning of a common noun like 'book' or a predicate like 'red' not as given by some discrete property or extension in the world, but rather as a complex, structured content which can be applied to the world in distinct ways. In this way, an utterance of 'book' in one context might mean a concrete object (as in 'She put the book on the table'), while in another it picks out an abstract idea (as in 'Her book was in every bookshop in London'), and in other contexts it might mean other things as well.

If this general idea were to prove correct then the worry would be, not (as it was in Chapter 3) that some sentences might fail to express propositions, but that *all* sentences fail to do so. For the kind of contribution which words make to the truth-conditions of larger linguistic units in which they occur would be underdetermined outside a context of use. So in the next two chapters I want to turn to look more closely at the fundamental issue of word meaning, asking whether it is right to think of lexical content in the atomistic, context-insensitive way that minimalism assumes (and even contextualists of Recanati's 2004, 2010 stripe allow) or whether the alternative picture indicated here (of lexical content as providing an indeterminate fragment of meaning which stands in need of application through use) is in fact to be preferred.

CHAPTER 5

The Ontological Argument Against Minimal Word Meanings

Minimal semantics is primarily a theory about semantic content for sentences—the kind of thing it is, how it is determined and how it relates to the meanings of utterances. However it should be clear that the theory also embodies some fundamental assumptions about the nature of word meanings. Recall that the third tenet of minimalism (as given in Chapter 1) was:

> (iii) There are only a limited number of context-sensitive expressions in natural language.

(iii) is explicitly about word meanings, so even at first blush it should be clear that minimalism involves claims about word meanings. Furthermore, if we reflect on minimalism's account of sentence meaning we can also see that a substantial view about word meaning is involved. Minimalism holds that the meaning of a sentence is exhausted by the meanings of its syntactically represented parts and the way they are put together, and that this meaning, for a well-formed sentence, is guaranteed to be truth-apt. That is to say, if you put enough words together in the right kind of way one can be certain of arriving at propositional content. Yet of course this can only be the case if word meanings are the kinds of things which, if one puts enough of them together in the right kind of way, then what one gets is propositional content.

The account of word meaning to which minimalism seems to be committed, then, apparently has two necessary features: first, as Dancy 2004: 197 points out, it is an atomic, context-independent conception whereby a token of a word type generally (e.g. when not an explicit indexical) makes the same contribution to any larger linguistic unit in which it occurs.[1] Second, this conception of word meaning is, in some broad sense, referential or world-involving. For the contents which sentences express to be truth-evaluable it seems clear that they must be 'about the world' in some sense. That is to say, the concepts involved in spelling out semantic content for the minimalist must bottom-out at some point in some kind of a connection to the world, they cannot be wholly internally individuated.[2]

One way to think of lexical content on the minimalist picture then is in terms of broadly referential lexical axioms such as:

> 'Barack Obama' refers to Barack Obama.
> 'Donostia' refers to San Sebastian.
> 'red' is true of red things/refers to the property of being red.

These axioms are 'broadly referential' in the sense that (whether they make use of a relation like reference or something like satisfaction) they pair an expression of a natural language on the left-hand side with an element of the non-linguistic world on the right-hand side. (There is a wrinkle here: it might be that word meanings are concepts and it is these concepts which stand in relation to objects in the world/have their content given by things in the world. However, while this seems right to me, I'll tend to gloss over the point in what follows, talking of words relating

---

[1] Dancy 2004 stresses the atomic nature of lexical content on the minimalist picture, however it is not obvious to me that this should be seen as an essential (as opposed to a likely) feature of any minimalist account of lexical content. Lexical content for the minimalist could, it seems, be given by a complex entity so long as (i) the full complex was always contributed to larger linguistic units in which the term appeared, and (ii) these complex definition-like meanings were ultimately constructed out of world-involving elements. The worry minimalism has with complex lexical entries is then two-fold: first, as we will see in Chapter 6 §1, it is common for accounts which allow lexical complexity to also allow that, on at least some occasions, a word only contributes part of its complex content to larger linguistic units (e.g. to accommodate the phenomenon of polysemy). So holding that word meanings are complex and that the whole complex must be contributed to larger linguistic units runs counter a main motivation for adopting complexity in the first place. Second, as we will see in Ch.6 §4, the move to complex lexical entries may also be thought to be problematic for independent reasons.

[2] The notions of internalism and externalism are vexed ones and there is, of course, a huge literature nudging up around the edges of this chapter. However in what follows I'm going to try to remain largely non-committal on the precise kind of externalism which minimalism should actually adopt (e.g. a broadly referential externalism, like that embodied in the axioms to be given above, or some more Burgean kind of social externalism, or some combination of the two). It seems to me that what minimalism is committed to is the idea that semantic contents are the kinds of things which can be true or false and to get this result what is needed is just some kind of commitment to 'weak externalism', construed simply, as Rey 2005 suggests, as the view that ascriptions of some content depend in one way or another on relations a computational system bears to things outside itself. That is to say, minimalism assumes a lexical semantics which contains some kind of symbol-world connection. What I'll be arguing for, then, is more a denial of internalism than a specific variety of externalism.

directly to features of an external world.) Such a model embodies what we might think of as an appeal to the common-sense objects of reference: the idea that there are objects and properties out there in the world which some of our terms somehow hook up with and that it is through standing in this kind of relation that at least some of our terms become meaningful. Leaving concerns about the unity of the proposition to one side, it seems clear, at least in principle, how combining enough of these kinds of meanings within an appropriate syntactic framework might lead to a truth-evaluable claim being expressed. (For discussion of the problem of the unity of the proposition, see, e.g. King 2007, Collins 2011.)

Of course, given such broadly referential axioms, it is obvious that words in general will make a stable contribution to larger linguistic units in which they appear: 'red' will always contribute, for instance, the property of *redness*, 'Barack Obama' will always contribute the same individual. Now, as we have already seen, this picture is rejected on an approach like Travis' occasionalism or Dancy's particularism. On these approaches, words do not make stable contributions to the propositions expressed by sentences containing them. Instead, words are held to have a kind of open-ended, holistic meaning which becomes determinate only within a specific context of use. As Travis 1997: 111 writes: "What 'is a fish' means may exclude the possibility of its being used to say something true of a piano", yet it certainly doesn't fix a determinate, context-independent contribution for 'is a fish' which could result in a univocal propositional content for a sentence like 'A shark is a fish'. The atomic, referential view of word meaning has also come under sustained attack in the work of Noam Chomsky and others who adopt the kind of semantic internalism Chomsky advocates. According to semantic internalism, it is wrong to think of words as having simple, broadly referential meanings, instead we should view word meanings as complex constructions of intra-linguistic features, where the precise combination of features conveyed by an utterance of a term may differ across different contexts. On this model, semantic content is (just as the minimalist holds) dictated by lexico-syntactic content but this entails, Chomsky argues, that such content is not also propositional, truth-evaluable content. As Collins 2007: 807–8 puts the point:

[W]e need to think again about the theoretical salience of notions such as proposition and truth conditions. Put in radical terms it is the very Frege-Russell conception of meaning as propositional (as truth-conditions) that is at fault... In short, as revealed by generative inquiry, it looks as if language narrowly construed is just not in the business of expressing propositions.

If we want semantics to run exclusively off syntactic form and lexical content then the Chomskian maintains that questions of external reference or satisfaction just drop out of the picture (at this level)— semantics as delivered by formal operations over syntax is necessarily insensitive to the vagaries of worldly extension.

In this chapter, then, I want to start by exploring the possible connections between semantic minimalism and Chomsky's semantic internalism, seeing why it might prima facie be tempting to think that the minimalist notion of semantic content should coincide with the internalist view offered by Chomsky. Then, in §2, I'll turn to look at the specific arguments Chomsky has offered against the possibility of, or need for, the kind of broadly referential account of lexical content which I've suggested minimalism tacitly embraces. The ontological arguments he offers will then be rejected in §3 where I'll argue, first, that simple referential lexical axioms remain possible (even given minimalism's commitment to what we might think of as a scientific approach to semantic theorizing) and, second, that such axioms (or at least, axioms which incorporate some kind of symbol-world connection) are required if we are to accommodate the explanatory work required of a genuine semantic theory. Finally, however, it will be noted that even if we reject the metaphysical arguments explored in this chapter there remains a second kind of argument for non-referential word meanings, which turns on the work required of lexical contents. Exploring this methodological argument for internalist word meanings and seeing how a broadly referential account of lexical semantics might accommodate it will be the subject of the final chapter.

(1) Semantic minimalism and Chomsky's semantic internalism

Recall that in the last chapter I suggested the minimalist should avoid the challenge to her approach from apparently intention-sensitive terms by admitting that speaker intentions have a role to play in fixing the referent of a context-sensitive term while denying that access to those intentions is required to grasp semantic content. In practice, I suggested this meant imposing a distinction between content and character at the level of thought (as well as language) and allowing that a subject can entertain a genuinely singular concept (one whose content is exhausted by the object in the world to which it attaches) even though her only way of identifying that object is under a linguistic description (the character of the concept) such as 'the actual object referred to by the speaker with this token of "that"'. However, many theorists have objected that an approach of this kind simply cannot give us an adequate picture of singular thought and the way in which referential expressions relate agents to their environment.

The worry is that, stripped of connections to abilities like non-linguistic identification, or re-identification over time, the content minimalism provides does not qualify as genuine singular content at all. Rather what it offers us is a mere placeholder for such content; a schema waiting for the world to fill it in.[3] Although I claimed in the last chapter that the truth-conditional contribution of a term like 'this' or 'that' was exhausted by the object to which it referred in a given context, since what the interlocutor is capable of consciously entertaining, on the basis of linguistic understanding alone, seems to be a character which is unchanged whether the term actually refers to α or β, or indeed to nothing at all, one might argue that it is this (object-independent) character which exhausts the minimal semantic content. Why, the question is, think that semantic content needs to take the extra step to involve the object itself, why not instead treat the step to the object as part of utterance-level, pragmatic content alone? In this way, semantic content itself could remain invariant across uses of that

[3] Peacocke 2008: 75 writes: "It is an overarching constraint on something's being a fundamental reference rule for a concept that, together with other information and conditions, it determine in various circumstances what are good reasons for making certain judgements containing the concept. An alleged fundamental reference rule that uniquely fixes an object, but does not contribute to the determination of reasons in this way, does not succeed in individuating a concept. Consider, for some particular object *x*, the alleged fundamental reference rule for an alleged singular concept *k* which states simply that: *k* refers to *x*. This proposed rule certainly determines a reference for *k*. But the rule does not contribute essentially to the determination of reasons in various circumstances for making judgements containing the alleged concept. The additional condition that *k is F (perceptually given)* may contribute to the determination of reasons for making judgements, but then the work is being done by the perceptual demonstrative *that F*. The referential dimension of a concept and its having a location in the space of reasons are coordinate elements in the nature of a concept. Neither can be fully elucidated without involving the other".

content to refer to different parts of the world: the sentence 'that is red' would be held to have an invariant (non-truth-evaluable) semantic content which could be used to talk about indefinitely many different things (different objects and, as will become clearer below and in the next chapter, different ways of being red).

Furthermore, this suspicion that minimal semantics might be best construed as dealing only with a pre-propositional fragment of content is reinforced by considering the extent of the common ground between the minimalist approach to semantics and the kind of semantic internalism advocated by Chomsky. For it seems that there is, from the outset, the kind of agreement in aims and objectives between minimalism and (this branch of) internalism which might make it natural to try to unite the two theories. As we have seen in this essay, according to minimal semantics, the aim of a semantic theory is to provide a formally tractable, recursive account of the literal meaning of the sentences of a natural language, where this does not commit such a theory to capturing an intuitive notion of what is said by an utterance of any such sentence (with the notion of what is said being treated as of pragmatic relevance only); for the minimalist, then, semantics in general aims to capture a content which is independent of the vagaries of a speaker and their context of utterance. This level of semantic content is held to be recoverable on the basis of lexicon and syntax alone, with everything found at the semantic level being contributed by something in the syntax of the sentence, and the apparatus taking one from the syntactic to the semantic can be modelled formally. Furthermore, at least according to the kind of minimalism espoused in this book, it is because semantic content is formally respectable in this way that its recovery in a subject can be underpinned by a dedicated semantics module in the mind of the language user (where the notion of a module is understood in computational terms, following Fodor 1983).

This picture, of semantic analysis as aiming at the context-invariant, syntactically mandated content of a sentence, which is (largely) uncontaminated by pragmatic processes, and which is underpinned by a cognitive module, echoes the kind of claims which Chomsky and others have made for semantic content. However, according to Chomsky, semantic content should be specified in entirely internal, non-referential terms: a theory of meaning need look no further than the limits of the individual mind. Contrary to Putman, then, meanings are in the head—if meanings are concepts then they are concepts whose content is independent of the world. On this approach the proper subject of semantic inquiry is the state of the agent's internal language faculty, so the study of semantics (along with the study of syntax or grammar) becomes entirely a branch of individual psychology. This is not to say that our language never makes contact with the world, but the referential properties of language emerge at the point of *use* not at the point of *meaning*. Thus Chomsky 2000: 36 suggests that:

[A] lexical item provides us with a certain range of perspectives for viewing what we take to be the things in the world, or what we conceive in other ways; these items are like filters or lenses, providing ways of looking at things and thinking about the products of our minds. The terms themselves do not refer, at least not if the term *refer* is used in its natural language sense; but people can use them to refer to things, viewing them from particular points of view—which are remote from the standpoint of the natural sciences.

So while a speaker might use a word with a given linguistic content to pick out some particular portion of the external world this use is not essential to the word's meaning what it does, the meaning was not caused by the object in the world it is used to talk about and the content will remain constant over different kinds of referential use.

The suggestion is then that when we turn to consider the kind of content that syntax and lexicon is actually capable of delivering for us, what we find is this kind of purely internal, non–truth-evaluable content; content which still requires application to a world through use before it is capable of yielding something which fits the profile of what we standardly think of as propositional content. As Pietroski 2005: 296 writes, it seems that we have a model of content as something which *constrains* but which does not *determine* the truth-conditions of what we say:

[M]eaning is less tightly connected to the truth (and ontology and alien interpretability) than a lot of work suggests; expressions have semantic properties; but these are intrinsic properties of expressions that constrain without determining the truth-conditions of utterances. One can say that semantics is a species of syntax on this view. But that is not an objection. Given how form constrains meaning in natural languages, perhaps we should indeed replace the idea that semantic properties are *not* syntactic properties with a suitably expansive view of syntax.[4]

So, the suggestion is, there is some reason, based on the minimal account of singular content offered in the last chapter together with a recognition of the shared aims and assumptions of minimalism and Chomsky-style internalism, to think that the content minimalism really ought to be dealing with is non-referential, internally specified content, something more like a flexible character-level content than a truth-evaluable, propositional content. In which case the assumption that minimalism can utilize apparently externalist notions like truth and reference (an assumption made, for instance, in Borg 2004a) must be revisited, with these notions either being dropped or given an internalist rendition (for the latter move, see Pietroski 2005b, Hinzen 2007).Yet, as noted at the outset, *if* this is the kind of content minimalism is genuinely offering us, then the approach once again fails to offer a genuine alternative to other competitors. For instance, according to contextualism, sentences are capable of delivering a fragment of meaning which then requires expansion or narrowing in context to yield a truth-evaluable content for an utterance. For the occasionalist too, though the claim is that it makes no sense to speak of meaning outside a context of use, still remarks such as 'blue' is used to speak of somethings being blue (Travis 2008: 154) might lead us to believe that they envisage some kind of content outside a context of use, though one which at most constrains (rather than determines) the truth conditions of what we say. Though the contextualist and occasionalist reasons for making these claims differ somewhat, the outcome remains the same: on neither school of thought does lexico-syntactic content alone get us to truth-evaluable semantic content. And this outcome is embraced on the current proposal to unite minimalism and internalism. For construed along internalist lines, it now turns out that minimalism is in fundamental agreement with these alternative accounts, for again syntactically determined content falls short of truly

[4] This conclusion is endorsed by Collins 2009: 55 who writes:"Semantic theory *does* target invariance in the interpretation of linguistic structure, but we lack good reason to think that such invariance answers our inchoate notion of what someone *says* as reportable in the third person. In short, it is not obvious that linguistic structures encode anything worth calling a proposition, minimal or not. This should hardly be a shocking conclusion if our aim is a *theory* as opposed to a high-level description of what is inter-personally available".Though note that minimalism, as construed here, is not a theory of *what someone says*.

propositional, truth-evaluable content, with this emerging only at the point of use. However, beyond a recognition of something of a shared outlook for minimalism and Chomsky-style internalism, we need to ask whether there are actually any arguments which show that the minimalist *must* or *should* follow Chomsky and reject the broadly referential view of word meaning which could stave off collapse into alternative accounts? According to Chomsky there certainly are such arguments, thus it is to these that we turn next.

(2) The arguments against minimal word meanings

Why might we think that simple, broadly referential, context-independent ways of specifying the meanings of simple, broadly referential, apparently context-insensitive words are not okay? Certainly, the kind of internalism about meaning sketched above does not appear to be the pre-theoretical position here, for it seems intuitively obvious that the meaning of a name like 'Ian Botham' is fixed by the person in the world it picks out, and that the meaning of a predicate like 'red' is given, say, by the property of redness had by some objects and not had by others. However, a moment's reflection shows us that any kind of simple-minded account of words whereby they are meaningful thanks to their relationship to things in the world must be mistaken. For even if it seems natural to assume that some words (say names) acquire meaning from the things in the world they pick out, lots of words simply don't seem to be connected to aspects of the external world in this way at all. For instance, we don't suppose that there must be unicorns or sakes in order for the expressions 'unicorn' and 'Jill's sake' to be meaningful (see Quine 1953; Hinzen 2007: 13).

What is more, the internalist argument continues, even the assumption that apparently uncontroversial referring terms like 'London' or 'Barack Obama' refer to objects in some mind-independent physical world begins to look problematic under pressure, for it is not obvious that the relata posited in the relevant referential axioms really exist (Stainton 2006 labels this 'the radical argument from ontology').[5] Thus given a putative referential clause, such as:

---

[5] Discussion in the next two paragraphs follows Stainton's 2006 very clear introduction of the issues.

(a)   'London' refers to London

where the expression on the left hand-side is supposed to name a
linguistic expression (in this case an English word) and the expression on the right introduces a real-world entity (in this case, the city
of London), there is, advocates of narrow semantics object, no such
word and no such object. Turning first to the linguistic side of the
relation: why might we be sceptical that there are words like
'London'? Well the first point to note is that the public languages to
which these words are supposed to belong themselves look pretty
suspect, for there are no clear individuation conditions for public
languages. Instead the distinctions between languages and dialects
are often vague and blurry. Why is it that we count the quite similar
and often mutually intelligible things said in the different countries
of Northern Europe as belonging to distinct languages (English,
French, etc.) rather than treating them all as variants within a more
general public language (Romance), yet we treat very different and
mutually unintelligible systems like Mandarin and Cantonese as
mere dialects of the more general language Chinese? It seems clear
that what drives the individuation of a language is not mind-
independent facts about objective states of affairs in the world but
rather a complex mish-mash of socio-economic factors (the kinds
of things which resist any purely scientific approach to understanding them).

The same sort of vagaries which beset language individuation also
crop up at the level of words. Thus we can ask whether we should
posit one word 'in' and allow that there are many different ways for
something to be in something else, or whether we should posit many
different words (one for each sense?) all of which happen to share an
orthographic presentation? And we can ask (in an example from
Stainton 2006: 918–19) whether there is one word pronounced
'fotoGRAFer' in India and 'foTAHgrafer' in Canada, or whether these
constitute two distinct words with the same meaning? It seems plausible to think that answering these and similar questions will be a matter of assessing our aims and interests in categorizing one way or the
other, rather than an attempt to limn some objective fact of the world.
So it seems that we lack the kind of clearly individuated, public words
which the left-hand side of the schema assumes.

Furthermore, the radical argument from ontology continues, we should be sceptical about the putative objects on the right hand side of (a) as well, for there are no physical, mind-independent entities of the kind such clauses require. As Jackendoff 2002: 303 notes: "[It is often asserted] that we refer to 'objects in the world' as if this is completely self-evident. It *is* self-evident, if we think only of reference to middle-sized perceivable physical objects like tables and refrigerators. But as soon as we explore the full range of entities to which we actually refer, 'the world' suddenly begins to be populated with all sorts of curious beasts whose ontological status is far less clear". The problem can be highlighted by noting that a term like 'London' can be used to pick out many different facets of the city it is supposed to refer to, thus in some contexts 'London' picks out a physical location ('London is east of Oxford'), in some a governmental structure ('London has a Mayor'), and in some its inhabitants ('London is growing'). Indeed we can even run together such different aspects apparently without contradiction, as when we say that 'London is an ugly city but it is well run'. The problem is that there simply cannot be external, real-world objects which are capable of having all the properties the referent of 'London' is supposed to have. As Chomsky 2000: 37 writes:

Such terms as *London* are used to talk about the actual world, but there neither are nor are believed to be things-in-the-world with the properties of the intricate modes of reference that a city name encapsulates.

An internalist avoids this aspect of the radical argument for ontology since the expression on the right-hand side of a clause like ['London' refers to London] picks out not an external object but a world-independent concept. Thus as Hinzen 2007: 82 writes:

The conclusion here should be that London, while having uniquely physical and non-physical aspects, has *none* of them essentially: it remains stable and self-identical across changes in apparently *any* of the properties that we might predicate of it...There simply is no external object that we could point to and claim: *this* object is London, and it is the referent of the word *London* no matter what predication it is a part of, and it determines the meaning and how we use it to refer... The only thing that remains stable in perspectivally different acts of reference to the 'same thing' *is* the concept we have of that thing, and that concept alone.

The above scepticism about the physical status of the ordinary objects of reference is reinforced by noting that object individuation is interest-relative. For instance, as Carnap 1937 observed, if we ask how many objects are in a given box it seems that there is no simple right or wrong answer to be given. Instead the answer we should give depends on the conceptual framework we are working with: if we are counting only 'middle sized dry goods' then one number is appropriate, but if we use a different conceptual scheme, say one which posits existence for mereologies, then some quite other number may well be appropriate. Yet if we can only count objects by adopting a particular conceptual scheme then this once again undermines the idea that there are objective, mind-independent objects of reference simply sitting around in the world, quite independent of us, waiting to be called upon by our language.

Finally, we might note along with Sosa that to admit objects of reference as objective parts of the external world is to submit the world to a kind of ontological explosion. Thus Sosa notes that we might introduce the term 'snowdiscall' into our language to refer to a collection of snow which has a shape somewhere between a ball and a disc; so every snowball is a snowdiscall but not every snowdiscall is a snowball. Further, each snowball and snowdiscall in turn must be a distinct entity from the piece of snow which comprises it since they have different persistence conditions—squashing a piece of snow will suffice for the destruction of a snowball but not the destruction of the piece of snow which constituted it. But now Sosa 1993: 620 notes:

[T]here are infinitely many shapes S1, S2,..., between roundness and flatness of a piece of snow, and, for each *i*, having a shape between flatness and *Si* would give the form of a distinctive kind of entity to be compared with snowballs and snowdiscalls. Whenever a piece of snow constitutes a snowball, therefore, it constitutes infinitely many entities all sharing its place with it. Under a broadly Aristotelian conception, therefore, the barest flutter of the smallest leaf hence creates and destroys infinitely many things, and ordinary reality suffers a sort of 'explosion'.

So, the radical argument from ontology concludes, clauses like (a) cannot form the basis of a semantic theory as there are simply no objects available to play the role of the required relata.

While the radical argument from ontology claims that there are no such things as ordinary words or ordinary objects of reference for those words, there is also a second, more modest, argument against referential content available. According to this 'moderate argument from ontology' (Stainton 2006), while 'London' and London do exist, they exist only as mind-dependent entities. They are thus not the kind of objects which can figure within a rigorous science of language. As Stainton 2006: 925–6 puts the argument:

[B]eing objective and ignoring interest-relative distinctions, the 'scientific perspective' cannot see entities whose individuation conditions inherently involve complex-human interests and purposes...[G]ranting that what common sense 'sees' is perfectly real, we still arrive at the same conclusion...that a comprehensive science of language cannot (and should not try to) describe relations of semantic reference, i.e. word–world relations. That is because the things which manage to *be*, on this more moderate view...are nevertheless not real *in the right sort of way*. Hence they cannot be 'seen' from the scientific perspective.

That this is Chomsky's position seems evident when he writes 2000: 138–9:

It is not that ordinary discourse fails to talk about the world, or that the particulars it describes do not exist, or that the accounts are too imprecise. Rather, the categories used and principles involved need not have even loose counterparts in naturalistic inquiry.

So, the moderate argument from ontology concludes that semantic content, if it is to be scientifically respectable, must be non-referential.

Finally, it may be thought that the explanatory burden facing a semantic theory can be specified in purely internal terms. For instance, an adequate semantic theory for English needs to explain (in Pietroski's 2005 example) why there is no reading of the sentence 'The Senator called an oilman from Texas' whereby the Senator (rather than the call or the oilman) is from Texas. Yet explaining this doesn't require a complicated theory about the way words and objects hook up but rather a theory about the internal structures and content which influence semantic interpretation.[6] As Pietroski 2005: 263–4 notes:

---

[6] This goes back to the point with which this chapter began: the idea that the minimalist's account of singular content is best understood in internalist terms, for what is required to explain the behaviour of a referential expression is content at the level of character not content at the level of worldly extension. Collins 2009: 63 suggests it is the explanatory redundancy of the external dimension to meaning, from the point of view of semantics, which is at the heart of arguments for internalism.

[I]nteresting phenomena—relevant to theories of meaning, since they bear on linguistic understanding—are often due to subtle interactions between lexical items and natural composition; and explaining such phenomena typically requires substantive (non-disquotational) hypotheses about lexical meanings and composition principles.

If the arguments of this section are correct then it seems not only that a semantic minimalist *should* accept the internalist rendition of semantic content but that she *must* adopt it. For either there are no such things as the words and objects the referential perspective presumes, or words and objects do exist but are individuated via appeal to human interests and are thus not the right kind of things to figure in a science of language. On the other hand, however, it also seems that the move to an internalist semantics might leave the explanatory burden of our semantic theory unchanged for the work our theory must do can be characterized in purely internal terms (this concern will be the focus of the next chapter). Yet if it is right that a minimalist must adopt the internalist view of semantic content then it is in fact, as argued above, far from obvious that she can be a minimalist at all. For if what sentences literally express is content which still requires application to a world via use prior to achieving truth-evaluable status, it seems this is tantamount to a rejection of minimalism. If minimalism is to survive, then, the arguments against referential lexical content must be rejected.

(3) Rejecting the arguments against minimal word meanings

Turning first to the objection that the referential picture can't apply across the board: it is not obvious that an advocate of referential content should feel particularly discomforted by this point. First, what referential accounts of lexical content demand, it seems, is that *for at least some expressions* what they mean is given by features of the agent's environment, but this clearly leaves room for other types of expression in natural language whose meaning is delivered in other ways.[7] What we

---

[7] Of course, an opponent might go on to argue that the way in which these non-externalist terms come to be meaningful could be extended to cover all terms in a natural language, in which case referential lexical semantics would prove otiose, but showing this obviously requires much more work from the internalist.

are concerned with in preserving the minimalist assumptions about word meaning is that lexical content be specifiable in a context-invariant, truth-conducive way and taking word content to be given by objects and properties in the world is just one (intuitively appealing) way (potentially among many ways) of doing this, but it need not be the model all word meanings follow. Second, as we will see below, we need to be clear about exactly what is involved in the claim (integral to broadly referential accounts of lexical content) that words get their meaning from facts outside the agent. For at least some varieties of this kind of approach might be applicable to all terms in a natural language. Specifically, if one were to opt for the kind of social externalism promoted by Burge 1979 then semantic externalism might be thought to hold true for a majority of natural language terms, not merely those which intuitively appear 'world-directed'. So, without further support, worries about the limitations of the referential approach do little to promote the internalist cause. However further support for semantic internalism is, of course, in the offing here in the form of the two internalist arguments from ontology, so let's consider these now.

According to the radical argument from ontology there are no such things as public words or the ordinary objects of reference, so referential clauses stated in terms of such entities are destined to be empty. Yet we might ask what motivation the radical argument has for setting the standards for existence so high, for as Stainton 2006: 921 notes:

[P]erfectly real objects can be quite hard to individuate/count, and can be norm-bound. They need not require a 'robust divide', but can rather be objectively different only in degree, with human interests settling the kind-divide between them. One could thus allow that there is such a thing as English...and that the nature of English and the words/sentences in it depend on a host of complex relations (political, military, historical, religious, etc.)—including even explicitly normative ones having to do with 'correct speech'...[T]his does not make English and its elements unreal.

It seems that this kind of approach could also extend to the objects on the right-hand side of clauses like ['London' refers to London], allowing that, in at least some cases, human interests and actions do have a role to play in individuating the ordinary objects of reference without this making them unreal. Thus it could be that, in part, what makes something a chair is it's makers intention that it be used as a chair. Or again what makes something London is in part agreement among a community of speakers that a current object is the same as that previously called 'London'. Yet it doesn't follow from this that there are no such things as chairs or London. If this is right then the radical argument from ontology can be rejected on the grounds that it sets existence conditions for both words and objects too high.

Furthermore, in response to the Carnapian concern that object individuation is dependent on the kind of conceptual framework the counter adopts, it seems that an externalist might admit this point without it undermining their essentially realist world-view.[8] For while *recognizing* objects may well be a perspective-relative matter this doesn't mean that there is not an objective world underpinning that perspective. As Sosa 1993: 608 notes:

[F]rom the fundamentally and ineliminably perspectival character of our thought it does not follow that reality itself is fundamentally perspectival. Everything that is true relative to a perspective and everything that is false relative to a perspective may be as it is as a necessary consequence of the absolute and unperspectival character of things.... [O]ur perspectival references and truths may be seen to derive necessarily from absolute and unperspectival reality.

Finally, in response to Sosa's concern about ontological explosion, we need to be careful about where we locate the point of detonation here. For though it is right that our *conception of reality* expands when we admit snowdiscalls and all the other possible objects of reference this is not the same as *reality itself* expanding. Snowdiscalls exist because their grounds for existence do (i.e. collections of snow of the relevant shape) and when we come to recognize them what we see in the world expands but reality remains unchanged. It seems then that the radical argument from ontology, with its strong conclusion that both 'London' and London fail to exist, can be rejected by the externalist: public words and the ordinary objects of reference they pick out may be individuated with respect to human interests and beliefs but this doesn't entail that they do not exist nor that there is no objective reality underlying our perspectival conceptions.

[8] Following Davidson 1974, we might also reject the idea that Carnapian counters really have different conceptual schemes here, since everything statable in one scheme can be translated into the other and a statement and its translation must be true or false together (i.e. the same statement can't be true relative to one conceptual scheme and false relative to another).

At this juncture, however, the internalist can turn to the moderate argument from ontology, pointing out that, while all this may be true, it provides no succour to the minimalist who wants to hold on to semantic externalism. For such perspectival, interest-relative objects are not what externalism promised us nor are they the kinds of things which can figure in a science of language. So, to the extent that minimalism holds semantic content to be scientifically tractable, referential accounts of lexical content must be abandoned. Once again however it seems that this line of argument can be queried. For a start it's simply not all that clear what externalism promised us at the outset concerning the ordinary objects of reference. It is true that in Putnam's classic externalist thought experiment 'water' was held to refer to H_2O—a purely objective stuff picked out via the (non-interest relative) vocabulary of physics—but it is far from clear that this was supposed to be the model for an externalist explanation of all natural kind terms, let alone all expressions in natural language. For instance, on Burge's social externalism, what matters for the meaning of the term 'arthritis' is the meaning assigned to this expression by experts in the community, namely, *a condition resulting in a painful inflammation of the joints.* This is clearly a broadly referential proposal even though we have not specified the content of the expression in terms of the basic vocabulary of physics. A non-internalist approach holds that, for an expression e, e's content is fixed (in part) via an appeal to facts about an agent's environment, either their physical environment or the community of speakers to which they belong. Yet it seems that *this* could hold true whether the content thus fixed is spelt out via an objective language of science, like H_2O, or via talk of some more human-relative feature of reality like chairs, or even entirely abstract objects, like numbers. Non-internalism need not, it seems, be taken as simply co-extensive with some kind of brute physicalism. So objects individuated via appeal to human propensities could play a role in a broadly referential account of linguistic content, but could such an account still fall within the remits of *science*?

Chomsky 2000: 21 is adamant that it couldn't:

To be an Intentional Realist, it would seem, is about as reasonable as being a Desk- or Sound-of-Language- or Cat- or Matter-Realist; not that there are no such things as desks, etc, but that in the domain where questions of realism arise in a serious way, in the context of the search for the laws of nature, objects are not conceived from the peculiar perspectives provided by the concepts of common-sense. It is widely held that "mentalistic talk and mental entities should eventually lose their place in our attempts to describe and explain the world" (Burge 1992). True enough, but it is hard to see the significance of the doctrine, since the same holds true, uncontroversially, for 'physicalistic talk and physical entities' (to whatever extent the 'mental'-'physical' distinction is intelligible).

So must a genuine science of language be prohibited from talking about both beliefs and desires and chairs and tables? I think not, for it seems that a non-internalist could in fact accept Chomsky's claims about the requirements of science and the nature of the ordinary objects of reference *without* being forced to accept the conclusion that a science of language must be blind to common-sense categorizations. Specifically, it seems that we might agree with Chomsky that it is in part human interests which individuate (some of) the objects of common sense and allow that a purely scientific account of such human-relative individuation is impossible (since it would need to be a 'science of everything' as Chomsky says), and yet still hold that the vocabulary of common sense could play a role in a genuinely scientific explanation of linguistic abilities. The move here would be to bracket the properties appealed to by common-sense categories separately from issues about what makes something instantiate this property (with this latter issue being a potentially non-scientific, interest-relative matter).

On this approach, a scientific study of semantic content would be required to deliver a genuinely explanatory and predictive theory which showed how complex surface behaviour (e.g. subjects' ability to acquire language given only limited evidence, to recover the literal meaning of an indefinite number of sentences, and to use language to communicate) was the result of a less complex underlying structure together with systematic rules for manipulating that structure. Thus an account which took the meanings of primitive expressions as basic and provided rules of composition for those terms (and a canonical method for delivering the meanings of complex expressions from those rules together with the meanings of primitives) would count as scientifically respectable on the current view, even if it incorporated axioms utilizing the categories of common-sense. For the properties denoted by common-sense terms like 'desk' or 'chair' can be counted as perfectly respectable properties (i.e. one can be a realist about them) and this is all that is required for a scientific study of semantics. Of course there are murky questions lurking here about what makes something a desk or a chair and answering such questions may well require some kind of unsystematic, unscientific approach making reference to community norms and human interests, but these questions are not ones which get voiced or require answering from within the semantic domain. On this conception, then, a semantic theory is required to specify that 'London buses are red' means that *London buses are red*. It is not expected to tell us why 'red' means *red* and not *blue*, nor is it required to guarantee that every subject who grasps this semantic information knows what is required to make something a bus, nor must they be able to tell, for every object they encounter, whether or not it is a bus (a point returned to below in §4).

The move here is analogous to the one suggested in Chapter 4 for providing a minimal account of the semantic content of directly referential expressions, like demonstratives. For demonstratives I argued that all that is required to grasp the semantic content of an utterance like 'That is red' is that a subject introduce a syntactically triggered singular concept relating to this token of 'that' which has as its content the object referred to by the speaker (where which object this is is settled by appeal to the speaker's referential intentions). Furthermore, a subject should be deemed capable of doing this *even if* she can conceptualize of that content only under the token-reflexive description *the actual object referred to by the speaker with this token of 'that'*. Similarly, then, for understanding general terms, like 'chair', what is required is that the subject deploy a general concept of the relevant property (*chairhood*) and this is something she can do *without* engaging in questions about what makes something a chair. It follows, then, that there may be cases where semantic information alone is insufficient to allow a subject to decide, for some object, whether or not it instantiates the property in question (i.e. whether or not it is a chair) and answering this question may thus require a non-semantic (and probably non-scientific) inquiry.

It seems to me then that the argument that a scientific methodology demands we excise chairs and tables from our referential canon is not well founded. The radical argument from ontology can be rejected as it sets the standards for existence claims too high, while the moderate argument from ontology can be rejected since it conflates questions of concept content with questions of how we identify objects as falling under those concepts.[9] Instead it seems to me that we might allow reference and extension identification to remain as murky as we like without this preventing the common sense properties we use for categorizing the world from entering into genuinely explanatory hypotheses about linguistic content.

This leaves us with the final challenge from the last section, that the explanatory burden of semantics is purely internalist in nature, so that any appeal to externally characterized content is otiose from the point of view of semantic theorizing. So, is it right to think that a theory couched in purely internalist terms could be adequate to the explanatory role proper to a semantic theory? Well (along with many other theorists), I think not. A first point to note is that if there is *any* external dimension to meaning then externalism must be right. For a properly nuanced externalist account could in principle explain all internally specified requirements on a semantic theory, while the converse does not hold. Furthermore, the idea that there must be *some* externalist dimension to semantic content seems extremely attractive. For a start it is unclear how an internalist system gets beyond the level of syntax to that of genuine content in the first place. As Fodor 1990: 98–9 notes "words can't have their meanings just because their users undertake to pursue some or other linguistic policies; or, indeed, just because of any purely *mental* phenomenon, anything that happens purely 'in your head'. For 'John' to be John's name, there must be some sort of *real relation* between the name and its bearer ... something has to happen *in the world*".[10] If we want our

---

[9] We might also note Williamson's 2008: 223–4 objection that the kind of judgement scepticism which seems to underlie this rejection of common-sense ontology itself undermines the empirical evidence and methodology at play in scientific theories. As he writes 2008: 223: "Judgement skeptical arguments apply to standard perceptual judgements, on which the natural sciences systematically depend: microscopes, telescopes, and other scientific instruments enhance ordinary perception but do not replace it, for we need ordinary perception to use the instruments. If the contents of those perceptual judgements concern ordinary macroscopic objects, they are vulnerable to judgement skepticism about common sense ontology. If so, the empirical evidence for scientific theories is threatened. To assume that the evidence can be reformulated without relevant loss in ontologically neutral terms, in the absence of any actual such reformulation, would be optimistic to the point of naïvety".

[10] This is to embrace Lewis's 1972: 169 oft-quoted aphorism that "semantics with no treatment of truth conditions is not semantics". See also Wiggins' 2001: 12 admonition "Let us forget once and for all the very idea of some knowledge of language or meaning which is not knowledge of the world itself" (quoted in Williamson 2008: 20).

words or thoughts to have content at all—to move beyond syntax to semantics—it seems that the requirement to let the world in at some point in the specification of that content is inescapable. Furthermore, as many theorists have argued, if we want to account for the possibility of error (and the normative dimension of linguistic meaning in general) this seems to require us to posit an external dimension to semantic content. When someone learns that 'contract' means *mutual agreement* rather than *written agreement*, they take themselves to be corrected about the meaning of the term, yet this behaviour only makes sense given the externalist perspective that what matters for word meaning can lie outside the individual (the example is from Higginbotham 2006, though the point is of course well known—see Wittgenstein 1953, Putnam 1975, Dummett 1978, Burge 1979, Kripke 1980). As Lassiter 2008: 608 notes: "it is possible for speakers to be simply *wrong* in their use of language because a language exists independently of its speakers. In contrast, under the individualist view, 'incorrect usage' is a murky social concept, usually a simple failure of communication or a *faux pas*". If we want to account for the fact that there is such a thing as being right or wrong about what our words mean, it seems to me that we have no option but to allow an externalist dimension to semantic content.

That words connect to the world is not, then, explanatorily redundant for semantics. However perhaps there is more to say here. For even if we disagree with Chomsky, Pietroski and others that the explanatory burden on semantics is *entirely* internalist in nature, still it might be the case that there is a *significant* internalist explanatory burden on semantics. If this is right, and if a broadly referential account of lexical content were to prove inadequate to the task of accommodating this internalist burden, then we would seem to reach a stalemate. Internalist accounts of word meaning fail to capture meaning (as opposed to syntax) at all and they fail to explain the normative dimensions of linguistic content, but non-internalist, broadly referential accounts, on the current suggestion, fail to accommodate the significant internalist work a semantic theory must do. In the next chapter, then, we will need to explore the internalist explanatory burden on semantics and assess the extent to which a referential lexical semantics might be able to bear this burden.

(4) Conclusion

There are arguments which seem to show that semantic minimalism should concern itself with an entirely non-referential, world-independent account of semantic content: first, we find between minimalism and the kind of semantic internalism espoused by Chomsky a surprising degree of common ground, which might lead us to expect that the two approaches should also share a common view of the nature of semantic content itself. Second, the kind of minimalist account of semantic content for indexicals and demonstratives recommended in Chapter 4 raises the concern that what minimalism is really offering us is a character-level account of content, rather than one which is genuinely object-involving (§1). Furthermore, if Chomsky is to be believed, it is only the kind of narrow, non-referential notion of content which he recommends which can meet the demands on a scientifically respectable study of semantics (§2). However I've tried to suggest that these arguments are mistaken (§3). First, the arguments concerning the requirements of science can be rejected, for though the categories of common-sense may not figure in fundamental physics, this does not rule out the possibility of their figuring in a systematic, explanatory and computational study of semantics. Second, although much of the work a semantic theory needs to do may be specifiable in internal terms, not all of it is. Specifically, it seems that if we want to move beyond the level of syntax to semantic content at all (avoiding the kind of solipsism Fodor warns of) and to capture the normative dimension of linguistic meaning we must look to the world not merely to the individual's mind.[11] My claim is then that the minimalist need not and should not give up on referential lexical semantics. Word meanings can be construed as the kind of discrete, context-independent entities which, when strung together in an appropriate syntactic framework, are capable of delivering a truth-evaluable claim, just as minimalism contends.

[11] See, for instance, Fodor 2008: 16, n.28: "Even these days it's not unheard of in cognitive science to opt for a real, honest-to-God, ontological solipsism, according to which there just *isn't* anything that's not mental. Sometimes I think that maybe Jackendoff holds that; in my darkest moments I think maybe even Chomsky does". This point resurfaces in Chapter 6, §2.

CHAPTER 6

The Methodological Argument Against Minimal Word Meanings

In the last chapter we looked at, and rejected, the ontological arguments which Chomsky and others have offered against the atomistic, broadly referential account of lexical content which minimalism seems tacitly to assume. However, as noted at the close of the last chapter, Chomsky and others opt for the kind of internalist construal of lexical content which they do, not just because of putative problems with alternative accounts but also because of the positive reasons they see as demanding non-referential lexical axioms. The positive argument for internalist lexical contents is that if a semantic theory is to do the work required what is needed is not an account of how a word hooks up to some feature of the world but rather an account of how that word relates to other intra-linguistic items. So in this chapter I want to look at what this intra-linguistic work might be, why it is supposed to push us away from the sorts of simple, common-sense, broadly referential accounts of word meaning which could underlie minimalism, and how the advocate of broadly referential word meanings might respond.

The structure of the chapter is as follows: in the next section I'll focus on the internalist or intra-linguistic burden for semantics, looking at the kinds of features which have been taken to support a move away from simple referential lexical axioms and towards an alternative position. As we will see, the internalist burden emerges in two key areas: first, predicting and explaining syntactic transactions and, second, accommodating semantic relations. Once we are clear on the burden itself, however, it will then appear that there is an apparently straightforward and appealing way to meet this explanatory demand by 'splitting the atom of word meaning', as Pinker 2007 puts it. That is to say, we might reject the idea that the lexicon is a mere list of word-denotation pairs and instead maintain that the meanings of even simple words are structured, complex entities. Thus, in §3, I'll look at two ways of spelling out this general idea—the approach of 'lexical semantics', common in linguistics, and that of 'inferential role semantics', common in philosophy—and see how they succeed in capturing the intra-linguistic data. However, both lexical semantics and inferential role semantics have been subject to vociferous criticism from Jerry Fodor and Ernie Lepore, thus in §4 we will examine their objections. I'll suggest that while the criticisms they offer of the two accounts do hold good, they also serve to highlight the fact that the kind of lexical complexity assumed in the two accounts is not the only kind of lexical complexity one might allow. For one could reject the idea, common to both lexical semantics and inferential role semantics, that the complexity found in the lexicon is meaning constituting. That is to say, one could posit complexity within the lexicon even while hanging on to the idea that word meanings are primitive, atomic elements. In §5 I'll look at two ways to spell out this idea: the appeal to so-called 'meaning postulates' and the appeal to what I'll term 'organizational lexical semantics'. I'll argue that it is this final position which provides the advocate of referential lexical semantics with the most attractive way to accommodate the internal burden outlined in §1. Finally, however, we will need to ask whether the kind of organizational lexical semantics advocated in this chapter is consistent with the overarching minimalist approach to semantics advocated throughout this book. This will lead us to reconsider the minimalist response to incomplete expressions (explored initially in Chapter 3) and the relationship between minimalism and approaches to semantics which allow that the semantic content of a sentence may fall short of being truth-evaluable. Thus the chapter will close by re-examining the notion of propositionalism and arguing, once again, that there are good reasons to preserve the minimalist assumption that all well-formed sentences are capable of yielding truth-evaluable semantic content.

(1) The intra-linguistic burden for semantics

A feature which we might expect a semantic theory to explain is, in my terminology, an *intra-linguistic* or *internal* feature if it concerns properties of, and relations among, expressions rather than appealing to a relation between a word and some aspect of the external, non-linguistic world. So, for instance, in the sentence 'Pietersen runs' the fact that 'Pietersen' is the subject of the sentence and that 'runs' is a verb count as internal facts, while the fact that 'Pietersen' refers to *Pietersen* counts as an external fact. The concern then, as raised by theorists like Chomsky and Pietroski, is that concentration on the externally determined properties of natural language expressions blinds the referentialist to the real explanatory work to be done on the internal side. As Pietroski 2005: 263–4 writes:

One way or another, we need to capture the following idea: the meaning of 'easy' is lexicalized so that when this word combines with 'to please' and 'John' constraints on grammatical structure and compositional semantics conspire to ensure that John is said to be an individual who is easily *pleased*; while the meaning of 'eager' is lexicalized so that when this word combines with 'to please' and 'John', John is said to be an individual who is eager to be a *pleaser*. We want to know more about these facts, which seem to be symptoms of how lexicalization interacts with (syntactic and semantic) composition in natural language. But just saying that 'easy' has the semantic properties that it has, or that 'eager' applies to what it applies to, tells us nothing about how 'easy' and 'eager' differ in a way that 'easy' and 'hard' do not . . . So a theory with axioms like '*easy* means EASY' or 'x satisfies *easy* iff x is easy'. . . may be a poor theory of meaning. Even if such axioms/theorems are true, it is a tendentious hypothesis that they are formulated in the right way for purposes of explaining how humans understand language.[1]

If this is correct, then either (as Chomsky et al. propose) a referential semantics for words proves redundant (since all the explanatory work required can be done by a theory which makes no appeal to word-world connections) or, at the very least, a referential lexical semantics needs to incorporate in some way information and structures which are capable of meeting the internal explanatory demand. Before we come to the question of how a referential semantics might meet the demand, however, let's try to get a little bit clearer on

---

[1] To advertise in advance, the strategy of this chapter is to agree entirely with Pietroski here up to the first lacuna. The claim will be, then, that the first part of the quote does not entail that a theory with referential axioms will be a poor theory of meaning.

exactly what the demand is. What is the internally specifiable explananda that Chomsky and others take to drive us to a non-referential lexical semantics?

Perhaps the most obvious point to start with here is the argument from proper names, for it is of course widely held that Frege showed that the meaning of a name cannot be given simply in terms of denotation or extension. The problem Frege famously noted is that sometimes we cannot exchange co-referring terms *salva veritate* in intentional contexts: swapping 'Hesperus' for 'Phosphorous' in 'Alf believes that Phosphorous is seen in the evening' may well result in a change of truth value for the sentence despite the fact that Hesperus is Phosphorous. Prima facie, then, the behaviour of proper names shows us that we must appeal to something other than worldly extensions in our account of the meaning of these expressions. We must move away from the primitive idea that the lexicon is a simple list of words and objects, and allow instead that word meanings are in some way complex (either complex combinations of denotations and descriptive material, or complex structures which make no appeal to denotations at all). Now there is, of course, a vast literature surrounding the correct treatment of proper names, and not everyone accepts that this is the take-home message of Frege's problem, but the point I want to stress here is the form of the argument: something in the behaviour of certain natural language expressions apparently shows us that word meanings cannot simply be denotations (i.e. that referential lexical semantics is wrong or inadequate) and the natural response is to posit some alternative, complex kind of content at the lexical level (i.e. taking the meaning of a name to be given by both a sense and a reference, or indeed by a complex descriptive sense alone).[2] As we will see, these two factors—the internalist explanatory need and the move to complicate lexical entries in response to it—emerge in a range of other settings as well.

For instance, as noted in the quote from Pietroski above, it seems that a semantic theory ought to explain the kinds of readings which sentences can and can't give rise to. So, consider the following well-known examples:

---

[2] See Salmon 1986 for an example of someone who rejects the claim that Frege Arguments show us the meaning of a proper name must be more than mere denotation.

1.   Ted is too clever to catch Jim.
1*. Ted is too clever to catch.
2.   Alfie is eager to please.
2*. Alfie is easy to please.

Here, despite the surface similarities of each pair of sentences, very different readings are required. For while Ted and Alfie are the agents of (1) and (2) respectively, in (1*) and (2*) they do not play this role at all (with (1*) stating that Ted is too clever *for someone* to catch, while (2*) is read as claiming that Alfie is easy *for someone* to please). However, if we want to explain these differences in the thematic roles played by the expressions it looks as if we will need to appeal to more than the syntactic structure of the sentence and the denotational content of the terms involved—knowing, say, just that 'easy' picks out the property of *being easy* doesn't seem to help here. Instead, then, it seems we need to know something about how the content of a term can affect the structure of a sentence, and this seems to suggest that the lexical content for the terms involved should be construed more richly than as simple word-denotation pairs.

The idea that explaining the syntactic behaviour of expressions and the readings sentences admit of requires us to look beyond the denotational content of a term is reinforced by considering other patterns of syntactic distribution. For instance, consider the kind of evidence about English verb behaviour collected by Levin 1985, 1993, and surveyed in Pinker 2007: 103–7 (from whom the following examples are taken). First, consider conative constructions such as 'Jill cut at the rope'. Here we find that some expressions participate in the conative form while others resist it:

Claudia kicked at the cat.
Vince hit at the dog.
* Nancy touched at the cat.
* Rhonda broke at the rope

It seems that conative constructions are admissible with verbs like 'hit' or 'cut' but that they are ill-formed with verbs like 'touch' or 'break'. The difference between verbs which enter the conative ('hit', 'chip', 'chop', etc.) and those which don't ('kiss', 'pat', 'rip', 'smash', etc.) seems to be, as Pinker 2007: 103 puts it, that 'the eligible verbs signify a kind of motion resulting in a kind of contact'. That is to say, 'hit', 'kick' and the other participating verbs care about the *kind* of motion which precedes the contact—something is a kick or a hit not merely if it makes a specific kind of contact but also if it involves a certain kind of motion beforehand. Verbs like 'touch' and 'break' on the other hand are not sensitive in this way. All that matters for touching or breaking is the end result—the kind of contact made with an object not the movement that led to that contact. Or again, take the following alternation:

> I hit the wall with the bat.
> I hit the bat against the wall.
> She bumped the table with the glass.
> She bumped the glass against the table.

This alternation resists verbs of breaking and of touching:

> I cut the rope with the knife
> ⋆ I cut the knife against the rope.
> She touched the cat with her hand.
> ⋆ She touched her hand against the cat.

In these cases participating verbs involve motion followed by contact (as in the conative construction) but not motion followed by contact followed by a specific effect (cutting, or breaking, say), nor contact without motion, i.e. without prior change of location (as in kissing or touching). The suggestion is then that there are non-arbitrary patterns of syntactic distribution for natural language expressions (see Levin 1993 for many more examples of this kind) and, prima facie, this is the kind of thing we might expect a semantic theory to explain and predict. However, it also seems clear that a theory which treats the lexical content of expressions as exhausted by their denotational content will be unable to capture these non-arbitrary patterns. Nothing in the claim that 'cut' means *cut* seems able to explain why 'I cut at the chain' is admissible but '⋆I cut the knife against the chain' is not.

So, purely referential axioms for words look problematic in the face of data concerning the syntactic interactions of expressions: saying that 'easy' picks out the property of being easy, or that 'hit' picks out the property of hitting, seems totally inadequate to explain the kinds of interpretations these expressions admit of and the kinds of complex intra-lexical relations they enter into. Furthermore, it seems that such axioms are also shown to be inadequate by consideration of certain intuitively semantic relations, such as synonymy, analyticity, entailment, and polysemy. For instance, intuitively it seems we want a semantic theory to reveal when two terms are synonymous, e.g. showing that 'bachelor' means the same as 'unmarried man', or that 'vixen' means the same as 'female fox'. Clearly, however, this is something which goes beyond a straightforward appeal to denotation, since two expressions can have the same extension (indeed, necessarily the same extension) and yet still fail to be synonymous: 'cordate' and 'renate' agree in extension, yet they do not mean the same thing. So the synonymy of 'bachelor' and 'unmarried man' can't simply be a result of the fact that every bachelor is an unmarried man and vice versa. Rather to capture the synonymy here it seems that we want an analysis of the meaning of 'bachelor' which shows it as somehow containing the elements *unmarried* and *man*, yet clearly this would be to reject the idea that word meanings are given simply via denotation.

Just as a broadly referential account of word meaning seems destined to miss the synonymy of certain terms, so it also seems destined to miss the analytic nature of certain inferences. So, for instance, take the move from 'x is a bachelor' to 'x is an unmarried man', or from 'x is red' to 'x is coloured'. In each case the moves are intuitively analytic, they seem to be guaranteed just by the meanings of the terms involved. Yet it is not clear how this intuitive analyticity could possibly be captured by a theory that claimed that word meanings are exhausted by their referential properties, for nothing in the claim, say, that 'bachelor' picks out the property of *bachelorhood* seems to underwrite the inference from 'x is a bachelor' to 'x is unmarried'. Or again, it seems we can infer from 'x chased y' to 'y was followed by x', or from 'x is a dog' to 'x is a mammal', yet any classical account of validity which looks just to the logical form of the sentences paired with the referential properties of the expressions involved will apparently miss the intuitive validity of these arguments.

A third semantic relation which is relevant here is that of polysemy, or the distinction between what is sometimes called *contrastive* and *complementary* ambiguity (Weinreich 1964). In the former camp fall terms with a single surface presentation and multiple meanings where those meanings seem completely arbitrary and unrelated. In these cases, as with the meanings assigned to 'bank' of *edge of a river* and *financial institution*, an explanation in terms of homonymy—allowing a single surface presentation to map to two or more distinct lexical entries—seems fitting. However a natural language like English also contains a vast number of words with a single surface presentation and multiple meanings where those meanings seem related to one another in non-arbitrary ways. This is the phenomenon of *complementary ambiguity* or polysemy. So, consider the concrete and abstract senses of a term like 'book', as in 'the book weighs two pounds' versus 'the book is in every shop in the country', or the different interpretations of 'good' in 'a good car' versus 'a good child', or the different senses of 'keep' in 'keep a pet', 'keep the money' or 'keep a crowd happy' (Jackendoff 1992: 37–9). Or again, there seems to be a quite general mechanism (sometimes referred to as 'the universal grinder') which allows a count noun to become a mass term (so, from Pinker 2007, 'she loved her cat' and 'after reversing, there was cat all over the driveway'). Prima facie, then, it seems we should expect a semantic theory to capture the relations of meaning we witness among polysemous terms and the general mechanisms which seem to underpin their introduction. Yet, as Pustejovsky 1995: 53–4 notes '[f]or all of these cases, [referential lexical axioms] would simply list the alternative structures along with their apparently distinct but related meanings. The fact that these senses are so related, however, suggests that this approach is missing the underlying generalization behind these syntactic forms'. On the contrary, then, Pustejovsky 1995: 39 suggests what we need is a theory which can accommodate the creative use of words (the fact that words can assume new senses in novel contexts), the permeability of senses (the fact that word senses overlap and reference each other) and the fact that a single word sense can have multiple distinct syntactic forms. Capturing these features will, he suggests, push us away from a simple denotational account of word meaning and towards a view of lexical meanings as complex, structured entities.

It is, then, in the fields of syntactic behaviour and semantic relations that I think we find the main weight of the internalist burden on semantics and thus the main arguments against a simple referential lexical semantics (of the kind we might expect a semantic theory like minimalism—which predicts truth-evaluable status for the contents recovered on the basis of syntactic forms and lexical content alone— to utilize). To do the work a semantic theory is required to do, the argument is, we do not need axioms which simply pair words and denotations, rather we need lexical entries which are themselves complex and rule-governed. In the next section I will turn to the question of how an advocate of referential lexical semantics might begin to meet this explanatory challenge, however before this let's note one last problem for the referential account. This final argument concerns so-called 'impossible words': these are words which do not occur in any natural language, despite their having apparently cogent meanings. So for instance, there is no natural language verb 'to cow', such that we could say:

3.   *It cowed a calf

meaning that *a cow had a calf* (the example is from Hale and Keyser 1993: 60). Or again, although we can say 'Mary broke the desk', there is no verb 'blik' where 'the desk bliked Mary' means that the desk was broken by Mary. As Johnson 2004: 334 notes:

> The absence of the word *blik* does not appear to be an accident, in the way that it is an accident that there is no noun that picks out one's tallest friends relatives. Instead, the absence of the verb *blik* appears to be due to the more general fact that whenever a transition verb of English expresses a relation between the doer of an action and the thing that is acted upon . . . the former is the subject of the verb and the latter is the object.

Clearly, if it is not an accident that natural language fails to contain words like 'cowed' and 'blik' then some explanation of these absences is required, but once again, if word meanings are given simply in terms of denotation, then it is unclear how we are to meet this explanatory demand. Nothing in the claim that the meaning of a verb is given by the relation in the world that it picks out reveals why, in a sentence of the form 'xVs y', x is always the subject and y is always the object.

So, the claim is that referential lexical semantics neglects the very real internalist burden on a semantic theory. That is to say, such an account fails to predict or explain what readings can and cannot be given to sentences, it fails to predict or explain the complex patterns of syntactic distribution we witness for natural language expressions, it fails to capture intuitively semantic relations like synonymy, analyticity and polysemy, and it fails to explain why 'impossible words' are impossible. When we turn to examine the work a semantic theory must do what we find is that it is not to be done by appeal to how words connect to objects (i.e. not by a semantic theory that contains axioms like ['e' refers to *e*]). It seems, instead, that there are two distinct ways we might seek to capture the internalist burden on semantics: on the one hand, we might, roughly speaking, take stuff out of lexical concepts and make them *thin* enough to do the work required. On the other hand, we might stick stuff into lexical concepts and make them *fat* enough to explain intra-linguistic facts. In §3, I'll turn to the (more common) idea that what these arguments point towards is the need to treat word meanings not as brute, atomic entities but as complex, structured entities, where the precise configuration of complex properties a word contributes to the larger unit in which it occurs may differ across different contexts of use, but before this let us consider the less-well-trodden path which claims that what we need is to make lexical concepts thinner rather than fatter.

(2) The thin approach to carrying the intra-linguistic burden

According to the thin solution, the proper response to the need to accommodate the intra-linguistic burden on semantics is to strip content out of lexical concepts and treat them as partial 'shadows' of full-blown concepts, where these somewhat spectral lexical concepts are specifically designed to explain intra-linguistic facts rather than to deliver truth-evaluable content. So, for instance, Pietroski 2010 proposes what he terms 'monadic I-concepts', which are designed to figure within the semantic theory of an I-language (following Chomsky's terminology). As he writes, 2010: 247–8:

Acquiring words is a process in which prior concepts—of a diverse and perhaps incommensurate sort—are used to make concepts that exhibit the format required by the composition operations that correspond to phrasal syntax... [The human faculty for language] generates expressions that direct the construction of systematically combinable concepts that exhibit distinctive formal properties and [that] having such concepts makes it *possible* for us to form truth-evaluable judgements given some additional cognitive talents. But our words are not true of the things we talk about.

Now, any version of the thin solution will clearly carry a significant part of the explanatory burden outlined above—for after all, lexical concepts on this kind of approach just are designed to accommodate facts about possible and impossible readings of sentences or about the syntactic distribution of expressions. However, whether or not the thin approach can carry the whole of the burden remains something of an open question. For instance, it is not clear that the skinny, pared-down concepts the approach posits will retain enough content to explain semantic relations such as synonymy and analyticity, nor do thin concepts look like good candidates to explain Frege cases. Furthermore, there remain theory-internal issues which any such approach will need to answer, e.g. concerning the relationship between full concepts and I-concepts (one might be concerned, for instance, about a risk of deviant causal chains if what ties a full concept to an I-concept is held to be something to do with causal ancestry).

However, the concerns that are perhaps most pressing here are rather more theory-external and concern the fundamental question (noted at the close of the last chapter) of whether or not it can be right to treat the *entire* explanatory burden on semantics as internalist in nature, as the thin approach supposes. Fully addressing this issue would clearly take us too far afield in the current context, but the points to consider here are the ones non-internalists have traditionally urged on internalists, for instance concerning normativity (how do we account for the apparent fact that there is such a thing as going wrong with language if a semantic theory is only answerable to internal, individualist constraints?) and whether any account which doesn't 'get to the world' can in fact qualify as an account of *semantic* content at all, as opposed to a description of some level of syntax. This latter worry might be thought to be a purely terminological one (I think Pietroski would tend to view it in this way), however I don't think that it is, for the question is whether, in the absence of external reference, what we have can ever move beyond the level of formal symbols to the level of representational content at all. This echoes a point made by Fodor 2008: 53, n.4, who writes:

It's possible to find philosophers and (more often) linguists who endorse a reference-free semantics...But I don't understand how a semantics can avoid lapsing into idealistic solipsism unless it recognizes some sort of symbol-world relation.

This seems to me to be a fundamental worry for any version of the thin approach and I think it is enough to push us towards looking for some alternative way to bear the explanatory burden.

(3) The thick approach to carrying the intra-linguistic burden: lexical complexity

One way to think about capturing the explanatory burden outlined in §1, then, is to reject the conception of the lexicon as a simple list pairing words and denotations and instead opt to put *more* content into lexical concepts to allow them to do the work required. To see how such a thick approach might go, and how it might meet the internal demands on a semantic theory, I want in this section to look at two specific versions of the general idea that word meanings are complex entities: first, the idea from lexical semantics that word meanings are bundles of semantic features, and, second, the idea from inferential role semantics that the meaning of a word is constituted by its inferential relations.[3]

(3.1) Lexical semantics

According to lexical semantics, word meanings decompose into sets of more primitive semantic features. So, for instance, the meaning of a verb like 'to cut' is said to be composed out of elements such as + CONTACT and + MANNER OF MOTION, while 'dog' decomposes into elements like + ANIMAL, + TYPICALLY BARKS,

---

[3] There is at least one other approach which belongs to this general category of accounts which posit structured, complex word meanings. This is the approach of prototype theory which treats meanings as statistical constructs, such as prototypes or stereotypes. Although such an approach clearly constitutes a rival to inferential role semantics and lexical semantics, it also shares with them the fundamental assumption that it is word meanings themselves which are complex (i.e., that the meaning of an apparently simple word is structured). Since it is this shared assumption which will be rejected in what follows, I will not consider prototype theory separately here.

+ TYPICAL PET, etc.[4] Now, whether this decomposition is supposed to be total or not (i.e. whether word meanings are held to be nothing over and above sets of semantic features) is something of a moot point, for at least some advocates of lexical semantics seem happy with the idea that the decompositions are merely partial. Thus Pinker 2007: 107 writes: 'Of course, many verbs, like *kiss* and *chip* and *snap*, do have a nugget specific to them, but it doesn't exhaust the verb's meaning or affect its syntactic behaviour' (see also Pinker 1989: 167 and Konrfilt and Correra 1993: 83; for the converse view that decompositions must be total see Jackendoff 2002, Chapter 11). However it is not obvious that an account which posits less than total decomposition will be able to do the work required (this is a point to which we will return below). Be this as it may, though, if these are the kinds of features which are hidden below the surface of a verb like 'to cut' then the superficially peculiar behaviour of this expression in various syntactic environments becomes entirely transparent. It is because the meaning of 'cut' specifies that it is a + MANNER OF MOTION verb that it will take part in conative constructions, and it is because this feature is shared with the meanings of 'hit' and 'kick', but not with those of 'touch' or 'stroke', that the former but not the latter are similarly syntactically permissive. So by treating word meanings as complex bundles of semantic features we are able to predict and explain the non-arbitrary patterns of syntactic distribution witnessed in §1.

Furthermore, treating the meaning of a term as decomposing into semantic features and structures allows us to capture (at least some of) the evidence surrounding semantic relations. So, for instance, recall the problem of polysemy, whereby some expressions admit of multiple interpretations but where these distinct readings seem related to one another in principled ways, as in the abstract and concrete senses of 'book'. As noted in the last section, polysemy seems to pose a challenge for a simple referential lexicon. However, if we treat word meanings as

---

[4] I will use capital letters to denote semantic features, whereas I use italics to denote ordinary concepts. This typographical distinction is supposed to mark the fact that, while undoubtedly sharing some commonality of meaning with the concepts associated with their natural language counterparts (so that CAUSE shares at least some content with *cause*), still the labels introduced in lexical semantics are technical terms. They stand for primitive semantic items which may relate only indirectly to notions picked out in ordinary language. So, for instance, see Pinker's 2007: 100–1 claim that the decompositions in lexical semantics are not equivalent to dictionary definitions.

composed of bundles of semantic features then it seems we have an easy explanation of these things. As Chomsky 2000: 15–16 notes:

Investigating language use, we find that words are interpreted in terms of such features as material construction, design, intended and characteristic use, institutional role, and so on. Things are identified and assigned to categories in terms of such properties—which I am taking to be semantic features—on a par with phonetic features that determine its sound. The use of language can attend in various ways to these semantic features. Suppose the library has two copies of Tolstoy's *War and Peace*, Peter takes out one, and Jack the other. Did Peter and John take out the same book, or different books? If we attend to the material factor of the lexical item, they took out different books; if we focus on its abstract component, they took out the same book. We can attend to both material and abstract factors simultaneously, as when we say that 'the book that he is planning will weigh at least five pounds, if he ever writes it,' or 'his book is in every store in the country.' Similarly, we can paint the door white and walk through it, using the pronoun 'it' to refer ambiguously to figure and ground. We can report that the bank was blown up after it raised interest rates, or that it raised the interest rate to keep from being blown up. Here the pronoun 'it,' and the 'empty category' that is the subject of 'being blown up', simultaneously adopt both the material and institutional factors.

This general idea—that polysemy can be explained and accommodated by treating lexical entries as complex bundles of semantic features, with certain elements of that bundle being stressed or depressed in a given use of the term—has been pursued in detail in Pustejovsky 1995, where word meanings are decomposed into structured forms made up of multiple interacting levels of semantic representation (see also Jackendoff 1990, 1992). For instance, Pustejovsky 1995: 58 proposes that the lexicon needs to contain an 'argument structure', specifying the number and type of arguments an expression takes, together with a 'qualia structure' representing the different modes of predication of which a term admits. These levels are then connected by various kinds of semantic transformation rules which capture the generativity of the lexicon. So, considering the two senses of 'bake'—its change of state sense (as in 'he baked a potato') and its creative sense (as in 'he baked a cake')—Pustejovsky 1995: 123 proposes that 'the complements carry information which acts on the governing verb, essentially taking the verb as argument and shifting its event type'. Thus he writes, 1995: 124:

[W]e can derive both senses of verbs like 'bake' by putting some of the semantic weight on the NP. This view suggests that, in such cases, the verb itself is not polysemous. Rather, the creative sense of 'bake' is contributed in part by the meaning of 'a cake', by virtue of it being an artifact.

As we will see below, there remain questions to be asked about Pustejovsky's specific proposal, but in principle at least it seems clear that lexical semantics, with its appeal to complex structures of semantic features below the surface of apparently simple expressions, seems well placed to accommodate the various gradations of meaning relations we find between homonyms, at one end of the scale, and synonyms, at the other.

Furthermore, although advocates of lexical semantics have been less exercised by semantic relations like synonymy and analyticity, it seems clear that the approach might accommodate these relations as well. Thus, if the decomposition into semantic features is held to be total (i.e. if the meaning of an expression is exhausted by a bundle of semantic features) then two terms will be synonymous just in case they decompose into all and only the same elements. On the other hand, an inference will count as analytic just in case it rests on some element in the sub-lexical content of an expression. So, for instance, the theory will clearly count the inference from 'A kicked B' to 'A made contact with B', and perhaps from 'A painted B' to 'A is an animate agent' (see Pinker 2007: 101–2), as analytic. Whether the theory can explain paradigm analytic inferences, like the move from 'x is a bachelor' to 'x is unmarried', will depend on exactly what semantic primitives are admitted (i.e. whether 'bachelor' is thought to decompose into a semantic feature like + UNMARRIED, or some other, more basic feature shared between 'bachelor' and 'unmarried man'), but once again, if we are supposing that word meanings decompose entirely then the promise that all intuitively analytic inferences will be captured certainly seems to be there.[5]

Finally, we might note that, at least prima facie, lexical semantics seems to offer us an attractive explanation of why certain words fail to appear in any natural language despite having apparently cogent

---

[5] See the Introduction to Jackendoff 1990 for discussion of which semantic features might count as genuinely primitive. Johnson 2004 suggests that not all analytic inferences will be captured via lexical semantics; he thus tentatively suggests recognizing distinct varieties of analyticity, one based on semantic features and one based on a philosophical notion like conceptual containment.

meanings. For the advocate of lexical semantics can claim that words like 'cowed' and 'blik', introduced in §1, are impossible since they would be the result of lexicalizing prohibited structures. So, for instance, it seems reasonable to expect that the items which can be successfully lexicalized must themselves be genuine constituents. That is to say, while phrases can be lexicalized a part of a phrase cannot. Yet this sort of quite general prohibition would seem to explain why there are no verbs like 'to cow' where 'It cowed a calf' could mean that a cow had a calf, since this would require the lexicalization of a phrasal fragment, namely 'cow had' (see Fodor and Lepore 1999: 126). Furthermore, this general idea that impossible words are impossible since they would require the lexicalization of structures which are in some way illegal would seem to provide a fertile ground for explaining a wide range of impossible words (see Hale and Keyser 1993).

So, treating word meanings as composed of semantic features would be one way to handle the intra-linguistic data here. If word meanings decompose into sets of more primitive semantic features we can apparently explain patterns of syntactic distribution, semantic relations and impossible words. However, taking word meanings to be bundles of semantic features is just one way to go here. Alternatively, as is common in philosophy, we could take word meanings to be constituted by a term's inferential relations.

(3.2) Inferential role semantics

Inferential role semantics is an approach which can be applied either directly to words or to concepts (or to both) and it is, of course, a kind of use-based approach to meaning—it tells us that words (and/or concepts) get their content from the way in which they are used by people, specifically, in this case, via the way in which they are used in inferential manoeuvres.[6] However, within the broad church of inferential role semantics there are many distinct positions available. For instance, different stances can be taken on the way in which inferential moves constitute content. On the one hand, the constitution claim might be held in a strong form, whereby word meaning

[6] As such then, inferential role semantics gives us an answer to the origination question of where linguistic meaning comes from—what is it that turns a lifeless physical item (marks on a page, soundwaves, etc.) into a representational sign? This is particularly clear in the work of Robert Brandom.

is taken to be nothing over and above a collation of inferential relations. Alternatively, a weaker claim might be made, say that inferential relations form part of the meaning of a term (with other properties, like how a word interacts with other systems, e.g. the visual system, also having a role to play (see Harman 1999, McCulloch 1995). Another variety of weaker claim has it that inferential properties fix the meaning we associate with a term (i.e. determining that 'dog' means *dog*) though meanings themselves are then allowed to be atomic, non-inferential elements; this position is taken by Horwich 1998 (see also Pagin 2006: 218–9). A further crucial question (and one to which we will return below) is that of *which* inferential relations are relevant: is it the *totality* of inferences which can be made on the basis of a term which determines its meaning or is it rather some sub-set of *core* relations? And is it the inferential moves that a subject is *licensed* in making or those she *actually* draws which count? Answering these, and other, questions, will clearly deliver distinct versions of the approach, but for the moment I want to leave these issues open and consider simply how inferential role semantics, in its most general form, is capable of shouldering the intra-linguistic burden.

Turning first to the need to accommodate semantic relations, the advocate of inferential role semantics is clearly very well placed to explain these. For instance, since it is held that the meaning of 'bachelor' is in part constituted by a subject's willingness to infer from 'x is a bachelor' to 'x is unmarried' the analyticity of this inference is guaranteed (as is the move from 'x is a dog' to 'x is a mammal', etc.) for it is the meanings of the terms involved alone which serve to support the inferences in question. Furthermore, since the meaning of 'bachelor' is presumably exhausted by the inferential relation '∀x (x is a bachelor)↔ (x is an unmarried man)' the intuitive synonymy of the terms also seems to be explained. Finally, although advocates of inferential role semantics have been less concerned with the notion of polysemy, it is, I think, clear that there is a way for the approach to ground this notion as well. For an advocate of inferential role semantics could hold that the different senses for, say, 'lamb' result from the fact that there are distinct sets of inferential relations pertaining to each sense. So, for instance, depending on the sense intended for a token of 'lamb' it might license inferences from 'the lamb looked lovely' to either 'an animal looked lovely' or to 'a foodstuff looked lovely'. However, the relatedness of the two senses of the term would be reflected in the large common ground of inferences both senses support, e.g. the fact that, whichever sense is intended, it would be correct to infer from our target sentence to 'the progenitor of that was a sheep'. So, inferential role semantics looks very well placed to accommodate intuitively semantic relations of the kind looked at in §1.

With respect to the issue of syntactic behaviour, this again is not something which has served as a primary motivation for inferential role semantics and thus it is not entirely clear what an advocate of the position would want to claim. However, it does seem that the account can provide an explanation of the behaviour in question. For instance, one possible route would be to point to the fact that speakers are not willing to infer from, say, 'Mary cut the rope with her knife' to 'Mary cut her knife against the rope'. Thus the inferential profile of a term like 'cut' (and thus the meaning of the term, according to inferential role semantics) might be thought already to contain the information about which syntactic environments are licensed for that expression and which are not. Alternatively, it could be argued that something in the inferential role of the expression would match the kind of semantic features appealed to by lexical semantics. So, for instance, the fact that someone could infer from 'Mary cut the rope with the knife' that 'Mary moved the knife in a particular way with respect to the rope, resulting in a particular effect on the rope' might be thought to mirror the claim in lexical semantics that 'cut' is a verb which specifies a manner of motion. If this is right, then the explanatory resources of inferential role semantics with respect to patterns of syntactic behaviour would mirror exactly the explanatory resources of lexical semantics.

For both inferential role semantics and lexical semantics, then, the general claim is that the buck doesn't stop with words, instead, we can delve deeper: we can look into the content of a word and there find significant structure and content. It is at this level of content—within a term's lexical entry—that we find the wherewithal to accommodate what I have been calling the intra-linguistic or internal burden for a semantic theory. That is to say, where we find the content needed to explain semantic relations like synonymy and polysemy, together with the complex network of syntactic transactions into which terms enter and the restrictions on admissible interpretations which expressions carry with them into sentential constructions. However, as we will see, the idea that we can treat the meanings of even apparently simple words in our language as complex has been vociferously opposed by Jerry Fodor and Ernie Lepore.

(4) Fodor and Lepore's objections to lexical complexity

Structured meanings apparently provide us with an elegant way to meet the internalist burden on a semantic theory, so why shouldn't an externalist (or anyone else for that matter) adopt them? Well, the concern raised by Fodor and Lepore in a number of works is simply that no account of lexical complexity is feasible in practice. A first problem to note concerns the question of whether word meaning can really be captured via an appeal to some structure of more basic elements. For there is what we might term 'the problem of residual meaning': for instance, what could we add (except for *red* itself) to + COLOUR TERM to get to the meaning of 'red'? Or again what kind of basic semantic feature could capture the difference between terms like 'incredulous' and 'amazed'?[7] Words seem to possess core elements to their meanings which are not obviously to be captured in other terms. Furthermore, this initial worry with the idea of lexical complexity is reinforced by Fodor and Lepore's central objection, which is that all approaches positing lexical complexity turn out (contrary to the suggestion of §3) to be inadequate to the explanatory task for semantics.

The central charge is that all such accounts (perhaps barring a straightforward appeal to defining descriptions, see Fodor 1998: 44)

---

[7] Fodor, Fodor and Garrett 1975: 527. Pinker 2007: 100–1 argues that the problem of residual meaning does not hold: 'The problem with this argument is that a definition (which admittedly is always incomplete) is not the same thing as a semantic representation. A definition is a dictionary's explanation of the meaning of an English word in conceptual structure (the language of thought), processed by a system of the brain that manipulates chunks of conceptual structure and relates them to the senses. Definitions can afford to be incomplete because they leave a lot to the imagination of a speaker of the language. Semantic representations have to be more explicit because they *are* the imagination of the speaker of the language. Fodor's attack on complex semantic representations depends on confusing them with dictionary definitions'. However, it is not obvious how claiming that semantic representations cannot afford to be incomplete answers the worry that they will be, unless they at some point reuse the very concept they are aiming to explicate. Jackendoff 1990: 37–8 and 2002: 334–5 also objects to the residual meaning problem on the grounds that it confuses lexical decomposition with dictionary definitions.

fail the compositionality constraint on natural languages. The problem, to which compositionality is supposed to be the answer, is the well-rehearsed fact (noted in Chapter 1, §1) that we need to account for the creativity of natural languages, i.e. the fact that we seem able to produce and understand an indefinite range of novel sentences. One can comprehend the meaning of a sentence one has never encountered before just so long as one knows the meanings of the parts and their mode of composition. In connection with this, natural languages also seem to be productive, in that we can, in principle at least, produce and understand an indefinite number of novel sentences: for instance, as pointed out in Chapter 1, if someone understands 'the father of Aristotle was Greek', we can predict that they will also understand 'the father of the father of Aristotle was Greek', and it seems only to be limitations arising from features of our performance (rather than limitations emerging from our linguistic competence per se) which might stop of us from grasping the meaning of a similar sentence constructed using some larger number of iterations of 'the father of'. Finally, our understanding of natural language is systematic: if someone understands 'Jack loves Jill' then they will also understand 'Jill loves Jack'. The only explanation of these properties, at least according to Fodor and Lepore, is in terms of compositionality. We can account for the creativity, productivity and systematicity of a language if we hold that the meaning of a complex expression is determined by the meanings of its parts and their mode of composition.

The main charge against accounts which endorse lexical complexity then is that they fail to be compositional. As Fodor and Lepore 2002b: 3–4 write:

The line of our argument is that since mental representation and linguistic meaning are *de facto* compositional, we can reject out of hand any theory that says that concepts (/word meanings) are Xs unless Xs are the sorts of things for which compositionality holds. That is, there must be a distinction between primitive and complex Xs and the syntactic/semantic properties of the latter must be inherited from the syntactic/semantic properties of the former. Otherwise, *the proposed identification of concepts (/word meanings) with Xs is* ipso facto *refuted,* however attractive it may otherwise appear. It's our belief that, of the various familiar candidates for concepthood, only very few—perhaps only one—can meet this compositionality constraint... If that's right, then, compositionality tells us what concepts and word meanings are.

The concern then is that if the meaning of, say, 'dog' is given in part by a semantic feature like + TYPICAL PET then this doesn't seem to be a feature which gets contributed to the meaning of a complex expression like 'wild dog'. So, Fodor and Lepore argue, if the totality of an expression's inferential roles or semantic features are taken to constitute its meaning—if the account is what we might term a 'global' one—then the approach is non-compositional.[8] On the other hand, if one tries to isolate just *some* of the inferential relations which an expression takes part in, or some of the semantic features it possesses, and hold just these core elements to constitute meaning (in the sense of contributing to the content of complex expressions which contain the term) then this will be analogous to drawing an analytic/synthetic distinction: the inference from 'x is a dog' to 'x is an animal' is taken to be a core, meaning constituting inference because it is analytic, while the inference from it to 'x is my favourite kind of animal' is taken to be an arbitrary, non-meaning constituting inference because it is synthetic. However if this is the route the advocate of inferential role semantics wants to take then, Fodor and Lepore argue, they are in trouble because, as they hold Quine to have shown, there is no analytic/synthetic distinction available to play this role (see also Williamson 2008 for a compelling critique of the kind of conceptual necessity required for a workable analytic/synthetic distinction).[9] That is to say, there simply doesn't seem to be any principled way to hold apart meaning-constituting inferences from non-meaning-constituting ones.

---

[8] They also note other apparently unpalatable consequences of the claim that *all* the inferences in which a term participates are meaning constituting. For instance, this seems to entail that any difference in the belief set between two agents (or one agent over time) will result in a difference of word meaning. So if you and I disagree over whether cats make good pets, it turns out that we don't really disagree at all since we simply mean different things by the term 'cat' (i.e. we are willing to make different inferential moves on the basis of 'x is a cat'). Recently some theorists (e.g. Pagin 2006) have objected to Fodor and Lepore's argument, claiming that an advocate of global inferential role semantics can allow that inferential sets map many:one to meanings. In this way slight differences in belief sets will *not* impact on meanings: you can believe that cats make good pets and I can disbelieve this without this entailing that we mean different things by 'cat'. This move, however, seems to depend on there being a principle which tells us when a difference in a belief set will result in a difference of meaning and when it won't, and this may be thought to require exactly the same kind of appeal to meaning constituting versus non-meaning constituting inferences that non-global inferential role semantics makes use of. The concern then is that the response of Pagin and others here runs the risk of collapsing global inferential role semantics into a local form of the kind considered in the text above.

[9] Not all advocates of inferential semantics do want to take this route, e.g. Block 1998 defends the possibility of a global approach where all inferences are meaning-constituting.

Now in recent work there has been a great deal of debate about what exactly the compositionality constraint commits us to and whether or not lexical complexity falls foul of a properly stated version of compositionality, and I think this is not an issue we can hope to reach a final pronouncement on here (for relevant work, see, e.g. Horwich 2002, Pagin 2006, Jönsson 2008, for an overview see Hinzen et al. 2012). However, the point I want to highlight here is that it seems we might simply circumvent this entire discussion.[10] For an important point to note is that all the objections raised thus far are objections to the idea that lexical meanings decompose into simpler constituents and there is no reason to think that all lexical complexity must be of this form. I'll return to this point below (at the end of the current section) but before discussing this we should note that Fodor and Lepore also raise a number of worries specifically for lexical semantics and it will be important to have all their objections to lexical complexity before us when we come to evaluate any alternative approach. So let's close this section by looking at their specific objections to lexical semantics.

Fodor and Lepore's main concern with lexical semantics is simply that there is no motivation for the approach. First, they contend that the syntactic patterns highlighted in so much work on lexical semantics do not demand the kind of semantic-level explanation the theory posits and, furthermore, that the explanatory mechanisms deployed in lexical semantics are not in fact capable of explaining anything. Second, they suggest that the arguments surrounding lexical generativity, deployed by Pustejovsky and others, fail to show lexical (as opposed to phrasal) generativity. Third, they claim that the arguments about impossible words also fail to motivate lexical semantics in any way. Turning first to the proposed explanation of patterns of syntactic behaviour, Fodor and Lepore contend that it is simply not obvious that there really are two issues—the syntactic *and* the semantic—to be settled here. That is to say, there is no reason to think that there is a semantic dimension to the problem over and above the recognition of syntactic behaviour. Thus considering lexical semantics' explanation for the difference in syntactic behaviour between 'devour' and 'eat' they suggest, 1998: 101: '[p]erhaps

---

[10] As Fodor 1998: 46 puts it: 'We have, as things now stand, no account of what makes an inference a defining one, and no idea how such an account might be devised. That's a serious reason to suppose that the theory of content should dispense with definitions if it can'.

the intuition that "devour", but not "eat", is *semantically* completive is just a hypostatic misconstrual of one's *syntactic* knowledge that the first but not the second verb takes a mandatory direct object' (see also Fodor 1998: 58). Their suggestion then is that there need be *no* semantic property which underpins a given grouping of expressions in terms of their syntactic behaviour. The terms in such classes may behave in the ways they do simply because it is in their syntactic character to do so and not because there is any commonality of meaning between them. So, they argue, pointing to such syntactic facts can do little or nothing to motivate the existence of lexical complexity.

Furthermore, they suggest, *even if* it were the case that such facts required semantic level explanation lexical semantics is unable to explain them. For the technical terms the theory employs are themselves unexplained, thus analyses offered in terms of them are essentially empty. So, for instance, in discussing the examples from Levin and Pinker above it was suggested that lexical entries might contain features like + /- MANNER OF MOTION or + /- CAUSE, yet the concepts in play here are not supposed to be those associated with their ordinary language counterparts. Instead these semantic features are technical constructs whose existence is supported by the explanatory work they can do. This has led Fodor and Lepore to object that lexical semantics lacks any real explanatory force, since the central notions it deploys are entirely opaque. As they write, 2005: 353, n.1: '[The claim] is that because they are theoretical terms, the justification for postulating CAUSE and the like is theory-internal, i.e. it depends on arguments-to-the-best-explanation. That, however, is beside the point. The question isn't whether postulating the concept CAUSE is *justified*; the question is *what the concept CAUSE is*' (see also Fodor 1998: 59). The worry is that, deprived of any explanation of the content of the notions used in the theory (like CAUSE), it is simply impossible to assess whether we have a genuine explanation (rather than simply a relabeling) of the syntactic patterns in question. So, the first objection to lexical semantics is that facts about syntactic distribution may not require semantic level explanation after all and that if they do lexical semantics is anyway unable to offer a genuine explanation of them.

A second concern with the motivation for lexical semantics concerns the kinds of arguments involving polysemy and supposed lexical generativity deployed by Pustejovsky and others. So, considering Pustejovsky,

Fodor and Lepore note that the proposed approach to polysemy seems simply to 'kick the problem upstairs from the semantics to the ontology' (1998: 105). That is to say, the approach replaces the question 'is a given term polysemous or homonymous?' with the question 'are two elements in the world the same or different?' So, for instance, we are supposed to treat 'bank' as homonymous but 'bake' as univocal since, intuitively, there is a single kind of activity in 'bake a cake' and 'bake a potato' but two activities in 'bank a cheque' and 'bank a plane'. Yet as Fodor and Lepore 1998: 105 object this doesn't seem to get us very far:

> Patently this question why the two kinds of baking count as one process but the two kinds of banking don't is just the polysemy problem all over again … Whereas we used to worry about how to count senses, we are now invited to worry about how to count processes.[11]

Furthermore, there is a concern over what exactly is supposed to be generative on a lexical semantics approach. The official line is that the lexicon itself is generative, so that, say, 'bake' has a meaning which is affected by the terms with which it is concatenated. In this case, in a context where 'bake' appears concatenated with 'cake' the lexical content contributed by 'bake' is the creative sense *made by baking*; whereas, when concatenated with 'potato' the lexical contribution made by 'bake' is *heat up*. Notice, however, that this is not the only way to read Pustejovsky's position, for it could be that 'bake' has a univocal meaning and that that very meaning is what it contributes to VPs in which it appears, with this single meaning being expanded or affected by the NP with which it appears. In this case, though 'bake' means *bake*, 'bake a potato' and 'bake a cake' can mean different things. Yet on this second model what we have is not a generative lexicon but the generativity of complex VPs, but, as they write (1998: 111–2):

> It's news if the *lexicons* of natural language are generative; lots of people (ourselves included) think they are more or less lists. But it's no news that VPs are

---

[11] Furthermore, Pustejovsky's intuition that there is a single, univocal sense for 'bake' looks doubtful anyway since the phrase 'bake a cake' is itself ambiguous. Although the standard reading of 'bake a cake' involves the creative sense it is also clear, as Fodor and Lepore note, that one can bake a cake in the sense familiar from potatoes—that is to say, one can put a pre-existing cake in the oven and bake it (though the results are unlikely to be very rewarding from a culinary perspective). Yet, if 'bake a cake' retains two possible readings, despite 'bake' being concatenated with an artefact term, then this undermines Pustejovsky's claim that 'bake' is not itself ambiguous.

generative, or that their semantics must somehow integrate the meaning of a verb with the meaning of its arguments.

The worry is then that advocates of lexical semantics need to show that the former version of the position is the one required, so that the lexicon itself is genuinely generative, but it seems that all the evidence is capable of showing is that the latter position holds, i.e. that complex expressions have complex meanings. So the phenomenon of polysemy does not, contrary to earlier suggestions, provide strong motivation for the kind of lexical complexity posited in standard lexical semantics.

Finally, turning to impossible word arguments, Fodor and Lepore object that the central idea of lexical semantics—that words have complex structures—in fact provides no explanation of the inexistence of the words in question. So, for instance, to return to the example of 'to cow' looked at above: here the suggestion on behalf of lexical semantics was that such a verb is impossible since it seeks to lexicalize something which is not a genuine constituent, namely the partial phrase 'cow had'. However, Fodor and Lepore object that even if it is right that 'to cow' cannot be the result of a process of lexicalization, this alone doesn't explain its absence from our language, for it leaves open the possibility that such a term could be introduced as a primitive. That is to say, nothing in the account so far rules out the possibility that 'to cow' is an undefined lexical term. As Fodor and Lepore 1999: 126 write:

By definition, impossible word arguments purport to explain intuitions of the form 'there couldn't be a word *w* that means "e"' by showing that [e] couldn't be a derivational source for *w*. But, on the face of it, that doesn't show that there couldn't be a word that means *e*; the most it could show is that if there is a word that means *e*, then it must be primitive. We assume . . . that the intuition about ['to cow'] is that it is *impossible*—and not just that *if* it is possible then it is underived.

Note that Fodor and Lepore are not here arguing that any lexicon does or could contain a verb like 'to cow', rather their point is that appealing to the supposed complexity of lexical items doesn't seem to explain the fact that lexicons *can't* contain verbs like 'to cow', for as long as it is *possible* for at least some words to be introduced into the lexicon without this being the result of lexicalizing pre-existing structures, 'to cow' could be one of these. Thus, again, the existence of impossible words provides no motivation for lexical semantics.

So, Fodor and Lepore's case against lexical semantics is that it is fundamentally unmotivated: first, the appeal to patterns of syntactic distribution assumes the need for a semantic level explanation of these syntactic facts but this would seem to beg the question in favour of semantic (i.e. lexical) complexity. Instead, the patterns of syntactic distribution might be just that—syntactic patterns in need of no semantic explanation. Furthermore, the putative explanation of these patterns from lexical semantics turns out, on closer inspection, to be empty for it rests on technical terms which remain undefined. Second, the approach to polysemy doesn't seem to take us very far in cataloguing the polysemous versus the homophonic expressions and claims for lexical generativity actually seem to reveal the generativity of phrases not words. Third, contrary to the claims of its advocates, the theory appears incapable of explaining the non-existence of impossible words. Taken together with Fodor and Lepore's earlier objections to lexical complexity per se (i.e. that definitions don't, in general, work as replacements for words and that accounts which posit lexical complexity fail to be compositional), these points seem to show that lexical semantics, and indeed any approach which proposes meeting the internalist burden on semantics by treating word meanings as complex, is in trouble.

However, we need to be clear about the *kind* of lexical complexity against which Fodor and Lepore's arguments are levelled. For their arguments all attack the idea that *word meanings decompose*—that underlying the apparently unitary form of a noun like 'dog' or a verb like 'hit' is a complex structure which gives or fixes that term's meaning. But of course we might envisage other kinds of complexity in the lexicon, specifically we might allow additional complexity that is not located *within* the meaning of a word. In this case, although the lexicon would be held to contain information above and beyond a mere list of word-object pairs, this information would not play a role in constituting the meaning of an expression, and thus word meanings per se could remain as atomic, basic elements. In the next section I want, then, to turn to consider two such versions of lexical complexity: the adoption of so-called 'meaning postulates' and a move to what I'll term 'organizational lexical semantics'. The former approach retains the idea that word meanings are non-complex but allows additional content to be meaning constituting in the sense that, if additional information about a word meaning *e* makes reference to some other word meaning *e**, then it will not be possible for a subject to possess *e* without also possessing *e**. The latter approach rejects both the idea that word meanings are complex and that additional lexical information is meaning constituting. I will argue that it is this last, weak notion of lexical complexity which gives the advocate of a referential lexical semantics the most attractive way to capture the internal burden. Our question then will be whether it is an avenue open to the advocate of minimal semantics.

(5) Organization of the lexicon

As noted in the previous section, Fodor and Lepore's objections hold only against a specific kind of lexical complexity—namely the proposal that word meanings are themselves complex—and it seems we might reject this idea whilst still admitting some form of complexity into the lexicon. So the question now is 'how can we admit of lexical complexity while still hanging on to the idea that the meaning of a word is atomic?' One established way in which we could do this would be to follow Carnap 1952 in allowing for meaning postulates. A meaning postulate is a conventional rule which attaches to an expression and which captures certain logical relations which that term enjoys. So, for instance, we might treat the term 'red' as having a primitive, undefined meaning but then postulate the following rule:

$$\forall x \ (x \text{ is red} \rightarrow x \text{ is coloured})$$

Given the existence of this meaning postulate, the analyticity of 'x is red therefore x is coloured' is assured, for the validity of the argument is grounded in the meaning convention we have adopted. Notice that this move is entirely compatible with the idea that the meanings of the words involved are atomic elements, for though the inferences embedded in the meaning postulates place constraints on concept possession (i.e. on what one needs to know to know the meaning of, say, 'red' or 'bachelor'), they don't place constraints on concept constitution (the explanation of analyticity is thus in terms of logical relations and not something like concept containment). This is a point Fodor 1998: 63 has been keen to emphasize:

> Linguistic features can perfectly well attach to a lexical item that is none the less primitive at *every* level of linguistic description. And it is only the weaker assumption that the facts about dative movement support, since the most these data show is that the syntactic behaviour of lexical items is determined by their semantics *inter alia*; e.g. by their semantic features together with their morphology. So Pinker's argument for definitions doesn't work *even on the assumption that 'denotes a prospective possession' and the like are bona fide semantic representations.* THE MORAL: AN ARGUMENT FOR LEXICAL SEMANTIC FEATURES IS NOT IPSO FACTO AN ARGUMENT THAT THERE IS LEXICAL SEMANTIC DECOMPOSITION.[12]

In a footnote he adds:

> Compare: no doubt, the lexical entry for 'boy' includes the syntactic feature + Noun. This is *entirely* compatible with 'boy' being a lexical primitive at *every level* of linguistic analysis. Saying that lexical items *have features* is one thing; saying that lexical items *are feature bundles* is quite another.

So, it seems we could adopt meaning postulates and thus admit certain kinds of complexity within the lexicon while still rejecting the idea that word meanings decompose (see Montague 1970). Thus we find modern-day advocates of meaning postulates like Barbara Partee 1995: 328 writing:

> The central issue... [is] whether all lexical meanings can be fully analyzed via 'lexical decomposition' into some sort of presumably universal semantic 'atoms', representing basic or primitive concepts. That view, while appealing and recurrent, may well be too strong; and the notion of meaning postulates is offered as a technique for capturing significant generalizations about extractable regularities within lexical meanings without presupposing total decomposability... [O]n the antidecompositional view, some lexical items have idiosyncratic 'residue' parts of their meanings that cannot reasonably be analyzed further into compositions of simpler parts. Meaning postulates can then express whatever regularities there are to be found without entailing

---

[12] Pinker 2007: 107 writes: 'concepts like "motion," "contact," and "cause-and-effect" sort verbs into crisscrossing classes, and thereby must be components of the verbs' meanings. This implies that these words *have* meanings, which implies that they need not be innate'. But it is not clear that, in order to sort verbs, these elements must be *part* of a word's meaning. For instance, we can sort objects into those which lie within five miles of the Eiffel Tower and those which don't, but such sorting doesn't seem to require that the properties by which we sort form a constitutive part of the objects thereby sorted.

that what can be said about the meaning of a given item with meaning postulates should be supposed to exhaust its meaning.

However, although meaning postulates offer one possible route for lexical complexity without meaning decomposition, it is not obvious that it is the route we should pursue. For instance, Quine 1953 famously objected that it is not possible to ground a notion of analyticity in adopted logical conventions in the way the meaning postulates approach supposes. While Fodor (though originally an advocate of meaning postulates, see for instance Fodor, Fodor and Garrett 1975: 519) has also argued that adopting meaning postulates is unattractive. The problem which exercises him is that the approach breaks the connection between the structure of a concept on one hand and its possession conditions on the other (see Fodor 1998: 63). This seems problematic, for while it is clear why possession of the concept *unmarried* should be a precondition for possession of the concept *bachelor* if the former concept is a proper part of the latter concept, it is much less clear why possession of the former should be a precondition for possession of the latter when the latter is held to be an atomic concept. Why, we might wonder, if the meaning of 'dog' is given by an atomic, undecomposible concept (and where the content of this concept is fixed by appeal to things in the world), should it only be possible to possess this concept if one also possesses certain other concepts (like *animal*)?

There are then prima facie problems with the move to adopt meaning postulates, but perhaps these could be overcome by weakening the appeal to lexical complexity still further, taking the additional information required to carry the internal burden on semantics to be constitutive of neither concept content nor concept possession. Perhaps (following Fodor's 1998: 65 suggestion above) we could simply allow that the lexicon contains additional information above and beyond a mere list of word-denotation pairs but maintain that this additional information doesn't constitute the meaning of a word nor does it impose any conditions on the possession of that word's meaning, instead it imposes constraints on our competence with the word. The thought is that the additional information emerges as part of the organizational structure of the lexicon, telling us *something about* the meaning of words but where this information is in addition to, and extraneous to, word meaning per se. In this way we could adopt a broadly referential account of word meaning (in at least some cases) but posit an additional level of lexical organization which is capable of grouping word-meaning pairs into different categories.[13] So, for instance, a noun like 'dog' could be marked as, say, + AGENT, + ANIMATE, but these properties of the expression do not constitute part of the word's meaning, instead indicating the *kind* of expression the word is by revealing the categories into which it falls. The additional content emerges then not within the meanings of words themselves but within the organization of the lexicon.[14]

To borrow Fodor's terminology, the proposal is that lexical items *have* complex semantic features but not that lexical items *are* bundles of these features. So, for instance, it might be right to treat 'hit' as a + MANNER OF MOTION, + CONTACT expression and having these properties would see 'hit' as being assigned to the same lexical category as words like 'kick' and 'chop'. However, on the current account, it would nevertheless be possible to know the meaning of

---

[13] Collins 2011b briefly considers, and rejects, an apparently somewhat similar approach which he refers to as 'split lexical items'. His concern with the approach he considers is that it treats one element as giving the meaning of an expression and the other as purely non-semantic, structural information. His objection then is that structural information also contributes to our understanding of meaning for expressions. This objection would not, I think, hold against the current proposal, which sees both 'structural' and atomic elements as part of the lexicon, i.e. as part of our grasp of the meanings of expressions broadly construed. The approach is also similar, I think, to the kind of 'dual content' approach to concepts of Prinz 2002 and Weiskopf 2009, whereby concept content is held to have a dual aspect made up of, on the one hand, referential content and, on the other, descriptive (or, as Weiskopf calls it, cognitive) content. (Though note that these authors are not concerned specifically with lexical concepts and there are significant issues, beyond the scope of the current work, to be addressed in widening discussion from lexical concepts to concepts in general.) It is interesting to note, however, that Weiskopf presents his theory as lying in opposition to atomism, while I present organizational lexical semantics (OLS) as in general agreement with conceptual atomism. The difference comes about because Weiskopf treats the descriptive content as part of the content of a concept, while OLS places it outside concept content as part of the broader framework into which concepts are embedded. However, Weiskopf 2009: 142 stresses that, on his model, descriptive content does not determine reference (e.g. one might have the concept *cat*, which picked out cats, even though the properties one associates with cats, i.e. the descriptive content of the concept, fails to be satisfied by cats). Furthermore, Weiskopf wants to allow that there is (often) no privileged piece of information which a subject must possess in order to have a given concept (although one must think of cats as having some property to have the concept *cat*, there may be no particular property it is necessary to think of them as having). So, on this model the descriptive element does not determine reference nor concept possession. Given these features, it seems to me that the difference between an account like OLS which advocates conceptual atomism but which allows an additional descriptive element which is external to concept content per se and an account like Weiskopf's which posits dual aspect content for concepts is probably, to some degree at least, terminological.

[14] There are clear parallels here to the approach of 'semantic nets' in AI, see, e.g. Simmons 1973, and to certain varieties of lexical semantics (namely those which preserve a clear role for the 'root' element of an expression, see Levin and Rappaport-Hovav 2005). I introduce the label 'organizational lexical semantics' not, then, because I think of the position as startlingly new, but rather because I want to make explicit the commitments of this kind of approach to lexical semantics (i.e. to stress it's anti-decompositional and structural nature).

'hit' (e.g. know that 'hit' refers to *hitting*) without knowing these additional facts (i.e. without knowing that 'hit' is a + MANNER OF MOTION verb). Someone who didn't know these additional facts would thus be likely to make mistakes about the kinds of syntactic environments in which the term could appear, e.g. mistakenly holding that 'Jack hit at Jill' is improper. But these would be errors in a subject's competence with an expression, they would not be revelatory of an error concerning their grasp of the meaning of the term. In this way, the patterns of syntactic distribution noted in §1 could be explained and predicted on the basis of an expression's lexical category and profile, without us treating word meanings as complex. We might also note that the concern that definitions always miss some aspect of meaning drops out of the picture here, for to repeat, there is nothing definitional about the current approach. Word meanings are non-decomposed primitives not definitions (dictionary or otherwise), so there is no question of something being missed in the meaning. Now, the flip side of this is obviously that we can't explain the way in which the meanings of new terms are acquired in terms of learning definitions. Thus the current picture must, it seems, follow Fodor in claiming that word meanings are not learnt. However, as Fodor has stressed, not being learnt is not the same thing as being there at birth—it may be that word meanings are acquired through our transactions with the world, which trigger the acquisition of concepts we can label, in which case word meanings are not learnt but neither are they innate (in the sense of 'being there from birth').

This kind of 'organizational lexical semantics' (OLS) makes space for information in the lexicon beyond mere word-denotation pairs, but without treating word meanings as complex, it thus avoids Fodor and Lepore's main objection—based on compositionality concerns—to inferential role semantics and standard lexical semantics. Indeed, it seems that, despite their concerns about extant varieties of lexical complexity, Fodor and Lepore are in fact pretty sanguine about the need for the kind of lexical complexity organizational lexical semantics posits. They write (1998: 112):

[T]hough we take the question to be largely moot, we are inclined to think that the exigencies of the compositionality problem really do require that lexical entries cannot specify only denotations; not even assuming that denotation is all there is to content.

Thus, Fodor and Lepore suggest a composition rule for 'want' of the form: if the constituents of VPi are ('want X NP'), then the interpretation of VPi is *wants to have F(X)*. They then note (1998: 115):

[A]ccording to this proposal, 'want' never means (denotes) anything except a relation between a creature and a state of affairs; not even in 'wants a beer' (i.e. not in expressions where the surface complement fails to denote a state of affairs). Therefore, 'want' is not polysemous; its *content* (unlike the logical form of its hosts) is absolutely context-invariant… The cost of this univocality is complex lexical entries, which determine not only the content of an item but the host's logical form.

'Want' means *want*, then, but the lexicon contains more information than this, containing in addition rules which tell us the kinds of arguments the term can take and the rules of composition relevant to those different arguments. As on the current proposal, this additional information is not meaning constituting: one could know the meaning of 'want' without knowing the kind of arguments the expression requires. This ignorance would no doubt be reflected in all kinds of errors but it seems they would be errors about how 'want' works not about what 'want' means.

Similarly, then, an advocate of OLS might seek to explain the very different meanings for 'John is eager to please' versus 'John is easy to please' by positing associated information attaching to the key terms which dictates how to construct logical forms for these sentences. These rules of construction would simply require that John plays a subject role in the former sentence and an object role in the latter. In this way, though 'easy' simply means *easy,* and all that is required to understand the term per se is to grasp the concept, still full competence with the term entails an understanding of how it contributes to sentences in which it occurs (and this requires grasp of associated lexical information).[15] In this way, the advocate of OLS might hope to explain possible and impossible interpretations of sentences while retaining the idea that the meanings of apparently simple words are simple atomic concepts.

---

[15] Kent Bach (pc) notes an alternative explanation in terms of the fact that while 'easy' is a property of actions, 'eager' is a property of agents, and this difference alone might be responsible for explaining the different logical form constructions. However this kind of explanation would still, it seems, require this fact about the properties to be represented somewhere within the lexicon.

However, despite the fact that Fodor and Lepore are, at heart, open to the possibility of some kind of lexical complexity, it seems unlikely that they would want to embrace the kind of picture suggested here, which sees semantic features of the kind appealed to in standard lexical semantics incorporated as part of the principles of categorization within the lexicon. For recall their objection that the technical terms employed in lexical semantics in general are empty and are thus incapable of explaining anything. However, it seems to me that this objection ignores the fact that the assignment of semantic features to expressions depends on the kinds of objects and properties in the world which they specify. Thus, it is because of the kind of activities that hitting, kicking and chopping are that it may be right to treat the verbs that specify them as having the semantic feature + MANNER OF MOTION. So while it is right to recognize that the labels for semantic features are technical terms, whose meaning is not equivalent to their natural language counterparts, nevertheless it seems to me to be a mistake to think that this necessarily robs the concepts of all content. It is what is in common between hitting and kicking, but not between hitting and touching, that gives content to the semantic feature in question. However, responding to Fodor and Lepore's challenge in this way might well be thought to deliver us straight into another of their objections. For now we might wonder, if it is at heart knowledge about relations and objects in the world which is operative here, why think that this knowledge requires *semantic* representation at all?

This objection emerges in two ways: first, why think the syntactic behaviour witnessed requires semantic level explanation at all (as Fodor and Lepore note, perhaps the recognition that 'devour' but not 'eat' requires an object is a purely syntactic realization, with no semantic underpinning at all)? And, second, how do we know which elements of world knowledge deserve representation at the lexical level—why should the fact that kicking involves a manner of motion be lexically represented but not, presumably, the fact that being kicked is often painful?

With respect to the first objection—that the patterns of syntactic distribution might be nothing more than syntactic peculiarities of the terms involved—it seems to me that this objection (though one I feel some sympathy with) is not fully compelling. For though we might be forced ultimately to concede that what look like non-arbitrary patterns

of syntactic behaviour are in fact no more than the syntactic eccentricities displayed by individual expressions, it seems that this conclusion
should be a last resort not an initial move. As theorists, we should try to
explain what look like principled patterns of behaviour if we can; prima
facie, the syntactic behaviour in question deserves explanation and this
would seem to require appeal to some kind of semantic similarity or
difference between the terms involved. Furthermore, OLS is motivated
by a range of apparently intra-linguistic features which stand in need of
explanation and, even if, ultimately, we decide that facts about syntactic
distribution require only syntactic level explanation, this would still
leave other facts (e.g. about possible and impossible readings of sentences) in need of explanation and in these cases it is hard to see that
anything short of a genuinely semantic level explanation will suffice.

However, and this brings us to the second objection above, if we are
explaining syntactic behaviour via appeal to semantic features and we
are allowing that the semantic features posited are contentful at least in
part due to the kinds of things in the world picked out by the terms to
which those semantic features attach, we might well wonder what this
explanation buys us over one which simply appeals directly to our
knowledge of things in the world (i.e. which doesn't try to make the
explanation a *semantic* one). That is to say, if it is because of the kind of
relation which hitting is (i.e. that it requires a specific kind of motion)
that the term 'hit' takes part in conative constructions, why think that
this feature requires lexical representation rather than just being part of
an agent's general world knowledge (i.e. part of their knowledge about
hitting rather than 'hitting')? This is a point Fodor 1998: 112 stresses with
respect to meaning postulates:

Imagine two minds that differ in that 'whale → mammal' is a meaning postulate for one but is 'general knowledge' for the other. Are any further differences between these minds entailed? If so, which ones? Is this wheel
attached to anything?

This is a serious question for anyone who wants to posit lexical
complexity while simultaneously rejecting the idea of lexical decomposition, because without a principled answer to the question of
which information is part of the lexicon, and why, the position looks
vacuous. The risk is that either everything will end up counting as
lexical information, or nothing will.

However, I think there is an answer we can give on behalf of the current proposal, which is that information counts as part of the categorizing lexical content associated with a term just in case it is either a feature which firm, type-level lexical intuitions attach to a term or it is a feature which is capable of affecting that term's syntactic behaviour.[16] This is to embrace Higginbotham's 1989: 470 idea that:

What is crucial to the design of language is not some distinction, however drawn, between properly semantic information, on the one hand, and empirical or collateral information, on the other, but rather the distinction between information that has systematic grammatical effects and information that does not.[17]

The suggestion is then that, for whatever reason, some of the properties of objects and events have been co-opted for lexical representation—they figure as features associated with words not only as part of our general knowledge about the non-linguistic items those words represent. It is the realization of these features within the lexicon which explains how and why they come to have an impact on the syntactic behaviour of expressions. It is because hitting is a relation which involves a certain kind of movement and because this sensitivity is lexically marked (e.g. by the fact that 'hit' is categorized as a + MANNER OF MOTION verb) that 'hit', along with 'kick' and 'chop', take part in conative constructions. On the other hand, it is because the information that dogs typically have four legs forms part of our general knowledge about dogs, and not part of our lexical knowledge about 'dog', that this information does not have any impact on the syntactic behaviour of the linguistic item 'dog'.

It should be clear then that although the current proposal allows more content into the lexicon than a purely denotational account of word meaning, still the additional content which it admits is itself pretty limited. Specifically, there will be no expectation that appeals to lexical information can support our intuitive judgements of analyticity. For although a notion of analyticity constructed just on the kinds of

---

[16] Jackendoff 2002 notes but ultimately rejects this view, arguing that 'we must consider the domain of linguistic semantics to be continuous with human conceptualization as a whole' (282). Instead he suggests capturing facts about the syntactic/semantic interface in terms of interaction rules: 'The subset of semantic features relevant to the grammar is just the subset that is (or can be) mentioned in phrasal interface rules—the part of conceptualization that is "visible" to these rules' (291).

[17] See also Pinker 1989.

semantic features deployed within organizational lexical semantics might capture *some* intuitively analytic inferences (say, the move from 'x hit y' to 'x made (physical) contact with y', or perhaps from 'x chased y' to 'y was followed by x', or 'x painted y' to 'x is an animate agent'), many of the inferences it would support as valid are not intuitively analytic at all (e.g. the inference from 'x hit y's arm' to 'y's arm is a part of y', on the assumption that the relation of 'being a part of' affects syntactic behaviour; see Johnson 2008 for some evidence for this claim). Furthermore, many (perhaps most) intuitively analytic inferences will not be captured at all on the current approach (e.g. the inference from 'x is a bachelor' to 'x is unmarried', the inference from 'x is a dog' to 'x is a mammal', and the inference from 'x is red' to 'x is coloured'). Instead the advocate of organizational lexical semantics must follow Fodor 1998: 74 in locating the support for these inferences in our world knowledge and not in our knowledge of meaning:

> The problem for informational semantics comes not from intuitions that the connection between *being Tuesday* and *coming before Wednesday* is *necessary*, but from intuitions that it's *constitutive* in the sense that one can't have one of the concepts unless one has the other. Compare *water is H20* and *two is prime*. Presumably though both are necessary, neither is constitutive. Accordingly it's possible to have the concept WATER but not the concept HYDROGEN, and its possible to have the concept TWO but not the concept PRIME. All of this is perfectly OK as far as informational semantics is concerned. It's perfectly consistent to claim that concepts are individuated by the properties they denote, and that *the properties* are individuated by their necessary relations to one another, but to deny that knowing about the necessary relations among properties is a condition for having the concept.

So, if Fido is a dog, then, necessarily, Fido is an animal, but this is a fact about the world not about our language.[18]

Organizational lexical semantics does not, then, suffice to capture all of what I've been calling the internal burden on a semantic theory. On the positive side, it might help to explain certain linguistic properties, for instance it might help to reveal the kinds of arguments an expression requires, which syntactic alternations a term will participate in, and the

---

[18] For Fodor's attempt to explain our (mistaken) intuitions of analyticity, see 1998: 82–3. See also Williamson 2008 for arguments against conceptual necessity and analyticity.

kinds of readings sentences will or will not admit of.[19] Furthermore the approach might make some headway in explaining the impossibility of at least some impossible words. For instance, there might be a prohibition on words whose meaning would require categorization in a way not permitted by the language, e.g. it might turn out simply to be a rule of categorization that there can be no non-ergative transitive verbs (i.e. terms—like 'bake', 'boil' and 'burst'—where there is no change in the role of the subject in the move from a transitive to an intransitive form) which are also not marked for agency, so the attempt to introduce such a word would be doomed to failure.

On the negative side, however, as noted the approach can take us only a very little way down the road of explaining intuitively semantic properties like analyticity and synonymy. For while the theory might predict the validity of a move like 'x hit y therefore x made contact with y' it cannot explain the putative semantic validity of the move from 'x is a dog' to 'x is an animal'. OLS looks to the world, not to our language, for support for this latter kind of inference and in doing so it rejects the idea that this kind of relation is properly an internal one after all—what carries this inference through is, organizational lexical semantics claims, facts about dogs not facts about the word 'dog'. Perhaps however, to return to the main theme of this book at last, this is something that will please some. For instance, given the general thesis of semantic minimalism that a semantic theory is only a very small part of what one needs to know to operate successfully within the world, the idea that many of our most fundamental inferences rest not on our knowledge of language but on our knowledge of, and interaction with, our environment should come, it seems, as no surprise.

The outcome of our extended discussion of the content of the lexicon is, then, that a referential lexical semantics could accommodate that portion of the internalist burden which it may be genuinely right to place at the door of semantics. If we allow that word meanings themselves are atomic but also that our lexicon itself is complex, in the

---

[19] Furthermore, we might think that given the kinds of constraints on referential lexical content imposed by theorists like McDowell 1977, whereby it is required that referential content be represented in a form appropriate to a subject, we can go some way towards ameliorating the problems surrounding exchange of co-referring terms. Picking up on the minimal account of singular content outlined earlier (Chapter 4), the claim would be that the meaning of 'Hesperus' and 'Phosphorous' differs since each term relates to distinct concepts (i.e. concepts with different, token-reflexive characters), even though these concepts share a content (i.e. refer to the same external object).

sense of imposing categories on words, then, I suggest, we can accommodate both concerns about features like compositionality, etc. (which push us towards atomic word meanings) and concerns about facts like possible versus impossible readings (which push us towards a degree of lexical complexity). Thus it seems to me that some kind of organizational lexical semantics provides the most attractive model to pursue if we are seeking to accommodate the internal burden on semantics. However there remains a final key question to address: could a semantic minimalist consistently adopt the model provided by organizational lexical semantics?

(6)   Minimal semantics and organizational lexical semantics

To begin with, it looks as if organizational lexical semantics might be a very good thing for minimalism. For as well as the kind of OLS manoeuvres sketched above, it seems that the approach might also create the space required to embed some of the kinds of approaches to incomplete expressions mooted initially in Chapter 3. So, for instance, recall the proposal from Chapter 3, §3.4 that a sentence like 'Flintoff is ready' might be treated as expressing the proposition that *there is something for which Flintoff is ready*. On the current OLS model, this proposal has the following form: 'ready' always means *ready*, the content of this expression is exhausted by the property in the world to which it refers. However, the term 'ready' gets categorized within our lexicon as belonging to a set of two-place adjectives, a set of terms which require both a subject and an object. Thus information associated with the term itself tells us that the logical form of sentences containing 'ready' must always have the form __ *ready* __ (or equivalently $\exists x \, \exists y \, Ready \, \langle x, y \rangle$).[20] In sentences where only the first argument place is filled then the associated information kicks in to mark the missing argument place at the level of the logical form, so 'Flintoff is ready' has the underlying logical form '$\exists x \, Ready \, \langle f, x \rangle$'.

---

[20] Of course it may be objected that these two formulations are far from equivalent, with '__ ready __' merely marking gaps or places to be filled, while '$\exists x \exists y$ ready $\langle x, y \rangle$' wheels in serious additional machinery in the form of existential quantification. I'll return to this concern in the context of discussion of Bach's 'radical minimalism' in the next section.

It is this which explains the apparent sense of incompleteness that subjects experience given the sentence 'Flintoff is ready', produced with no supporting context. On the current model, the sense of incompleteness is explained by the fact that 'ready' is grouped within the lexicon with other two-place expressions, thus hearers tacitly recognize that the vocalized material fails to mark all the argument places associated with the terms in the sentence. It is this recognition of a disparity between vocalized constituents and the arguments to be found at the level of logical form which results in our sense of incompleteness.[21] Finally, notice that, just as with Fodor and Lepore's suggestion above for 'want', 'ready' on this proposal always denotes the same relation—the relation of *readiness*—which holds between a subject and the thing for which they are held to be ready. However the second argument place of this relation can be filled by objects or events, and OLS can allow that the rule for concatenating 'ready' with other expressions will be sensitive to the kind of object supplied. Roughly speaking, if the object is a noun phrase then the resulting sentence will have the form 'x is ready for NP', while if it is a verb phrase the resulting sentence will have the form 'x is ready to VP'. Yet this additional information about how to construct the logical form of sentences in which 'ready' appears is external to the meaning of 'ready' itself.

As we saw in Chapter 3, the same kind of proposal could also be made for gradable adjectives like 'tall'. An OLS approach with respect to these terms might hold, for instance, that 'tall' means *tall* though information associated with the lexical categorization of this term makes it the case that the logical form of a sentence like 'Ted is tall' is $[\exists x \text{ Tall} <t, x>]$. Here the relativization to some comparison class or standard

---

[21] Note, as stressed in Chapter 3, n.13, this holds only for cases of disparity between surface form and logical form where the additional syntactic elements are supplied by lexical content alone, rather than being recoverable from the context via ellipsis. So take the following two scenarios:

(1) Flintoff pulls up mid-run and begins rubbing his leg. Concerned, Pietersen runs over and says 'Can you carry on bowling?', to which Flintoff replies 'Yes, I'm ready.'
(2) Flintoff pulls up mid-run as above. As Pietersen runs over Flintoff says 'I'm ready'.

The claim is that in (1) the sentence Flintoff utters literally expresses the proposition that *Flintoff is ready to carry on bowling*, the value of the second argument required by 'ready' being recoverable directly from surrounding discourse. In (2), however, the sentence Flintoff utters literally expresses only that Flintoff is ready to do something, with the claim that he is ready to carry on bowling, ready to bowl the next ball to Tendulker, ready to go off for tea, etc, being purely pragmatic elaborations of the literal content of the sentence. Furthermore, the suggestion is that it is only in this second case, where the lexical category of 'ready' alone is responsible for the additional syntactic material, that subjects get a sense of incompleteness.

would be marked because 'tall' belongs to a category of two argument expressions. So, once again, a sentence where only the first argument place is filled, and where there is no possibility of a contextual recovery of the second argument via ellipsis, is heard not as ill-formed but as in some way incomplete. What we have on both these OLS proposals, then, is the positing of more material at the level of logical form than is transparent at the level of surface form. Given this, however, a serious question now seems to arise, for we need to ask whether such a move can actually be consistent with the tenets of minimalism?[22] Can one in fact consistently adopt minimal semantics on the one hand (as a theory about what sentence meanings are and how they are generated) together with organizational lexical semantics on the other (as a theory about what word meanings are and the kinds of information that might be associated with them)?

The reason one might be sceptical about the consistency of these views is, I believe, that minimalism as a theory tells one that the literal meaning (propositional content) of a sentence is to be recovered simply from the words a sentence contains and the way they are put together and it seems but a small step from here to the idea that the semantic content of a sentence can be directly read off its surface form. Thus it is easy to think that the existence of any semantically relevant material which is not made absolutely explicit in surface form must be entirely inimical to minimalism. Furthermore, in Chapter 1, minimalism was presented as lying in opposition to views like indexicalism and contextualism which hold that surface form is a poor guide to semantic form, since either there is more syntactic or lexical context sensitivity than we initially envisaged (indexicalism) or there is more content to the proposition a sentence literally expresses than can be traced to the lexico-syntactic form (contextualism). Yet now it seems we find OLS positing exactly the same kind of divergence between surface form and semantic form which we find in indexicalism and in contextualism. So, the thought is, wouldn't adopting OLS (at least in the form of the proposals above) strip minimalism of all that was characteristic of it, submerging it beneath the very positions it was supposed to be opposed to? On reflection, however, I think this worry turns out not to be well founded.

---

[22] I'm grateful to Lenny Clapp and an anonymous reader for stressing this question.

For, as argued in Chapter 3, I think we should see minimalism as growing up in response to approaches which claim that we need to increase context-sensitivity in order to deliver a semantics which tightly tracks our intuitions about speech act content (either increasing syntactically marked context-sensitivity, as in indexicalism, or admitting purely pragmatically required context-sensitivity, as in contextualism, or treating the contribution all words make to larger linguistic units as inherently context-sensitive, as in occasionalism). In opposition to this, the minimalist claims that it is not the job of semantics to capture intuitive judgements about speech act content. Rather a semantic theory should be in the business of capturing rule-based, recursive literal linguistic meaning (the kind of meaning which provides input to, but certainly does not fully determine, judgements about speech act content). Thus a minimalist semantic theory should require lexicon and syntax to fully determine semantics and it should rule out one-off intuitions about speech act content as reasons for making semantic or syntactic claims. Yet it should be clear that what motivates the move, via OLS, to allow hidden syntax is *not* a desire to cleave more closely to judgements of speech act content. Rather it is a desire to capture correctly the syntactic behaviour of expressions, recognizing that simple, referential lexical entries may not be the whole story in accounts of lexical content. Yet once we recognize that, to do what a theory of lexical semantics needs to do (in terms of capturing data about possible and impossible readings, syntactic distribution, etc.) we need an additional level of lexical complexity, then the door is at least open to a minimalist account which takes seriously certain intuitive judgements of language users (namely the incompleteness intuitions looked at in Chapter 3).

Furthermore, note that the intuitions which are relevant here are not the kind of one-off, on-the-fly intuitions about speaker meaning appealed to in context-shifting arguments. Rather they are type-level intuitions about the meanings of terms in our language (e.g. our sense that 'ready' is incomplete without two arguments) and it is clear that even the most austere formal semantic theory will need to let in some kind of appeal to what speakers think about and do with their words in the course of constructing a lexicon for a natural language (see Borg 2005). Finally, note also that the claim that these additional argument places are not obvious at the surface level is only partially correct. Of course they are not explicitly vocalized but, on the OLS account, they are explicitly provided by the terms in the sentence: it is because 'Flint-off is ready' contains the two-place expression 'ready' that it is to be understood as *Flintoff is ready for something*. Thus adopting OLS takes us only a very small step indeed away from the idea that minimalism takes the semantic content of a sentence to be something which can be read straight from its surface form. It certainly moves us no further towards the possibility of free pragmatic enrichment.

Minimalism, as I understand it then, should not be construed as the thesis that the semantic content of a sentence can never outstrip its vocalized constituents (a claim which would be made false, after all, by any genuine instance of ellipsis). Rather what minimalism should be held to claim is that the route to semantics runs along exclusively lexical and syntactic footholds and furthermore that judgements about one-off speech act content are the wrong kind of evidence to call into play to license syntactic or semantic claims. Minimalism doesn't seek to offer a semantic theory which faithfully shadows our intuitive judgements of what someone says when they utter a sentence and it is one of the main claims of the approach that the hunt for a semantic theory which might do this is both hopeless and unnecessary (see Borg 2004a, Chapter 2, §2.5) Yet seen from this perspective there is nothing inherently inconsistent in the combination of minimalism and a position on lexical complexity like OLS. Of course, what this does mean is that, if an approach like that suggested above were to be adopted for, say, 'tall' or 'ready', then the reasons in support of it could not turn on nonce judgements about speech act content.[23] We would need evidence in terms of type-level lexical intuitions and syntactic evidence such as binding, the control of PRO items, cross-linguistic evidence and, undoubtedly, behavioural syntactic tests yet to be developed. In the case of gradable adjectives, for instance, some mileage might be got out of an appeal to the possible aetiology of these expressions in their comparative cousins—if 'tall' were acquired via a grasp of the comparative form 'x is

---

[23] Though note that the claims might still be backed up by intuitions about strict or literal meaning. For instance, in arguing for a hidden existentially marked argument place over a hidden indexical, it might be relevant to note that contextually enriched readings are always cancellable. That is to say, a speaker can always reject without explicit contradiction an expansion of their words which explicitly mentions the contextually salient completion. A speaker who says 'Ted is tall' in context where all parties know that seven-year-olds are under discussion can always, it seems, continue 'though I mean tall for a four-year-old not a seven-year-old'. The cost here is apparently one of failure as a good communicative partner not outright contradiction; I return to this point below.

taller than y' this might give us grounds for thinking that gradable, as opposed to non-gradable, adjectives carried the memory of this two-place structure with them.[24] Or again, the distinction between predicative and attributive adjectives might be usefully brought into play, noting, for instance, that while one can legitimately infer from 'x is a red ball' that 'x is red' and 'x is a ball' one cannot infer from 'x is a good killer' that 'x is good' and 'x is a killer'. If this way of classifying adjectives were found to be robust it might help to provide clear, behavioural evidence to support positing a hidden argument place for one set of expressions but not the other.

In closing, I should note that I do think the jury is still out on whether, in any given case, the kind of OLS approach sketched above will prove correct. Indeed, it seems to me that the jury will require much more nuanced linguistic evidence to be provided before a decision can be made either way. Yet it does seem that OLS provides an avenue for exploration in the face of putatively incomplete expressions which is fully consistent with the tenets of minimalism. Furthermore, we should be clear that explanations of difficult cases via the mechanisms of OLS are just one possible recourse for minimalism. It has been a theme of this essay that minimalism should not be understood as committed to providing a single, unified solution to all those cases which prove difficult for the theory. Sometimes there may be sufficient lexical and syntactic evidence to motivate the kind of solution sketched above, sometimes there may be sufficient lexical and syntactic evidence to show that the expressions we are interested in really do make the grade as genuinely context-sensitive terms, and sometimes the right answer may simply be that the phenomenon in question trades on features of pragmatic, not semantic, content. What I want to suggest here is that minimalism in general is compatible with the deployment of this range of possible solutions—what matters for minimalism is not so much which answer is given in any case but what evidence can be brought to bear to support that way of accommodating the data. For it is by paying proper attention to the kinds of admissible motivations here that we will avoid the slippery slope examined in Chapter 1 (which saw the alternatives to

---

[24] It might also be that the gradable/non-gradable distinction cross-cuts expressions belonging to a single homophonic category. So, for instance, as we saw in Chapter 3, Kennedy and McNally 2010 argue for a semantic distinction within colour terms between, on the one hand, gradable readings and, on the other, non-gradable 'classificatory' readings.

standard claims about syntactically marked indexicality as launching one on an inevitable descent to occasionalism and use-based semantics).

(6.1) Minimalism and radical minimalism

There is, however, a final challenge to the OLS proposals outlined here which we need to consider. This objection stems not from the idea that the move risks merging minimalism with indexicalism or contextualism, but rather from the idea that the OLS proposals above are too profligate, that they seek to posit a something (an existentially bound or contextually controlled variable) when we should make do with a nothing (a gap, a hole, or an unassigned variable, something waiting to be filled prior to the recovery of a truth-evaluable entity). This is the challenge from Kent Bach's 'radical minimalism' and other approaches which allow for incomplete propositional radicals as the output of a semantic theory, with the propositions subsequently recovered via pragmatic enrichment (or some other kind of pragmatic process) being purely pragmatically conveyed contents (*implicitures*, to use Bach's terminology). In this way, a sentence like 'Flintoff is ready' would be viewed as semantically gappy, what it yields falls short of a proposition and the pragmatically completed proposition recoverable in context counts only as an aspect of speaker meaning not semantic meaning.

Now, as I've argued elsewhere (e.g. Borg 2004a) it seems to me to be a fine line (teetering perilously on the purely terminological) between radical minimalism (with its propositional radicals, implicitures and implicatures) and contextualism (with, to use the terminology of Sperber and Wilson, its incomplete logical forms, its explicatures and implicatures). For the three-fold elements of both approaches seem fundamentally the same, with the only significant difference coming in where one chooses to draw the line for literal meaning: at the propositional radical for radical minimalism, at the explicature/implicature for contextualism. Be this as it may, however, the point remains that, unless we can find a good reason to think that what OLS delivers in these cases is a filled argument place rather than merely marking a need or a gap, we remain open to the challenge that the moves above are fundamentally unmotivated. The motivation for marking an *argument place* is, the challenge goes, provided by intuitions of incompleteness, but what could motivate the stronger claim that that gap is filled?

I think there are two points to be made in response to this challenge. First, it does seem that certain aspects of our understanding of the terms in question are better explained by the OLS proposals mooted above than by the gappy radical minimalist/contextualist approaches. So, for instance, it seems that it is always possible to rescind from a contextually enriched interpretation of an utterance of, say, 'Flintoff is ready'. Even if being ready to bowl is clearly contextually salient, it is always possible to say 'Flintoff is ready, though I mean to have lunch not to carry on bowling' and the cost involved here seems to be one of communicative failure not literal contradiction. However, readings which make explicit the presence of an existentially bound variable in these cases apparently cannot be cancelled without contradiction: it is not possible to say without contradiction 'Flintoff is ready, though I don't mean ready to do or have anything'. Yet a reading which cannot be cancelled without contradiction would seem to have a good claim to being the literal meaning of the sentence in question. Furthermore, if literal meaning is gappy we might wonder why this gappy content can't be explicitly asserted? Why can't one explicitly deny the existentially bound reading and thereby assert simply the gappy content which radical minimalism predicts as the semantic content of this sentence? What we have on radical minimalism, it seems, is not merely the divergence between literal meaning and typical utterance meaning predicted by minimalism, but rather a radical separation of literal meaning and utterance meaning which makes literal meanings for putatively incomplete sentences unutterable, strangely ineffable.

It is also not obvious that a gappy-proposition approach can accommodate the gradations of judgement we apparently find in these cases. So consider the following:

4. *John devours.
5. *Ready to take the exam.
6. John is ready.

Ordinary speakers judge (4) to be ill-formed. (5), it seems, is also judged ill-formed, at least where it is not heard as a question ('Are you . . . ?') (6), on the other hand, is perfectly acceptable. Yet if all semantics delivers is gappy versus non-gappy contents we might wonder why the gaps in (4) and (5) lead to judgements of ill-formedness while the alleged gap in (6) leads at most to a judgement of incompleteness. On the other hand, on the OLS proposal we can accommodate these different judgements. First OLS can differentiate at least three categories of expression: those which require only one argument place (like 'dance'), those whose lexical entry specifies two argument places (like 'devour') and those whose associated lexical information classifies an expression as a two-place term (like 'ready'). So, it is the fact that 'devour' means *to devour something* which makes (4) genuinely ill-formed. Note the suggestion is that the requirement of, say, 'dance' for one argument place to be filled, while 'ready' requires two, stems from issues about lexical content, syntax and well-formedness, not from any concerns about the metaphysics of the properties picked out. That is to say, though both dancing and being ready no doubt require, as a matter of metaphysics, more than simply a subject, that this need is marked in our lexicon in one case but not the other is a matter of syntax not metaphysics. This realization is reinforced by noting that one and the same worldly happening may be lexicalized in different ways in different languages, so while 'hit' is a transitive verb of English, the counterpart term in Lhasa Tibetan is not, or again while the English term 'blush' describes a process, the Italian expression 'arrossire' is a change of state term (Levin and Rappaport Hovav 2005: 19–22). Clearly then, issues of metaphysics alone are not what are responsible for lexical realization.

Secondly, OLS can allow that the two argument places required by 'ready' are realized in different ways within the lexicon. The subject appears to be required as part of the lexical content of 'ready', for ordinary speakers judge statements like 'Ready for lunch' where the first argument is missing as genuinely ill-formed (at least, as noted above, where the sentence fragment is not heard as a question, i.e. 'are you...?' and there is no possibility of recovering a subject from the surrounding discourse via standard ellipsis). However they do not make this judgement with a sentence like 'Flintoff is ready', where the object is missing and there is no possibility of recovering it from the surrounding discourse. In this case all they get is some kind of sense of incompleteness. For OLS this difference can be taken to emerge from the fact that the first argument forms part of the lexical entry for 'ready' (to understand the term 'ready' one must know that it requires a subject), while the second argument place is marked by the lexical category to which 'ready' belongs (one can understand the term 'ready' without this knowledge). The fact that OLS can allow for the kind of fine-grained judgements between ill- and well-formedness which ordinary subjects seem willing to make might make the approach preferable to one which posits only a binary distinction between gappy and non-gappy propositions.

Gappy propositions have of course been the subject of a fair amount of discussion in philosophy of language (e.g. see Braun 1993) and it does seem to me that the minimalist is not currently in a position to rule them out entirely. Yet, as indicated above, it also seems to me that there is some evidence which points towards the need to posit a something rather than a nothing in these cases and, furthermore (and this brings me on to my second point), it remains, I think, very much a moot point whether a fairly fragile phenomenon like incompleteness can really be sufficient to motivate a move to gappy propositions. If, on balance, it were to turn out that the move to posit some kind of covert syntax in these cases could not be motivated, to my mind this should push us towards a rejection of incompleteness judgements as in any way semantically informative (i.e. as not showing that some expressions bring with them superficially unmarked argument places *and* as not showing that some sentences fail to express propositions). If our choices turn out to be between giving up on the propositional model of semantics simply on the basis of controversial incompleteness judgements versus accommodating intuitions of incompleteness in some other way (e.g. as expressions of concern about the triviality of the propositions expressed) it seems to me that the latter option is clearly preferable. For, as I stressed in Chapter 3, §3.1, there are serious questions to be asked about how robust judgements of incompleteness are and whether, in actual fact, they can ultimately succeed in delimiting some subset of all sentences for a distinctive semantic treatment. That is to say, if one opens the door to non-propositional semantics on the basis of expressions like 'ready' and 'tall' there must be, as Cappelen and Lepore 2005 stress, the very real fear that the project of propositional/truth-conditional semantics cannot be saved for any sentences at all and this (given the reasons voiced in Chapter 1 §1 in favour of propositional semantics in general) should make us very cautious about moving to sub-propositional semantics in the case of sentences containing incomplete terms.

Finally, notice that the way in which appeals to gappy propositions traditionally come about is with respect to empty names and other singular terms which fail to secure a referent. Yet admitting gappy propositions in respect of these cases would not, I think, be inconsistent with minimalism for in these cases, as we might put it, the problem lies with the world not with our language. Minimalism holds that all well-formed sentences are capable of expressing propositions relative to a context of utterance. That sometimes a well-formed sentence fails to express a proposition because the context it is relativized to fails to play ball, as it were, does not show minimalism's commitment to propositionalism is mistaken. If we hold that someone who is hallucinating the presence of a red dragon and who utters 'That is scary' (intending to refer to what they take to be a real dragon) fails to express a proposition, this will be because the singular concept introduced on the basis of this token of 'that' lacks content, the world can provide no object to which it refers. From the perspective of the language, everything is in place for a proposition to be expressed but the context doesn't play its part in providing a referent. In the case of putatively incomplete predicates, however, a move to gappy propositions is genuinely inconsistent with minimalism because in these cases the problem is alleged to lie with our language. When someone utters 'Flintoff is ready' (standardly) the world does play ball, there is something for which Flintoff is ready, but the claim of the radical minimalist is that our language fails to incorporate this element into its semantics. Minimalism can allow that some well-formed sentences fail to express propositions because their world lets them down, what it can't allow is that some well-formed sentences fail to express propositions because bits of language just aren't in the business of incorporating enough information to permit truth-evaluable claims to be made at the semantic level. So it is not gappy propositions per se with which minimalism has a problem, rather it is the move to allow gappy propositions in these cases.

In summary then: it seems to me that minimalism can and should allow for the possibility of semantically relevant material which is not explicitly voiced at the surface level. Thus there is nothing inconsistent in adopting minimalism together with the kind of OLS approach to putatively incomplete expressions explored above. The kind of OLS proposals considered do not increase the context-sensitivity of our language to enable our semantic theory to cleave more closely to judgements of speech act content and they respect the picture of meaning which lies at the heart of minimalism. What the motivating ethos of minimalism demands is that we provide a purely lexico-syntactic motivation for any claims about the lexico-syntactic constituents we posit, and thus that thought-experiments about what is said in specific contexts by utterances of, say, 'Flintoff is ready' be treated as irrelevant in determining the logical form and semantic content of this sentence. Yet OLS, just like minimalism, is committed to the principle of lexico-syntactic evidence for lexico-syntactic claims. What supports the OLS proposals is not one-off intuitions about speech act content but consideration of the syntactic behaviour of expressions. As we have seen, minimalism embodies a model which sees words in general as making a static, predictable and context-insensitive contribution to the literal, truth-conditional or propositional content of the well-formed sentences in which those words appear. All OLS adds to the minimalist picture is the recognition that sometimes the 'blob' of meaning contributed by a term to a sentence may come with more instructions than are realized in a simple specification of the referential content of the term. Yet nothing in this realization takes us away from the atomistic picture of word meaning inherent in the minimalist outlook or puts us on the slippery slope to indexicalism, contextualism, relativism or occasionalism.

(7) Conclusion

I've tried in this essay to make the case for a minimal semantics: a model of literal linguistic meaning which takes semantic content to be largely context-insensitive, a matter of word-reading not mind-reading, and thus open to capture via an encapsulated, computational mental module. I've suggested that, contrary to common claims, this kind of minimal approach to literal linguistic meaning possesses a fair degree of intuitive appeal and that it could underpin much of the work we require from our language (from providing a

clear boundary between semantics and pragmatics and thus capturing what speakers are literally committed to by the sentences they
speak, to delivering the fall-back content available when our grasp
of context is impaired, to accommodating judgements about properties like validity and contradiction). However, minimalism does
depend on the truth of propositionalism—the idea that all well-
formed sentences are capable of expressing truth-evaluable content
when relativized to a context of utterance—and propositionalism, as
we have seen, faces two significant problems. First, as looked at in
Chapter 3, there are some expressions in natural language which
seem in some way incomplete prior to contextual input, so for
instance, sentences like 'Flintoff is ready' and 'steel is strong enough'
seem to fail to express propositions until we know from a context of
utterance what Flintoff is ready to do or what steel is strong enough
for. Second, as looked at in Chapters 5 and 6, it may be argued that
the minimalist assumption that words make a discrete, broadly referential contribution to sentence meanings (a kind of contribution
which would allow appropriate concatenations of words to yield
propositional, truth-evaluable content) is mistaken. Perhaps instead
words should be taken to express an open-ended, indeterminate
fragment of content, something which requires fixing within a context of use prior to contributing to a truth-evaluable content. I've
tried to argue, however, that ultimately neither of these putative
problems suffice to show that propositionalism is false. With respect
to putatively incomplete expressions, if the lexico-syntactic evidence
warrants it, the minimalist may analyse them either as involving genuinely context-sensitive elements or as context-independent expressions whose contributions to the logical forms of sentences in which
they appear is more complicated than might initially have been
thought. Where the lexico-syntactic evidence does not warrant
either of these explanations, she will argue that the sentences do
express propositions as they stand, with all richer content being
merely a pragmatic not a semantic feature. On the other hand, with
respect to the internalist arguments against atomistic, broadly referential lexical axioms, the minimalist will contend that the ontological arguments that such axioms are impossible or unnecessary fail,
while the methodological arguments concerning the need to accommodate the intra-linguistic behaviour of expressions are ones which

can be met without jettisoning atomistic, referential lexical axioms. So neither argument forces one to give up propositionalism and thus neither forces the rejection of minimalism.

In the Preface I described the position minimalism wants to occupy as potentially precarious, since though we can clearly see the need for lexico-syntactically determined yet possibly non-propositional content and we can clearly see the need for pragmatically affected propositional content, the need for lexico-syntactically determined *and* necessarily propositional content is much less clear. Yet I believe that, on closer inspection, the position turns out not to be terribly precarious after all, for, as I've tried to suggest in this essay, there is simply no good reason to think that the lexico-syntactically determined contents (which all parties agree we need) must on some or all occasions fall short of propositional contents (barring cases of reference failure for directly referential terms). Contrary to well-publicized reports about their demise, it seems to me that minimal propositional contents are alive and well and have a good claim to being the semantic contents of natural language sentences.

For many people, however, perhaps their real, underlying problem with minimalism stems not from relatively technical objections concerning the existence of minimal propositions or the kind of work they can do. Rather their dissatisfaction with the approach comes directly from the fact that minimalism drives a wedge between literal sentence meaning and pragmatic speaker meaning, allowing that the former may fail to match the latter, and for many this is to demand the right to be called a semantic theory without taking on board any of the responsibilities associated with such a title. However, the claim from Chapter 1 on has been that allowing a semantic theory to step away from what the syntax and lexicon alone provide and towards what the speaker means will launch one on an inevitable descent to a full-blown use-theory of meaning, where the distinction between sentence level semantic content and pragmatic utterance level content is fundamentally blurred. The way to avoid this kind of collapse is to recognize that constructing a semantic theory is one kind of enterprise, while constructing a theory of speaker meaning and communicated content is quite another. Clearly ordinary subjects perform fairly impeccably both in understanding literal linguistic meaning and in understanding communicative acts and intentions, but that shouldn't confuse us into thinking that a single, undifferentiated competence necessarily underlies them both. As long as we keep focused on what it is proper to require a semantic theory to explain, then, there is no bar to treating semantic content as the content delivered by (a cognitive module utilizing) the kind of austere, formal, predominantly context-insensitive semantics we find in minimalism.

Bibliography

Arbib, M., E. Oztop, P. Zuckow-Goldring. 2005. Language and the mirror system: a perception/action based approach to communicative development. *Cognition, Brain, Behaviour* 3: 239–72.

Atlas, J. 1977. Negation, ambiguity and presupposition. *Linguistics and Philosophy* 1: 321–36.

Atlas, K. forthcoming. Whatever happened to meaning among the contextualists and anti-contextualists. In. K. Turner (ed.) *Making Semantics Pragmatic.* Elsevier: Oxford.

Avramides, A. (1989) *Meaning and Mind: an examination of a Gricean account of meaning.* Cambridge, MA: MIT Press.

Bach, K. 1992a. Intentions and demonstrations. *Analysis* 52:140–6.

—— 1992b. Paving the road to reference. *Philosophical Studies* 67 (3):295–300.

—— 1994. Semantic slack: what is said and more. In *Foundations of Speech Act Theory: philosophical and linguistic perspectives*, edited by S. Tsohatzidis. London: Routledge. 267–91.

—— 1999. The semantics–pragmatics distinction: what it is and why it matters. In K. Turner (ed) *The Semantics/Pragmatics Interface from Different Points of View.* Netherlands: Elsevier Science. 65–83.

—— 2001. You don't say? *Synthese* 128: 15–44.

—— 2006. The top ten misconceptions about implicature. In B. Birner & G. Ward (eds) *Drawing the Boundaries of Meaning: Neo-Gricean studies in pragmatics and semantics in honor of Laurence R. Horn.* Amsterdam: John Benjamins.

—— 2007. Regressions in pragmatics (and semantics). In N. Burton-Roberts (ed) *Advances in Pragmatics.* New York: Palgrave Macmillan.

—— 2007b. The excluded middle: minimal semantics without minimal propositions. *Philosophy and Phenomenological Research* 73: 435–42.

—— Minimalism for dummies. <http://userwww.sfsu.edu/~kbach/replytoC&L.pdf>

Baldwin, D & Baird, J. 2001. Discerning intention in dynamic human action. *Trends in Cognitive Sciences* 5: 171–8.

Baron-Cohen, S. 1995. *Mindblindness: An essay on autism and theory of mind.* Cambridge, MA: MIT Press.

Block, N. 1998. Holism, mental and semantic. Routledge Encyclopedia of Philosophy.

Bloom, P. 2000. *How Children Learn the Meanings of Words*. Cambridge, MA: MIT Press.

Borg, E. 2002. Pointing at Jack, talking about Jill: understanding deferred uses of demonstratives and pronouns. *Mind and Language* 17: 489–512.

—— 2004a. *Minimal Semantics*. Oxford: Clarendon Press.

—— 2004b. Formal semantics and intentional states. *Analysis* 64: 215–23.

—— 2005. Intention-based semantics. In E. Lepore & B. Smith (eds) *The Oxford Handbook of Philosophy of Language*. Oxford: Oxford University Press. 250–67.

—— 2006. Review of F. Recanati's *Literal Meaning*. *Mind* 115: 461–5.

—— 2007. Minimalism versus contextualism in semantics. In G. Preyer & G. Peter (eds) *Context Sensitivity and Semantic Minimalism: Essays on Semantics and Pragmatics*. Oxford: Oxford University Press. 546–71. Reprinted in M. Ezcurdia & R. Stainton (eds) *The Semantics-Pragmatics Boundary in Philosophy*, Oxford: Oxford University Press.

—— 2007b. If mirror neurons are the answer, what was the question? *Journal of Consciousness Studies* 14: 5–19.

—— 2009. On three theories of implicature: default theory, relevance and minimalism. *The International Review of Pragmatics* 1: 1–21. Reprinted in K. Petrus (ed) *Meaning and Analysis*, Palgrave, and A. Kasher (ed) *Critical Concepts II*, Routledge.

—— 2012. Review of F. Recanati's *Truth-conditional Pragmatics*. *The Times Literary Supplement*. February 13th issue: 24.

Brandom, R. 2000. *Articulating Reasons: An Introduction to Inferentialism*. Cambridge M.A.: University Press.Harvard University Press.

Braun, D. 1993. Empty names. *Nous* 27: 449–69.

Bridges, J. 2010 Wittgenstein vs. contextualism. In A.M. Ahmed (ed) *Wittgenstein's Philosophical Investigations: a critical guide*. Cambridge: Cambridge University Press. 109–128.

Burge, T. 1979. Individualism and the mental. *Midwest Studies in Philosophy*, 4: 73–121.

—— 1992. Philosophy of language and mind. *Philosophical Review* 101: 3–51.

Cappelen, H., & E. Lepore. 1997. On an alleged connection between indirect speech and the theory of meaning. *Mind and Language* 12: 278–96.

—— —— 2005: *Insensitive Semantics: a defense of semantic minimalism and speech act pluralism*. Oxford: Blackwell.

—— —— 2006. Reply to Bach. *Philosophy and Phenomenological Research*. 73: 469–473.

—— & J. Hawthorne. 2009. *Relativism and Monadic Truth*. Oxford: Oxford University Press.

Carnap, R. 1937. *The Logical Syntax of Language*. NY: Harcourt Brace

—— 1952. Meaning postulates. *Philosophical Studies* 3: 65–73.

Carpenter, M., J. Call, & M. Tomasello. 2002. A new false belief test for 36-month-olds. *British Journal of Developmental Psychology* 20: 393–420.

Carruthers, P. 1996. *Language, Thought and Consciousness: An essay in philosophical psychology*. Cambridge: Cambridge University Press.

Carston, R. 1999. The semantics/pragmatics distinction: a view from relevance theory. In K. Turner (ed) *The Semantics/Pragmatics Interface from Different Points of View*. Netherlands: Elsevier Science. 85–125.

—— 2002. *Thoughts and Utterances*. Oxford: Blackwell.

—— 2008. Linguistic communication and the semantics-pragmatics distinction. *Synthese* 165: 321–45.

—— 2008. Review of E. Borg's *Minimal Semantics*. *Mind and Language* 23: 359–67.

Cattaneo, L., Fabbi-Destro, M., Boria, S., Pieraccini, C., Monti, A., Cossu, G., and Rizzolatti, G. 2007. 'Impairment of actions chains in autism and its possible role in intention understanding', Proceedings of The National Academy of Sciences, 104 (45), 17825–30.

Chomsky, N. 2000. *New Horizons in the Study of Language and Mind*. Cambridge: Cambridge University Press.

Clapp, L. 2007. Minimal (disagreement about) semantics. In G. Preyer & G. Peter (eds) *Context-Sensitivity and Semantic Minimalism: Essays on Semantics and Pragmatics*. Oxford: Oxford University Press. 251–77.

Collins, J. 2007. Syntax, more or less. *Mind* 116: 805–50.

—— 2009. Methodology, not metaphysics: against semantic externalism. *Proceedings of the Aristotelian Society Supplementary Volume* LXXXIII: 53–70.

—— 2011. *The Unity of the Proposition*. Oxford: Oxford University Press.

—— 2011b. Impossible words again; or why beds break but not make. *Mind and Language*. 26: 234–60.

Corazza, E., Fish, W. & Gorvett, J. 2002. Who is I?' *Philosophical Studies* 107: 1–21.

Dancy, J. 2004. *Ethics Without Principles*. Oxford: Oxford University Press.

Davidson, D. 1967. Truth and meaning. *Synthese* 17: 304–23. Reprinted in Davidson (1984), *Truth and Interpretation*, 17–36. Page references to there.

Davidson, D. 1974. On the very idea of a conceptual scheme. *Proceedings and Addresses of the American Philosophical Association* 47: 5–20. Reprinted in Davidson 1984.

—— 1984. *Inquiries into Truth and Interpretation*. Oxford: Clarendon Press.

—— 1986. A nice derangement of epitaphs. In E. Lepore (ed) *Truth and Interpretation*. Oxford: Blackwell.

Davies, M. 1987. Tacit knowledge and semantic theory: can a five per cent difference matter? *Mind* 96: 441–62.

—— 2006. Foundational issues in the philosophy of language. In M. Devitt & R. Hanley (eds) *The Blackwell Guide to the Philosophy of Language*. Oxford: Blackwell.

DeRose, K. 1992. Contextualism and knowledge attributions. *Philosophy and Phenomenological Research* 52:913–29.

—— 2008. Gradable adjectives: a defense of pluralism. *The Australasian Journal of Philosophy* 86: 141–60.

—— 2009. *The Case for Contextualism*. Oxford: Oxford University Press.

Dowty, R. 1991. Thematic proto-roles and argument selection. *Language* 67: 547–619

Dummett, M. 1978. *Truth and Other Enigmas*. Cambridge, MA: Harvard University Press.

—— 1993. *Origins of Analytical Philosophy*. London: Duckworth and Cambridge MA: Harvard University Press.

Evans G. 1982. *The Varieties of Reference*. Oxford: Clarendon Press.

—— 1985. Does tense logic rest on a mistake? In his *Collected Papers*, Oxford: Clarendon Press. 343–63.

Fodor, J. 1983. *Modularity of Mind*. Cambridge, MA: MIT Press.

—— 1990. A theory of content and other essays. Cambridge, MA: MIT Press.

—— 1998. *Concepts: Where Cognitive Science Went Wrong*. Oxford: Oxford University Press.

—— 2000. *The Mind Doesn't Work That Way*. Cambridge, MA: MIT Press.

—— 2008. *LOT2*. Oxford: Oxford University Press.

—— Fodor, J. & Garrett, M. 1975. The psychological unreality of semantic representations. *Linguistic Inquiry* 4: 515–31.

—— & E. Lepore. 1998. The emptiness of the lexicon: reflections on Pustejovsky. *Linguistic Inquiry* 29: 269–88. Reprinted in Fodor & Lepore 2002b: 89–119. Page references to there.

—— —— 1999. Impossible words? *Linguistic Inquiry* 30: 445–53. Reprinted in Fodor & Lepore 2002b: 120–134. Page references to there.

—— —— 2002. Why compositionality won't go away: reflections on Horwich's 'deflationary' theory. In *Meaning and Representation*, Borg (ed). Oxford: Blackwell. 58–76.

—— —— 2002b. *The Compositionality Papers*. Oxford: Oxford University Press.

—— —— 2005. Impossible words: reply to Johnson. *Mind and Language* 20: 353–6

Frege, G. 1967. *Kleine Schriften*. Hildesheim: Olms.

—— 1884. *Die Grundlagen der Arithmetik: eine logisch-mathematische Unter-suchung über den Begriff der Zahl.* Breslau: W. Koebner. Translated by J. L. Austin as *The Foundations of Arithmatic: A Logic-Mathematical Enquiry into the Concept of Number.* Oxford: Blackwell. 1974.

Gallagher, S. 2001. The practice of mind: theory, simulation or primary inter-action? *Journal of Consciousness Studies* 8: 83–108.

—— 2005. *How the Body Shapes the Mind.* New York: Oxford University Press.

—— 2006. Perceiving others in action. *A lecture in the series Fondements cognitifs de l'interaction avec autri,* given at the Collège de France, Paris. Available online <http://pegasus.cc.ucf.edu/~gallaghergallo6ParisAS.pdf>

Gallese, V. & Goldman, A. 1998. Mirror neurons and the simulation theory of mind reading, *Trends in Cognitive Science* 2: 493–501

Garcia-Carpintero, M. 1998. Indexicals as token-reflexives. *Mind* 107: 529–63.

—— 2001. Gricean rational reconstructions and the semantics/pragmatics distinction. *Synthese* 128: 93–131.

—— 2006. Recanati on the semantics/pragmatics distinction. *Critica* 38: 35–68.

—— & M. Kölbel 2008. *Relative Truth.* Oxford: Oxford University Press.

Gauker, C. 2008. Zero tolerance for pragmatics. *Synthese* 165: 359–71.

—— first published online 2011. What Tipper is ready for. *Nous.*

Gibbs, R. 2002. A new look at literal meaning in understanding what is said and implicated. *Journal of Pragmatics* 34: 457–86.

Glanzberg, M. 2009. Implicit arguments and intentions. Presentation at CSMN workshop on *Contexts and Intentions,* Oslo.

Gleitman, L. 1990. The structural sources of verb meanings. *Language Acquisition* 1: 3–55.

Gopnik, A. (1988). Conceptual and semantic development as theory change. Mind and Language 3: 3: 197–217.

Gorvett, J. 2005. Back through the looking glass: on the relationship between intentions and individuals. *Philosophical Studies* 124: 295–312.

Grice, P. 1989. *Studies in the Way of Words.* Cambridge, MA: Harvard Univer-sity Press.

Gross, S. 2006. Can one sincerely say what one doesn't believe? *Mind and Language* 21: 11–20.

Hale, K. & S. Keyser. 1993. On argument structure and the lexical expression of syntactic relations. In K. Hale & S. Keyser (eds) *The View From Building 20. Essays in Honour of Sylvain Bromberger.* Cambridge, MA: MIT Press. 53–110.

Harman, G. 1999. *Reasoning, Meaning and Mind.* Oxford: Oxford University Press.

Hawthorne, J. 2004. *Knowledge and Lotteries*. Oxford: Oxford University Press.

—— & D. Manley 2012. *The Reference Book*. Oxford: Oxford University Press.

Higginbotham, J. 1989. Elucidations of meaning. *Linguistics and Philosophy*, 12: 465–517

—— 1994. Priorities in the philosophy of thought. *Proceedings of the Aristotelian Society Supplementary Volume* 68:85–106.

—— 2006. Languages and idiolects: their language and ours. In E. Lepore & B. Smith (eds) *The Oxford Handbook of Philosophy of Language*. Oxford: Oxford University Press. 140–50.

Hinzen, W. 2007. *An Essay on Names and Truth*. Oxford: Oxford University Press.

—— E. Machery & M. Werning (eds). 2012. *Oxford Handbook of Compositionality*. Oxford: Oxford University Press.

Horwich, P. 1998. *Meaning*. Oxford: Oxford University Press.

—— 2002. Deflating compositionality. In *Meaning and Representation*, edited by E. Borg. Oxford: Blackwell. 77–93.

Hurley, S. 2006. Active perception and perceiving action: the shared circuits model. In T. Gendler & J. Hawthorne (eds) *Perceptual Experience*. New York: Oxford University Press. 205–59.

Iacoboni, M., I. Molnar-Szakacs, V. Gallese, G. Buccino, J. Mazziotta, G. Rizzolatti. 2005. Grasping the intentions of others with one's own mirror neuron system. *PLoS Biology* 3, e79: 0001–0007.

Iacona, A. 2008. Faultless or disagreement. In M. Garcia-Carpintero & M. Kölbel (eds) *Relative Truth*. Oxford: Oxford University Press. 287–96.

Jackendoff, R. 1983. *Semantics and Cognition*. Cambridge, MA: MIT Press.

—— 1990. *Semantic Structures*. Cambridge, .MA: MIT Press.

—— 1992. Languages of the Mind. Cambridge, MA: MIT Press.

—— 1993. *Languages of the Mind: Essays on mental representation*. Cambridge, Mass: MIT Press.

—— 2002. *Foundations of Language*. Oxford: Oxford University Press.

Jaszczolt, K. 2005. Default semantics: foundations of a compositional theory of acts of communication. Oxford: Oxford University Press.

Jeshion, R. 2002. Acquaintanceless de re belief. In J. Campbell, M. O'Rourke & D. Shier (eds) *Meaning and Truth: Investigations in Philosophical Semantics*. New York: Seven Bridges Press, 53–78.

Johnson, K. 2004. From impossible words to conceptual structure: the role of structure and processes in the lexicon. *Mind and Language* 19: 334–58.

—— 2008. An overview of lexical semantics. *Philosophy Compass* 3: 119–34.

Jönsson, M. 2008. *On Compositionality: Doubts about the structural path to meaning.* Lund University PhD thesis.

Kamp, H. 1981. A Theory of truth and semantic representation. In J. Groenendijk, T. Janssen & M. Stokhof (eds) *Formal Methods in the Study of Language: Proceedings of the 3rd Amsterdam Colloquium.* Amsterdam: Mathematical Centre Tracts. 277–322.

Kaplan, D. 1977. Demonstratives. In *Themes from Kaplan*, edited by J. Almog, J. Perry & H. Wettstein. Oxford: Oxford University Press. 481–564.

—— 1978. Dthat. In P. Cole (ed) *Syntax and Semantics.* New York: Academic Press. 221–42. Reprinted in P. French, T. Uehling, H. Wettstein (eds) *Contemporary Perspectives in the Philosophy of Language.* Minneapolis 1979: 383–400.

—— 1989. Afterthoughts. In J. Almog, J. Perry & H. Wettstein (eds) *Themes From Kaplan.* Oxford: Oxford University Press. 565–614.

Katz, J. 1977. *Propositional Structure and Illocutionary Force.* New York: Thomas Y. Crowell.

Kempson, R. 1975. *Presupposition and the Delimitation of Semantics.* Cambridge: Cambridge University Press.

—— 1986. Ambiguity and the semantics-pragmatics distinction. In *Meaning and Interpretation*, edited by C. Travis. Oxford: Blackwell. 77–104.

Kennedy, C. & L. McNally. 2010. Color, context, and compositionality. *Synthese* 174: 79–98.

King, J. 2007. *The Nature and Structure of Content.* Oxford: Oxford University Press.

——, & J. Stanley. 2005. Semantics, pragmatics, and the role of semantic content. In *Semantics vs. Pragmatics*, edited by G. Szabo. Oxford: Oxford University Press. 111–64.

Kölbel, M. 2002. *Truth without Objectivity.* London: Routledge.

—— 2003. Faultless disagreement. *Proceedings of the Aristotelian Society* 104: 53–73.

—— 2008. Motivations for relativism. In M. Garcia-Carpintero & M. Kölbel (eds) *Relative Truth.* Oxford: Oxford University Press. 1–40.

Konrfilt, R. & N. Correra. 1993. Conceptual structure and its relation to the structure of lexical entries. In Reuland & Werner (eds) *Language and Knowledge 2: Lexical and Conceptual Structure.* Dordrecht: Kluwer.

Kripke, S. 1980. *Naming and Necessity.* Oxford: Blackwell.

Larson, R., & G. Segal. 1995. *Knowledge of Meaning.* Cambridge, MA: MIT Press.

Lasersohn, P. 2005. Context dependence, disagreement, and predicates of personal taste. *Linguistics and Philosophy* 28: 643–86.

Lassiter, D. 2008. Semantic externalism, language variation, and sociolinguistic accommodation. *Mind and Language* 23: 607–33.

Leslie, Alan M. (1987). "Pretense and Representation: The Origin of 'Theory of Mind' ". Psychological Review. 412–26.

Levin, B. 1985. Lexical Semantics in Review. Cambridge, MA: MIT Center for Cognitive Science.

—— 1993: English Verb Classes and Alternations: a preliminary investigation. Chicago: Chicago University Press.

—— & M. Rappaport Hovav. 2005. *Argument Realization*. Cambridge: Cambridge University Press.

Lewis, D. 1972. General semantics. In D. Davidson & G. Harman (eds) *Semantics of Natural Language*. Reidel: Dordrecht-Holland. 169–218.

MacFarlane, J. 2003. Future contingents and relative truth. *The Philosophical Quarterly* 53: 321–36.

—— 2005. The assessment sensitivity of knowledge attributions. *Oxford Studies in Epistemology* 1: 197–233.

—— 2007. Relativism and disagreement. *Philosophical Studies* 132: 17–31.

—— 2007a. Semantic minimalism and nonindexical contextualism. In G. Preyer & G. Peter (eds) *Semantic Minimalism: Essays on Semantics and Pragmatics*. Oxford: Oxford University Press. 240–50.

—— 2009. Nonindexical contextualism. *Synthese* 166: 231–50.

Marti, L. 2006. Unarticulated constituents revisited. *Linguistics and Philosophy* 29: 135–66.

McCulloch, G. 1995. *The Mind and its World*. London: Routledge.

McDowell, J. 1977. On the sense and reference of a proper name. *Mind* 86: 159–85.

—— 1978. On 'the Reality of the Past'. In C. Hookway & P. Pettit, eds., *Action and Interpretation: Studies in the Philosophy of the Social Sciences*. Cambridge: Cambridge University Press, 127–44. Reprinted in McDowell 1998, page references to there.

McGinn, C. 1981. The mechanisms of reference. *Synthese* 49: 157–86.

McGrath, M. 2005. Review of M. Kölbel *Truth Without Objectivity*. *Philosophy and Phenomenological Research* 71: 441–4.

Merchant, J. 2010. Three Types of Ellipsis. In F. Recanati, I. Stojanovic, N. Villanueva (eds.), *Context-Dependence, Perspective, and Relativity*. Mouton de Gruyter: Berlin.

Montague, R. 1970. English as a formal language. In B. Visentini et al. (eds) *Linguaggi nella Società e nella Tecnica*. Milan: Edizioni di Comunità. Reprinted in Montague (1974), *Formal Philosophy: Selected Papers of Richard Montague*. New Haven: Yale University Press. 188–221.

Moore, G. E. 1954. Wittgenstein's lectures in 1930–33. *Mind* 63 1–15 and 289–315. Reprinted in Moore 1959. *Philosophical Papers*. London: Allen and Unwin. 247–318.

Neale, S. 2007. Heavy hands, magic, and scene-reading traps. *European Journal of Analytic Philosophy* 3: 77–132.

Nunberg, G. 1993. Indexicality and deixis. *Linguistics and Philosophy* 16: 1–43.

Pagin, P. 2006. Meaning holism. In B. Smith & E. Lepore (eds) *The Oxford Handbook of Philosophy of Language*. Oxford: Oxford University Press. 213–32.

Partee, B. 1995. Lexical semantics and compositionality. In D. Osherson (general editor), in *Part I: Language*, L. Gleitman & M. Liberman (eds), *Invitation to Cognitive Science*, 2nd edition. MIT Press, Cambridge, 311–60.

Peacocke, C. 2008. *Truly Understood*. Oxford: Oxford University Press.

Perry, J. 2001. *Reference and Reflexivity*. Palo Alto, California: CSLI Publications.

Pietroski, P. 2005. Meaning before truth. In G. Preyer & G. Peter (eds) *Contextualism in Philosophy: Knowledge, Meaning, and Truth*. Oxford: Oxford University Press. 255–302.

—— 2005b. *Events and Semantic Architecture*. Oxford: Oxford University Press.

—— 2010. Concepts, meanings and truth: first nature, second nature and hard work. *Mind and Language* 25: 247–78.

Pinker, S. 1989. *Learnability and Cognition: the acquisition of argument structure*. Cambridge, MA: MIT Press.

—— 2007. *The Stuff of Thought: Language as a Window Into Human Nature*. London: Allen Lane.

Predelli, S. 1998a. I am not here now. *Analysis* 58: 107–15

—— 1998b. Utterance, interpretation, and the logic of indexicals. *Mind and Language* 13: 400–14.

—— 2002. Intentions, indexicals, and communication. *Analysis* 62: 310–16.

—— 2005. *Contexts*. Oxford: Oxford University Press.

Prinz, J. 2002. *Furnishing the Mind*. Cambridge, MA: MIT Press.

Pustejovsky, J. 1995. *The Generative Lexicon*. Cambridge, MA: MIT Press.

Putnam, H. 1975. The meaning of 'meaning'. In *Philosophical Papers, vol. 2: mind, language and reality*, pp. 215–71. Cambridge: Cambridge University Press.

Quine, W. 1953: *From a Logical Point of View*, Cambridge, MA: Harvard University Press.

Recanati, F. 1993. *Direct Reference: From Language to Thought*. Oxford: Blackwell.

—— 2002. Unarticulated constituents. *Linguistics and Philosophy* 25: 299–345.

—— 2004. *Literal Meaning*. Cambridge: Cambridge University Press.

—— 2006. Predelli and Garcia-Carpintero *on Literal Meaning*. *Critica* 38: 69–79.

—— 2007. *Perspectival Thought: A Plea for (Moderate) Relativism*. Oxford: Oxford University Press.

—— 2007b. It is raining (somewhere). *Linguistics and Philosophy* 30: 123–46.

Recanati, F. 2008. Moderate relativism. In M. Garcia-Carpintero & M. Kölbel (eds) *Relative Truth*. Oxford: Oxford University Press. 41–62.

—— 2010. *Truth-conditional Pragmatics*. Oxford: Oxford University Press.

Reimer, M. 1991. Do demonstrations have semantic significance? *Analysis* 51: 177–83.

—— 1992. Three views of demonstrative reference. *Synthese* 93 (3):373–402.

Rey, G. 2005. Mind, intentionality and inexistence. *Croatian Journal of Philosophy*, 5: 389–415.

—— 2006. The intentional inexistence of language - but not cars'. In *Contemporary Debates in Cognitive Science*, edited by R. Stainton. Oxford: Blackwell. 237–55.

Rizzolatti, G and Arbib, M. (1998). "Language within our grasp". Trends in Neurosciences 21: 188–194.

——, Fogassi, L. and Gallese, V. (2000), 'Cortical mechanisms subserving object grasping and action recognition: a new view on the cortical motor functions', in Gazzaniga M.S., (Ed.), The Cognitive Neurosciences, Second Edition (Cambridge, MA: MIT Press), 539–52.

Robbins, P. 2007. "Minimalism and modularity" in G. Preyer and G. Peter (eds.), Context-Sensitivity and Semantic Minimalism. Oxford University Press. (2007) 303-319.

Roeper, T. 1987. Implicit arguments and the head-complement relation. Linguistic *Inquiry* 18: 267–310.

Rothschild, D. and G. Segal. 2009. Indexical predicates. *Mind and Language* 24: 467–93.

Russell, B. 1911. Knowledge by acquaintance and knowledge by description. In *Mysticism and Logic*, edited by B. Russell. London: Allen and Unwin. 152–67.

—— 2006. Against grammatical computation of scalar implicatures. *Journal of Semantics* 23: 361–82.

Sainsbury, R.M. 2008. Fly swatting: Davidsonian truth theories and context. In Maria Cristina Amoretti & Nicla Vassallo (eds) *Knowledge, Language, and Interpretation. On the Philosophy of Donald Davidson*. Ontos Verlag (Frankfurt).

Salmon, N. 1986. *Frege's Puzzle*. Cambridge, MA: MIT Press.

Sauerland, U. 2004. Scalar implicatures in complex sentences. *Linguistics and Philosophy* 27: 367–91.

Schaffer, J. 2011 Contextualism for taste claims and epistemic modals. In *Epistemic Modality*, edited by A. Egan & B. Weatherson. Oxford: Oxford University Press.

Searle, J. 1980. The background of meaning. In J. Searle, F. Keifer & M. Bierwisch (eds) *Speech Act Theory and Pragmatics*. Dordrecht: Reidel. 221–32.

Simmons, R. 1973. Semantic networks: their computation and use for under-standing English sentences. In R. Schank & K. Colby (eds) *Computer Models of Thought and Language*. Freeman, San Francisco. 63–113.

Sinigaglia, C. 2008. Mirror neurons: this is the question. *Journal of Consciousness Studies*, 15: 70–92.

Soames, S. 2002. *Beyond Rigidity*. Oxford: Oxford University Press.

—— 2005. Naming and asserting. In Z. Szabo (ed) *Semantics vs. Pragmatics*. Oxford: Oxford University Press. 356–82. Reprinted in Soames 2009 *Philosophical Essays* Vol. I. Princeton: Princeton University Press, 251–277.

—— 2009. *Philosophical Essays Vol. I*. Princeton: Princeton University Press.

Sosa, E. 1993. Putnam's pragmatic realism. *Journal of Philosophy*, XC, 605–26.

Sperber, D. & D. Wilson. 1986. *Relevance: communication and cognition*. Oxford: Blackwell.

Stainton, R. 2006. Meaning and reference. In E. Lepore & B. Smith (eds) *The Oxford Handbook of Philosophy of Language*. Oxford: Oxford University Press. 913–40.

—— 2006b. *Words and Thoughts*. Oxford: Oxford University Press.

Stanley, J. 2000. Context and logical form. *Linguistics and Philosophy* 23: 391–424.

—— 2002. Nominal restriction. In G. Preyer & G. Peter (eds) *Logical Form and Language*. Oxford: Oxford University Press. 365–88.

—— 2002b. Making it articulated. *Mind and Language* 17: 149–68.

—— 2005. Semantics in context. In G. Preyer & G. Peter (eds) *Contextualism in Philosophy*. Oxford: Oxford University Press. 221–54.

—— 2005b. *Knowledge and Practical Interests*. Oxford: Oxford University Press.

Stern, J. 2006. Metaphor, literal, literalism. *Mind and Language* 21: 243–79.

Stokke, A. 2010. Intention-sensitive semantics. *Synthese* 175: 383–404.

Storto, G. & M. Tanenhaus. 2004. Are scalar implicatures computed online? *Proceedings of WECOL 2004*.

Szabo, Z. 2006. Sensitivity training. *Mind and Language* 21 : 31–8.

Taylor, K. 2001. Sex, breakfast, and descriptus interruptus. *Synthese* 128:45–61.

Travis, C. 1989. *The Uses of Sense: Wittgenstein's Philosophy of Language*. Oxford: Oxford University Press.

—— 1997. Pragmatics. In B. Hale & C. Wright (eds) *Companion to the Philosophy of Language*. Oxford: Blackwell. 87–107.

—— 2008. *Occasion-Sensitivity*. Oxford: Oxford University Press.

Umiltà, M.A., Escola, L., Intskirveli, I., Grammont, F., Rochat, M., Caruana, F., Jezzini, A., Gallese, V., and Rizzolatti, G. (2008), 'How pliers become fingers in the monkey motor system', Proceedings of The National Academy of Sciences, 105 (6), 2209–13.

Weinreich, U. 1964. *Webster's Third*: a critique of its semantics. *International Journal of American Linguistics* 30: 405–9.

Weiskopf, D. 2009. Atomism, pluralism and conceptual content. *Philosophical and Phenomenological Research* 79: 130–62.

Wettstein, H. 1981. Demonstrative reference and definite descriptions. *Philosophical Studies* 40:241–57.

Whiten, A. 1996. When does smart behaviour-reading become mind-reading?. In P. Carruthers & P. Smith (eds) *Theories of Theories of Mind*. Cambridge: Cambridge University Press. 277–92.

Wiggins, D. 2001. *Sameness and Substance Renewed*. Cambridge: Cambridge Univeristy Press.

Williamson, T. 2000. *Knowledge and its Limits*. Oxford: Oxford University Press.

—— 2005. Contextualism, subject-sensitive invariantism and knowledge of knowledge. *The Philosophical Quarterly* 55: 213–35.

—— 2005. Knowledge and scepticism. In F. Jackson & M. Smith (eds) *The Oxford Handbook of Contemporary Philosophy*. Oxford: Oxford University Press. 681–700.

—— 2008. *The Philosophy of Philosophy*. Oxford: Blackwell.

—— 2009. Replies to Kornblith, Jackson and Moore. *Analysis* 60: 125–35.

Wittgenstein, L. 1953. *Philosophical Investigations*. Trans. G.E.M. Anscombe.

Wright, C. 2007. New age relativism and epistemic possibility: the question of evidence. *Philosophical Issues* 17: 262–83.

—— 2008. Relativism about truth itself: haphazard thoughts about the very idea. In M. Garcia-Carpintero & M. Kölbel (eds) *Relative Truth*. Oxford: Oxford University Press. 157–86.

Index

Printed and bound by CPI Group (UK) Ltd, Croydon, CR0 4YY

24/11/2024

01793610-0008